# SPIRAL GUIDES

*t*®

C000076483

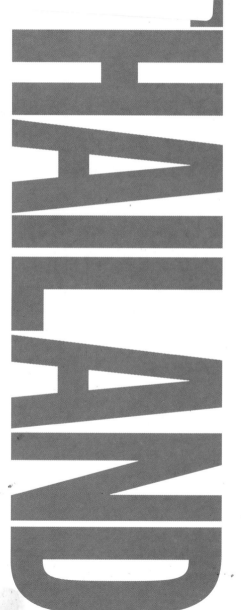

THAILAND

# Contents

## *the magazine* 5

✦ The Best of Thailand
✦ Spirit of a Nation ✦ A Festival Calendar
✦ What's Wat: A Temple Tour
✦ A Nation of Royalists
✦ "He Who is Awake" – the Thai Buddhist Faith
✦ View From a Mountain ✦ A Welcome Retreat
✦ "Same Same...But Different" ✦ Did You Know?

## Finding Your Feet 29

✦ First Two Hours
✦ Getting Around
✦ Accommodation
✦ Food and Drink
✦ Shopping
✦ Entertainment

## Bangkok 39

**Getting Your Bearings**
**In Three Days**
**Don't Miss** ✦ Grand Palace and Wat Phra Kaeo ✦ Wat Po
✦ Chao Phraya River ✦ Chatuchak Market
**At Your Leisure** ✦ 7 more places to explore
**Where to...** ✦ Stay ✦ Eat and Drink ✦ Shop
✦ Be Entertained

## Central Plains 63

**Getting Your Bearings**
**In Three Days**
**Don't Miss** ✦ Kanchanaburi Town ✦ Damnoen Saduak
Floating Markets ✦ Ayutthaya ✦ Sukhothai
**At Your Leisure** ✦ 7 more places to explore
**Where to...** ✦ Stay ✦ Eat and Drink ✦ Shop
✦ Be Entertained

## The North 87

**Getting Your Bearings**
**In Six Days**
**Don't Miss** ✦ Chiang Mai ✦ Trekking ✦ Mae Hong Son
**At Your Leisure**
✦ 6 more places to explore
**Where to...** ✦ Stay ✦ Eat and Drink ✦ Shop
✦ Be Entertained

## East Coast 109

**Getting Your Bearings**
**In Five Days**
Don't Miss ✦ Ko Chang ✦ Ko Samet
At Your Leisure ✦ 4 more places to explore
Where to... ✦ Stay ✦ Eat and Drink ✦ Shop
✦ Be Entertained

## Gulf Coast 125

**Getting Your Bearings**
**In Seven Days**
Don't Miss ✦ Hua Hin ✦ Khao Sam Roi Yot National Park
✦ Ko Samui Archipelago
At Your Leisure ✦ 5 more places to explore
Where to... ✦ Stay ✦ Eat and Drink ✦ Shop
✦ Be Entertained

## Andaman Coast 149

**Getting Your Bearings**
**In Seven Days**
Don't Miss ✦ Khao Sok National Park ✦ Ao Phang Nga
✦ Krabi ✦ Ko Phi Phi
At Your Leisure ✦ 7 more places to explore
Where to... ✦ Stay ✦ Eat and Drink ✦ Shop
✦ Be Entertained

## Walks and Tours 173

✦ 1 Bangkok's Chinatown
✦ 2 Mae Hong Son Loop
✦ 3 Krabi
✦ 4 Khao Sam Roi Yot National Park

## Practicalities 187

✦ Before You Go ✦ When to Go
✦ When You Are There

## Useful Phrases and Glossary 193

## Atlas 195

## Index 203

Written by Jane Egginton

Where to sections by David Henley and Andrew Forbes

Produced by Duncan Baird Publishers, London, England
Copy edited by Sarah Hudson
Verified by Lara Wozniak
Indexed by Marie Lorimer

American editor Tracy Larson

Edited, designed and produced by AA Publishing

Published in the United States by AAA Publishing,
1000 AAA Drive, Heathrow, Florida 32746
Published in the United Kingdom by AA Publishing

ISBN-13: 978-1-59508-113-1
ISBN-10: 1-59508-113-5

Cover design and binding style by permission of AA Publishing

Color separation by Keenes, Andover
Printed and bound in China by Leo Paper Products

10 9 8 7 6 5 4 3 2 1

A02354

*the magazine*

# The BEST of
# Thailand

Many of Thailand's highlights are not just the best of their kind in the country, but in the world. The white-sand beaches and turquoise waters rival those of the Caribbean; the historical cities of Sukhothai and Ayutthaya are World Heritage Sites; and the diving is some of the best on the planet.

Footprints on the shore, Ko Phuket

Lacquerware from Thai market

National Museum, Bangkok

## National Parks
Thailand has more than 80 national parks. **Khao Sok** (▶ 154) offers a real jungle experience with leopards, tigers, treehouses to stay in and the largest-known flower in the world, the *Rafflesia kerri meyer* or wild lotus (▶ 154). **Doi Inthanon** (▶ 99) has the highest mountain in the country, and **Thalay Ban** (▶ 167) is home to hundreds of species of bird life.

## Islands
It is impossible to pick the country's most idyllic island – there are so many – but there is one to suit everyone. **Ko Phi Phi** (▶ 162–163) is probably the prettiest, **Ko Phuket** (▶ 164) the most sophisticated and **Ko Jam** (▶ 165) one of the most remote.

## Buddha Statues
The most sacred Buddha statue in the country is the **Emerald Buddha**, in Bangkok's Wat Phra Kaeo (▶ 45). **Wat Traimit**, or the Temple of the Golden Buddha in Bangkok, is home to a solid gold Buddha, the largest in the world at 4m (13 feet) high.

## Markets
Although **Chiang Mai's night market** (▶ 93) is the most famous and most popular with tourists, **Chatuchak Market** (▶ 51) in Bangkok beats it hands down for number of stalls (more than 6,000), range of goods (from life-size fake trees to guinea pigs), price and all-important atmosphere.

## Museum
If you only go to one museum, make it the **National Museum** in Bangkok (▶ 52), housed in a former palace surrounded by

Elephant trekking in the north

Best diving: Ko Tao

Ancient site: Wat Sra Sri, Sukhothai

Hill-tribe village near Mae Hong Son

Thai massage on the beach

beautiful grounds. Its collections of memorabilia from the royal family as well as historical artefacts are among the finest in Southeast Asia.

## Journeys

For most visitors the most memorable journeys in Thailand are **treks** through jungle to hill-tribe villages in the north (► 95–97). Buzzing past **James Bond Island** in a traditional longtail boat in Ao Phang Nga comes a close second (► 156–158).

## Diving

Thailand's diving mecca is the small turtle-shaped island of **Ko Tao** (► 136). Those in the know go there for some of the cheapest and best diving in the world. **Pattaya** (► 120) is the unchallenged watersports capital of Thailand.

## Retreats

Riverside retreats are found throughout the country, from the peaceful towns on the northern border of the Mekong River to the floating lodges of **Kanchanaburi** (► 68–69). Even Bangkok's **Chao Phraya River** (► 49–50) offers relief from the city.

## Ancient Sites

The ancient cities of **Sukhothai** (► 75–77) and **Ayutthaya** (► 72–74) are both World Heritage Sites. Although Ayutthaya is magnificent and within easy reach of Bangkok, Sukhothai wins for its scenic qualities which hark back to a golden age.

## Villages

Charming villages abound in Thailand. The hill-tribe communities around **Mae Hong Son** (► 98–99) are invariably scenic and almost untouched by the 21st century. The floating Muslim fishing village in **Ao Phang Nga** (► 156–158) is unique.

## Thai Massage

If you only have one Thai massage, make it at **Wat Po** in Bangkok, the national headquarters for massage training (► 48). Thai massage is a combination of Western massage and foot reflex-zone massage. The highly trained masseurs and masseuses (usually the same sex as their client) are expert in reducing tension.

# Spirit of a Nation

There's a kind of magic to everyday life in Thailand. Buses, taxis and boats are draped with wreaths of jasmine flowers to appease the spirits and ensure a safe journey. Amulets – maybe a sacred gem or a tiger's tooth – adorn the necks of most Thais as protection against everything, from infertility to crop-destroying winds. Outside almost every building is a miniature wooden house on a pole, built as somewhere for displaced spirits to live.

A belief in animism (that inanimate objects have a soul) as well as in Hindu gods happily sits side by side with the Thais' Buddhist faith. The current king, Bhumibol, like those in the Chakri dynasty before him, is known as Rama, to align him with the ideal king in the Hindu epic *The Ramayana,* and he regularly uses Brahmin priests at royal ceremonies.

The Erawan shrine is a Hindu shrine outside the Grand Hyatt Erawan in Bangkok, built to placate the spirits when a series of construction problems blighted the building of the hotel in the 1950s. It receives a constant swarm of worshippers who believe it will bring them good luck. A shrine to phalluses in the grounds of the Hilton Hotel in Bangkok attracts those hoping for fertility – they come here to pay their respects and leave phallic offerings.

Despite the seriousness of these beliefs, however, Thais believe that whatever we do should be fun, or *sanuk*. This applies equally to work in a field or work in a bank. It is partly this philosophy that makes Thais smile, whatever the situation. They also highly value a "cool heart" or a calm manner. This means being discreet when it comes to displaying affection or emotion in public, using soft speech and avoiding becoming impatient or angry. The more you can achieve this, the more you are respected. On the whole Thais are incredibly tolerant – just so long as you don't disrespect their royal family or religion, and dress cleanly and neatly.

## SPIRITS AND SUPERSTITIONS

• Spirits are said to live in the doorsills of temples, so it is bad luck to step on them.
• Many Thai men, including monks, have tattoos to ward off evil spirits.
• Astrologers are regularly consulted to find an auspicious day for an important occasion, such as starting work on building a house or opening a business.

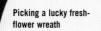

Picking a lucky fresh-flower wreath

# A Festival Calendar

Thailand's festivals are always colourful celebrations, whether their origins are in agricultural traditions, the Buddhist faith, the royal family or local gods and goddesses. Those mentioned here are the most important and take place nationwide, unless otherwise stated. Dates can differ from one year to the next, but local tourist offices are able to provide more information.

❖ **Festival of Flowers** – flower parades in February in Chiang Mai.

❖ **Chinese New Year** – Chinese fireworks in February or March.

❖ **Pattaya Festival** – April carnival in Pattaya.

❖ **Songkran** – celebration of the Thai New Year in mid-April. The biggest festival involves the washing of Buddha images and playful water fights, especially in Chiang Mai.

❖ **Visakha Bucha** – on a full moon in May the birth, death and enlightenment of Buddha (they all happened on the same day) are commemorated with candlelit processions.

❖ **Royal Ploughing Ceremony** – in early May the start of rice-planting is celebrated in Bangkok.

❖ **Rocket Festival** – in mid-May this festival features parades, folk dancing and handmade bamboo rockets in Yasothon, northeast Thailand.

❖ **Khao Phansa** – in July the retreat of the rains in Ubon Ratchathani is celebrated.

❖ **Narathiwat Fair** – at the end of September a local fair lasts a week in Narathiwat Province.

❖ **Vegetarian Festival** – at the end of September or beginning of October,

Right: A Chiang Mai girl at the Songkran water festival

Below: A giant Kratong (Songkran float) on Kamphaeng's River Ping makes a surreal spectacle

Background: Beauty queens parade at the Chiang Mai flower festival

vegetarianism is celebrated by the Chinese community in Phuket and in Trang.

❖ **Loy Krathong** – during November full moon tribute is paid to the Goddess of Rivers, Mae Kongkha, by setting sail small boats. All over the country, but best seen in Sukhothai.

❖ **River Kwai Bridge Week** – at the end of November or early December a sound-and-light show takes place with historical displays in Kanchanaburi Town.

❖ **King's Birthday** – King Bhumibol's birthday on 5 December is celebrated with a parade in Bangkok.

# ωβατ's ωατ: a τεμρλε τουρ

As the showcase for art and architecture, Thailand's 30,000 temple complexes (*wats*) feature high on any tourist itinerary. They are much more than simply places of worship.

Historically they were centres of education and some, especially those in rural areas, continue this role. **Wat Po** in Bangkok (► 47–48) was the first centre for public education and today houses the national headquarters for traditional Thai medicine and massage. Some, such as Krabi's **Wat Tham Seua** (► 161), surrounded by

**Far left: Detail at Wat Ming Meuang, Chiang Rai**

**A Budhha image at Wat Phra Singh, Chiang Rai**

## What's in a Temple?

At the heart of each temple complex is a *bot*, an ordination hall open only to monks who meditate and carry out ceremonies. It has eight surrounding stones, looking rather like gravestones. Decorated with carvings of Buddhist scenes, these sacred stones protect the consecrated ground on which the *bot* is built.

A *viharn* looks very similar to a *bot*, but is the assembly hall containing the Buddha image. This is where worshippers and visitors tend to head. Large *wats* may have more than one *viharn*. The *wats* are often dominated by cone-shaped towers known as *chedis* or *stupas* (in the north *thats*), containing Buddha relics or the remains of deceased local dignitaries. Additional elements may include a *mondop* to house a Buddha statue, a *ho trai* or library of holy scriptures and a *sala* for lectures or meetings.

limestone cliffs and tropical forest, are worth visiting for their scenic locations alone.

Many of the buildings' details are rich in symbolism. Roofs with three tiers symbolise the "triple gems" of Buddhism: the Buddha (the teacher), the Dhamma (the act of teaching) and the Sangha (the followers of the teachings). The reclining Buddha is usually shown with his head resting on a lotus. As a flower that germinates in mud but blossoms into a thing of great beauty, it suggests that Buddha is within us all. The *garuda* bird that is often seen supporting buildings in a temple complex is a royal Hindu symbol of strength. Rounded Khmer *prangs* (towers) symbolise Mount Meru, home of the Hindu gods, while large towering *chedis* were designed to stand as testament to the enduring stability of Buddhism.

## Temple Etiquette
• Remove shoes
• Do not expose legs or shoulders
• Never touch the head of a Buddha image
• Do not point your feet towards a person or a Buddha image
• Sit on the floor
• Never have your head higher than a monk's, or any Buddha image
• Women should not have eye contact with a monk

# Buddha images

Buddha images are not meant to be physical representations of the holy man, but of his teachings. They appear in one of only four postures, or *asanhas*. By far the most common is the sitting, or meditating, Buddha. The reclining Buddha represents his entering Nirvana, and in the standing or walking position he is descending from heaven. The hand gestures (*mudras*) of the Buddha are significant and distinguish one activity from another. The following are the most common hand gestures:

❖ *Bhumisparca mudra*: seated with the left hand in the lap and the right hand on the right knee with the tips of the fingers pointing to the ground. The Buddha is harnessing the power of the earth to meditate.

❖ *Abhaya mudra*: the Buddha teaching: standing with the palm of the right hand and sometimes both hands raised outwards.

❖ *Vitarka mudra*: the thumb and index finger of the right hand in a circle represent the teachings of the Buddha.

❖ *Dhyana mudra*: the meditation position: both hands in the lap with palms pointing upwards.

❖ *Abhaya mudra*: dispelling fear: the right hand is held up as if to say "stop".

## Hindu Gods

Alongside Buddhist iconography, Thai temples often incorporate the rather fantastical gods of the Hindu religion:

• **Vishnu** with four arms, usually wearing a crown
• **Garuda**, half-man, half-bird
• **Shiva**, a mythical creature like the *garuda*, with his four arms carrying different objects and showing gestures of peace and sacrifice
• **Ganesh**, with the head of an elephant

From top: the tiny famed Emerald Budda; A reclining image; a fasting Budda; a stucco relief of the Buddha in a sitting position

# A Nation of Royalists

Thais are utterly devoted to their royal family. Vast illuminated pictures of King Bhumibol and Queen Sirikit appear at the roadside and it would be hard to find a family that doesn't have at least one, if not several, framed photographs of the royal family in pride of place in their living room.

King Bhumibol, the much-loved current king

## Humanitarian Monarchs

King Bhumibol, or **Rama IX**, is the latest in the line of the Chakri Dynasty, which began in 1782. His great grand-father, **Rama IV Mongkut** (1851–68), spent 30 years as a monk, yet embraced modernism. **Rama V Chulalongkorn** (1868–1910) ended outdated medieval court rituals and established the first school system, a railway network and the country's first hospital. **Rama VI Vajiravudh** (1910–25) was committed to bringing Thailand in line with the western world. Thai people were known only by their first names until 1913, when Rama VI introduced surnames in an attempt at modernisation. He also made primary education compulsory and founded the first university. A respected author, **Rama VII Prajadhipok** (1925–35) set up the National Library, the Fine Arts Department and the National Museum.

So great is their devotion that at eight o'clock every morning in Bangkok's central train station, city commuters stop and stand in silence as the National Anthem is played out over the loudspeaker system. This performance is repeated again at six o'clock in the evening.

King Bhumibol's name means "the strength of the land", and he is regarded by his kingdom in a similar way as the Tibetans see their spiritual leader, the Dalai Lama, rather than any comparable monarch. Most Thais would agree with the Thailand tourist office website that describes him as a "paragon of virtue" and a "literary genius". This is partly due to history and a constitution that states that the king must be "enthroned in a position of revered worship", but it is also possibly because Thailand has never previously had a clear and consistent political leadership and has been dogged by

## The King and I

King Mongkut was unfairly portrayed as bad-tempered and naive in the fictionalised account of his court in the musical *The King and I*. The film is still banned in Thailand, along with the 1946 film *Anna and the King of Siam* and the more recent film *Anna and the King* starring Jodie Foster.

government corruption and incompetence.

Thailand had an absolute monarchy until 1932, when a *coup* established a constitutional monarchy, as in the UK. King Bhumibol was

**An image of King Bhumibol on Ratchadamnoen Avenue, Bangkok**

born in the United States, educated in Switzerland and came to the throne in 1946 – the country celebrated his Golden Jubilee in 1996. But unlike British royalty, the Thai royal family does not receive any money from the royal treasury. Their power cannot be ignored by politicians: in 1992 the prime minister and his opponent prostrated themselves at the king's feet on live television while he instructed them on how to deal with a national crisis. Chief executives of international companies

**Above: Bangkok's National Assembly**

**Left: Regal King Chulalongkorn (Rama V)**

## Public Holidays

❖ **Chakri Day**, 6 April, honours Rama I, the founder of the Chakri dynasty

❖ **Coronation Day**, 5 May, honours King Bhumibol and Queen Sirikit's coronation

❖ **The Queen's Birthday**, 12 August

❖ **Chulalongkorn Day**, 23 October, in honour of King Chulalongkorn, Rama V

❖ **The King's Birthday**, 5 December

reported being literally "floored" by his presence.

In King Bhumibol's opinion "a successful monarch must become the living symbol of the country. He must change with the country but at the same time keep the

spirit of the country", this is something that he, and his family before him, has somehow managed to achieve. King Bhumibol's older brother, Ananda, is credited with being responsible for establishing modern medicine in Thailand, and his mother founded the flying doctors to give medical assistance to remote parts of the country. Between them, King Bhumibol and Queen Sirikit have established over 4,000 projects to give assistance in rural areas, particularly in the poor northeast.

### Royal Etiquette

As a visitor to Thailand the worst thing you can do is criticise the royal family. The best course of action is not even to mention them – most Thai people do not think themselves worthy of discussing them in idle conversation. When a French visitor mildly criticised the Thai royal family on a flight to Bangkok in 1995 he was arrested on arrival.

Top: One of many shrines to King Bhumibol

Above: The Royal Guard Constitution Day Parade

In Buddhism there is no all-powerful God to look to – the religion dictates that every man and woman is responsible for what happens in the world and we all have the power within us to become a Buddha ourselves.

# "He Who is Awake"
## – the Thai Buddhist Faith

The first Buddha was simply a man who gained enlightenment. The name means "he who is awake". Buddhism is apparent in the golden spires of the thousands of temples and the saffron-robed monks, but essentially in the Thai people themselves. No fewer than 95 per cent of the country's 60 million inhabitants are Buddhist, and this is apparent in the gentle respect they show the world. They try to abstain from killing, stealing, sexual liberty, lying and taking intoxicants, and to carry out daily acts of kindness. Believing that suffering stems from desire, they hold that by

**Below: Monks parade through Wat Phra Kaeo, Grand Palace in Bangkok**

### It's a Monk's Life
In Thai culture, monks are greatly revered. The back seats in buses are reserved for them and they have access to a special orchid-covered area at Bangkok's airport. Nuns, who wear white, have no such status.

wisdom, compassion and mindfulness we can all reach Nirvana and the State of Enlightenment.

The shaved heads and yellow robes of Buddhist monks are everywhere. This is because most Thai men are ordained at some time in their life, even if only for a few days, and civil servants get three months off with pay to complete their ordination. Dan is a young novice monk studying English at university who says: "My father became a monk because it was the only way to learn to read and write. Ex-monks were popular choices for women looking for a husband because they were thought to be clever and calm. Now women are more likely to look to men with money."

Thai people are very practical in their beliefs. When they give alms in a monk's collection bucket it is to gain "merit", so they don't give anything unwanted. Curried chicken, teabags and toilet paper are the typically practical contents. Thai monks are equally practical and will share with everyone else in the temple. If they get too many gifts, they will sell them on to the next temple.

Above: Monks' robes drying in the sun

Left: Monks' buckets on sale in Bangkok

Above: Novice monks, Chiang Rai

Left: A shadow puppet maker in Nakhon Si Thammarat

## The Beginnings of Buddhism

According to Buddhist belief the Buddha was born as Prince Gautama Siddhartha in the 6th or 7th century BC. When he escaped the royal household at the age of 29 and encountered real poverty, he attempted to come to terms with it through meditation. Concluding that all is impermanent, he eventually achieved enlightenment and advocated the "Middle Way", which rejects the two extremes of austerity and indulgence.

# view from

## "My name is Atapa. I live in a hill tribe in the mountains...

**A Lisu girl in traditional dress**

Atapa is the name given to every eldest boy in a Lisu family. If I were a girl it would be Amema. My Thai name is Somsak. I am 25 years old, with six brothers and sisters. Tourists have been coming to my village for 12 years. In the high season they come every day. The first time I wondered where they came from, these people with big bodies and golden hair. Why don't they stay in the town where everything is nice? But they want to know how we live and they like our culture.

We feel that they are like guests here. The family who has them to stay is very proud because they have the income. The guide chooses which family, but usually it is the headman's. They do everything the guide requests and he says things like: "When I am coming, tell the villagers to weave costumes." The tourists like coca-cola

and beer, so we bring it from the town, but many of them complain because they don't want to see modern things in the village.

In January and February we are busy clearing the fields and in March and April we burn them. We are preparing so we can start to grow rice and corn which we plant in May and June. After that we weed, but we still have free time and in the first weeks of August we can celebrate the new corn. We take the corn and give some to the *shaman*, some to the spirit in the village and some to the spirit house outside the village. Every house has a shelf where you put vegetables and tea and whisky underneath at this time and also when it is New Year or someone is sick.

The *shaman* is the only person who can contact the

spirits. We go to him if someone is sick or if we want to know why we have a problem. Some villagers are tired because they work so hard. The *shaman* says they must offer the head and heart of the pig. It is cooked and given to the villagers at a party at the patient's house so they feel happy and better.

I am satisfied in my village. Many young boys in the village are not happy so they go to the town. But they are uneducated, so what can they do there? I have never seen anyone be successful

**Background:
The view from
Doi Inthanon,
Thailand's
highest peak**

**Opposite: Hill-
tribe children
at a local
village school**

**Above: Stars
and stripes of
hill-tribe crafts**

**Left: A
traditional Lisu
parade in
Chiang Rai**

but they don't want to come back because they think they will lose face in the village.

When people have children they hope it will be a girl because boys are likely to become drug addicts. Amphetamines are a big problem; opium is now too expensive. Before, everybody was happy if the silo was full of grain. They never suffer, they have enough. Now everybody worries about the younger people going to the town.

Sometimes the tourists swim in the river nude, do not wear good clothes and kiss. For us it is shameful to do that. We wait the whole year for New Year to have a chance to meet the girl who we like and hold her hand. The *shaman* decides how many days for celebration, but we normally dance for three days and three nights. Maybe we sleep for two or three hours and then start again. We begin at the *shaman's* house and then we go to every family who gives us whisky. If they take good care of us we stay longer.

**"If we decide to marry the girl we give her something like a deposit of 1,000 baht or if we have no money, a watch or a ring."**

We give it secretly, asking her to hold out her hand and send a friend with a vase and a bottle of whisky to the family of the girl. The family will say they need 20,000 baht to replace her, and as she has two older brothers she must pay a 5,000 baht fine for jumping ahead. The amount of money depends on how beautiful the girl is. It's a kind of game. They bargain and when they agree they all drink whisky."

**Whether for its sophisticated spa hotels frequented by models and film stars or its monastic-style meditation retreats, Thailand has long been a favourite with stressed-out Westerners.**

Serenity is a concept rooted in the country's sensibility and the Buddhist religion. Thai people are almost invariably calm and their approach to life is typified by the much used phrase "*mai pen rai*", or "never mind".

## Spa Hotels

Spa hotels are found in just about every corner of the country. If you don't want to pay for accommodation, many charge a set rate for day use or even just per treatment.

Spa hotels combine the ancient healing methods of the East – from India, China, Indonesia and Thailand – with modern rejuvenation techniques. You will find traditional massage alongside state-of-the-art flotation tanks, and contemporary dietary measures are just as likely to be prescribed as yoga, meditation techniques and herbal remedies.

Thailand's best spa hotels, all of which have a global reputation, are located at the beach or in the mountains. **Chiva Som** (73/4 Thanon

Relaxation at Chiva Som: From top: massage, flotation tank and yoga

## Real Retreats

For a genuine get-away-from-it-all you can't get much better than a meditation retreat. They may last for as long as a month, although 10 days is more typical and temples often offer an afternoon's instruction. The most common technique is **Vipassana**, which involves focusing on breathing techniques. Most retreats stipulate no talking and no eating after noon, as well as abstaining from all intoxicants and sexual activity. The World Fellowship of Buddhists (616 Sukhumvit Road, Soi 24, Bangkok, tel: 02 661 1284, fax: 02 661 0555) has information on English-speaking retreats throughout the country.

**The Banyan Tree** (33 Thanon Srisoonthorn, Cherngtalay, Amphur Talang, Phuket 83110, tel: 07 632 4374; www.banyantree.com) is in a beachside complex of international up-market resort hotels on the island of Ko Phuket (▶ 164–165).

Rice fields and grazing buffalo surround the **Four Seasons Chiang Mai** (▶ 104) in countryside on the very edge of Chiang Mai.

## Other Relaxations

Many people find peace in Thailand without checking into an expensive resort. Traditional Thai massage and foot-focused reflexology, available on almost every street corner, are blissful ways to break up a shopping or sightseeing trip.

Traditional Thai massage was established by monks who wanted to find a way of stretching and exercising after sitting for long periods during meditation. It is a lot more active than other forms of massage as the joints are manipulated as well as relaxed.

Petchkasem, Hua Hin, Prachmab Khiri Khan 77110, tel: 03 253 6536; email: reserv@chivasom.co.th; www.chivasom.com), in the royal resort of Hua Hin, means "Haven of Life" and is the undoubted queen of spa hotels, not just in Thailand, but all over the world. Its exquisite décor provides unadulterated luxury, yet it is purely inspired by nature. Guests sink into plunge pools filled with pink lotus flowers and are massaged in open-air pavilions, often surrounded by banana trees (▶ 142).

## Bliss on a Budget

Spa hotels come at a price that you may not find as relaxing as the treatments offered. Follow this fast track to tranquillity and Thai style without losing your serenity.

• A Thai massage or reflexology treatment can be had for little cost. Try to avoid establishments on obvious tourist corners and ask about qualifications.

• Essential oils and herbal teas such as chrysanthemum and jasmine are widely available and easy to take home.

• Strictly speaking, a spa hotel is one that uses water in its therapies, but you don't have to jump in a hydrotherapy bath or flotation tank. Water therapy can be gained by swimming, especially in the sea, as salt water is a natural detoxifier.

• Simple furniture, floor cushions and low futon-style beds are very much Thai style. Many Buddhists believe that only the Enlightened should raise themselves above floor level.

Opposite: A smiling spa assistant at Chiva Som

Right: Cycling on the sands

Below: Traditional pavilions built around a lake

# "Same same...
# but different"

"Same same...but different" is a phrase that Thais use time and time again.

It's an indication that things are often not what they seem in beguiling Thailand, blithely called the "Land of Smiles".

Lose your temper with a Thai and the chances are they will smile sweetly and walk away. It's an attitude that frustrates Westerners, but deeply rooted in Thai culture is the concept of "not losing face", or embarrassing yourself or others. The ease with which Thai people seem to handle difficult situations springs from the desire to avoid confrontation at any cost.

**Wherever you go in Thailand, you will be greeted with smiles**

## Forging Ahead

Although the government has clamped down on the sale of bootleg tapes, CDs and DVDs, markets all over the country are still full of stalls selling fake goods. Designer copies such as Louis Vuitton handbags and Rolex watches are snapped up by tourists, many of whom bring expensive suits from home to be copied at a fraction of the price by a skilled tailor. The culture of copying is such that Kho San Road even has adverts for "handmade passports".

Because of the very visible sex industry, people often assume that the country has a liberal attitude. But you will rarely see Thais of the opposite sex showing any kind of physical affection, and the older generation find those who do so offensive.

Young girls may dress provocatively in tourist bars, but many locals will not even take their clothes off to swim and are genuinely shocked at the sight of scantily clad tourists on the beach. Yet Thailand's transvestites (*katoeys*) – frequently mistaken for beautiful women – are widely tolerated, both in towns and villages, since transvestism isn't seen to have sexual connotations.

## Scams

Watch out for slick scams aimed at overseas visitors. A good rule is to be wary of anyone who approaches you to offer unsolicited information under the guise of being helpful; they will probably only be helping themselves. Report any incidents to the tourist police who can be reached from anywhere in the country by dialling 1155, or through any TAT office. Scams might take any form, but the following are worth looking out for:
• You may ask a taxi driver to take you to a hotel, but be told it is closed and taken to a different one which pays the driver a commission.
• Schemes involving fake jewels abound.
• Bangkok's Grand Palace (► 44–46) and Wat Po (► 47–48) are breeding grounds for those trying to nab first-time visitors; a popular line is to tell you they're closed and try to take you on a shopping tour.

Clockwise from above: Smiling passerby in Lam-pang; a T-shirt vendor, Bangkok's Bo Be Market; fried maggots – a local delicacy; gold sellers in Bangkok's Chinatown
Below: Thais enjoy the beach fully clothed, here at Bang Saen

- Thailand is the only Southeast Asian country never to have been colonised by a European power. As the word *Thai* means "free", Thailand literally translates as "the land of the free".

- The word *farang* is used to describe just about any foreign visitor to the country. It is not always implied as a derogatory term, and has its origins in the Thai word for "French", who were expelled from the country during the 17th century.

- Historically Thailand's kings gave sacred white (albino) elephants to their enemies. Being royal, the animals could not be killed or made to work, so the recipients then bankrupted themselves trying to keep them. The practice is said to be the origin of the term "white elephant".

- Thailand is the biggest exporter of rice in the world.

The original Thai flag featured an elephant

# Did You Know?

- The first hospital was not established until 1886 and even then it was amid much opposition because herbal remedies were favoured above Western medicine.

- Siam was the name used for Thailand by foreigners between the 12th and 20th centuries. It was only used by the Thai people for a short period from the 19th century to 1939, when the nation was given its current name.

- There are more than 1,300 varieties of Thai orchid.

- The original Thai flag depicted an elephant until it was mistaken by some Europeans as a rodent. The red, white and blue of today's flag represent the nation, Buddhism and the monarchy.

- Women play a powerful role in the economy and are frequently the ones who run businesses.

Most of the country's work-force labour in the fields

# Finding Your Feet

# First Two Hours

## Arriving by Air

Most overseas visitors arrive at Bangkok's International Don Muang, one of the busiest in Southeast Asia. Although only 25km northeast of the city, it will take at least an hour to get into the centre, depending on the traffic and how you travel.

Construction is underway for a second international airport, Suvarnabhumi Airport, 25 km (15 miles) east of the city. The huge new airport (the world's largest single building, with the world's highest control tower) was originally scheduled to open in Sepetmber 2005, but construction delays mean it will probably not be operational until late 2006.

## Airport Facilities

Facilities at the airport include a currency exchange, a post and telephone communications office and left luggage, all of which are open 24 hours. There is also the Thai Hotel Association reservations service, which can check on vacancies at their member hotels, a tourist office and several food outlets on the upper floors.

## Departure Tax

Note that on leaving Thailand you will be charged a 500 baht departure tax, for which credit cards are not accepted. For enquiries, tel: 02 535 1111.

## From the Airport to Bangkok by Taxi

- Travelling by **taxi** into town from the airport is probably the best choice after a long flight. The journey should take around 35–40 minutes.
- The taxi fare is 200–300 baht.
- Take a **licensed cab** from the booth outside the Arrivals hall.
- Ignore any **drivers who approach you directly**; they may be unlicensed and will almost certainly try to charge you an extortionate fare.
- You can take taxis with either a **fixed fare** (make sure you agree the fee in advance) or a **meter**. There's little difference in price, although in rush hour a metered ride can soon escalate.
- You will have to pay **tolls** into the city in addition to the fare, but they should be included in any flat rate quoted.

## From the Airport to Bangkok by Limousine

- Costing about **twice the price of a taxi**, taking a limousine is still a relatively reasonably priced option.
- As well as a little extra luxury, it means you can **avoid having to queue** for a taxi.
- Several companies operate from the **airport** – ask for details from the Tourism Authority of Thailand office.
- Make sure you **establish a price** beforehand.

## From the Airport to Bangkok by Airport Bus

- This efficient, frequent, air-conditioned service is in operation from **6 am to 11:30 pm**.
- Much more comfortable, and probably safer than catching the public bus, it is considerably **cheaper** than travelling by taxi.

■ Although the chances are the airport bus won't take you exactly to your destination, the service does stop at some of the city's **larger hotels**.

## From the Airport to Bangkok by Train

■ A fast **rail link** from the airport to central Bangkok is due to open in 2006. Journey time will be about 30 minutes, incorporating stops connecting with Bangkok's underground metro system and the Skytrain.

## Tourist Information

■ The **Tourist Authority of Thailand** is more usually known, and referred to throughout this book, as **TAT**.
■ The **airport office** is open 9 am–midnight.
■ The **central office** is located at 1600 Thanon Phetchaburi Makkasan, Ratchathewi, tel: 02 250 5500; open 8:30–4:30 and at the Thai Boxing Stadium, Ratchadamnoen Nok Avenue, tel: 02 281 4205; open 8:30–4:30.
■ There are TAT offices throughout the country. Consult the relevant chapter for details.

# Getting Around

*"Pai nai?"* ("Where are you going?") is the regular cry of taxi drivers and boatmen eager to sell you a ticket, but it's also a standard Thai greeting that translates as "How's it going?" or simply "Hello". Travelling around Thailand is surprisingly straightforward. Bus and train services are frequent and very reasonably priced. A little comfort can be had for a small price, in the form of first-class rail travel, air-conditioned buses and internal flights.

## Buses

■ **Air-conditioning** is essential in order to ensure a comfortable bus journey in Thailand, so it is worth travelling by the slightly more expensive air-conditioned **government or private buses** whenever possible, particularly at night.
■ The government service is known as **Bor Kor Sor (BKS)** and they come in several classes, from ordinary non-air-conditioned services for shorter journeys to comfortable air-conditioned superior ones for longer journeys. So-called VIP buses have reclining seats, hostesses who serve drinks or a refreshment station and toilets. They are excellent for overnight journeys as the seats can be reclined to near horizontal.
■ Superior buses for longer journeys tend to leave in the early morning or early evening, while ordinary buses leave throughout the day from the centre of towns at unfixed times.
■ The long-distance northern and southern bus terminals can be bewildering due to the number of ticket counters attached to different bus companies. If you arrive by taxi ask your driver to drop you at the ticket counter of the company offering a service to your destination. Many taxi drivers will accompany you to the relevant counter and even help you buy your ticket.Ticket counter staff are also invariably friendly and helpful.
■ Air-conditioned **mini vans**, available at busy tourist hubs like Khao San Road in Bangkok, may seem more convenient, but they rarely run on time, can be cramped and are a lot more expensive. You may be taken to a ferry company or a hotel that is not your choice, but which earns the bus company a commission. Often the services are illegal, with bad-tempered, overworked drivers who may have a poor safety record.

■ *Songthaews* are pickup trucks with two rows of bench seating that operate like buses, although if they are otherwise empty you can often charter the whole vehicle.

## Trains

■ Try to use the **well-run** train network wherever possible in Thailand as it's a comfortable way to travel, especially if you book an overnight sleeper.
■ There are **four train lines**, running from Bangkok to Chiang Mai (► 92–94) in the north, to Hua Hin, Surat Thani – jumping off point for Ko Samui (► 134–137) and the Malaysian border in the south (► 141) – and into the Isan provinces in the northeast. The northern line from Bangkok to Chiang Mai stops at Ayutthaya (► 72–74) and Lampang.
■ **Tickets** should be booked in advance, it is often worth paying a travel agency premium for them to purchase tickets for you to avoid the hassle of having to visit the station and then return to your hotel.
■ There are **three classes** (1, 2 and 3) and **three types** of train (Special Express, Rapid and Ordinary). First-class overnight accommodation is in two-berth sleeping compartments, second-class is in Pullman-style sleeping cars, third class in upright seats. Unless you value the privacy of first class, the second-class compartments are clean, comfortable and exceptional value. Dining cars are on most overnight trains, although a buffet service is provided on all.

## Domestic Air Travel

■ Domestic air travel is very **reasonably priced** in comparison with European or American fares.
■ The Thai government's deregulation policy has spawned several budget airlines which now fly from Bangkok to most tourist destinations at fares as low as 900 baht. **Thai International Airways** (tel 02 1566) maintains its dominance of the domestic network, and if you're planning your trip in advance it's advisable to reserve either with them or Thailand's number two, **Bangkok Airways** (tel 02 2655678), which has its own airport serving Sukothai. But if you want to take your chance, you can find excellent deals at the airport booths of the leading minor airlines: **Nok** (02 1318), **Air Asia** and Orient Thai's **One-Two-Go** (02 267 299).
■ A useful flight that can save time is the daily flight with Thai Airways from **Chiang Mai to Phuket**, stopping at Bangkok en route.
■ As flights are often booked up, especially at weekends and during holidays, **reserve ahead** as far as possible.

## Taxis

■ Always **agree a price** – you may have to bargain hard – or establish that the meter is used before getting in.
■ Some taxi drivers, especially at busy transport hubs and popular attractions, try to take advantage of tourists, quoting several times what the price should be. In general **avoid drivers who approach you** or at least try to find out what the price should be before negotiating.
■ Hiring a taxi even for a **trip of several hours** is worth considering, particularly if public transport connections are difficult, you want a bit of comfort, or local transport is inconvenient.

### Tuk-tuks

■ Three-wheeled, open-sided vehicles known as *tuk-tuks* provide a **cheap and fast** means of transport, particularly in Bangkok, but they are very noisy and the journey can be hair-raising.

■ *Tuk-tuks* don't have meters so it is vital to **agree a price** with the driver before getting aboard.

## Car Rental

■ Car rental is **relatively inexpensive** and available in most places in Thailand.
■ Negotiate a **discount** if you want the car for more than a day.
■ If you don't want to drive yourself, a **driver** can normally be engaged for around half the daily car-rental fee.
■ Ask to see **insurance details**. In the event of an accident you may be liable.
■ You will need an **international driving licence**, although more often than not it is not asked for.
■ Generally, arranging car-rental **from your own country** is more expensive than waiting until you arrive in Thailand.

---

**Driving Essentials**
■ Drive on the **left**.
■ Be prepared for a certain amount of **chaos**. There are very few rules of the road in practice, except for the one that says the bigger your vehicle the more rights you have.
■ Attitude to wearing **seatbelts**, keeping within the **speed limit** and **parking** tends to be rather relaxed.
■ **Flashing your lights** is a warning, not a signal that the coast is clear.
■ **Beeping the horn** is not aggressive, but an indication that you are about to overtake.
■ **Kilometre markers** are found along bigger highways.

---

**Car-Hire Companies**
The following companies in the UK cover the main tourist destinations in Thailand:
■ Avis: 0990 900500
■ Budget: 0800 818181
■ Hertz: 0990 996699

---

**Admission Charges**
The cost of admission for museums and places of interest featured in the guide is indicated by the following price categories.

**Inexpensive** = under 50 baht
**Moderate** = 50–100 baht
**Expensive** = over 100 baht

# Accommodation

Accommodation opportunities in Thailand are many and varied, although you will find the distribution rather uneven. Bangkok, Chiang Mai, Phuket and Ko Samui have a choice of everything, from cheap and cheerful guesthouses to luxury hotels that have often been voted the best in the world. In other places, such as Ayutthaya and Sukhothai, the choice is not nearly as good. Thailand's tourist season runs from November to March and bookings are essential at this time for the more expensive hotels and resorts. Bangkok has a vast array of accommodation. If you're splashing out there's only one place to go – the Oriental (➤ 54 and 57), regularly voted one of the world's top hotels.

## Guest Houses
- **Quality** varies, but most are clean and well maintained.
- In Bangkok's **Khao San Road** area a very basic room can be found for as little as 100 baht. Similar prices can be found in Chiang Mai, but standards at this cheap end are higher in Chiang Mai.

## Luxury Hotels
- Considering the quality available all over the country, **prices** for hotels are **very reasonable** compared to just about everywhere else in the world.
- Many of the luxury hotels are run by well-known **international chains** and offer all the amenities and facilities found in their western branches, often at half the price.

## Resort Hotels
- Many of Thailand's resort hotels double as spas and health centres.
- **Standards** are extremely high.
- Be aware that Thais will sometimes use the word "resort" for any hotel or guest house located **outside a town** or built-up area.

## Laundry
- Just about every hotel and guest house offers an efficient, clean and inexpensive laundry service. Clothing is returned washed, dried and ironed within 24 hours, although a faster service is available on request.

## Toilets
- **Western-style toilets** and bathroom facilities are increasingly the norm, but anywhere outside Bangkok and at smaller or older hotels you will encounter squat toilets, and water and a jug rather than toilet paper.

## Booking
- It is advisable to **book ahead** for the large Bangkok hotels, although Bangkok is overflowing with high-quality rooms.
- It is also a good idea to book hotels in advance in Chiang Mai, on Ko Phuket and in Pattaya **during festivals** (➤ 10–11) and in **December**, which is at the height of the tourist season.

## Tax and Tipping
- Luxury hotels generally charge a 10 per cent **service charge** and 7.5 per cent **government tax**.
- **Tipping** is not a requirement but is obviously appreciated.
- Guest houses and more reasonably priced hotels do not charge any tax, nor is tipping required.

> **Prices**
> The following symbols refer to the average cost of a double room.
>
> £ under 1,000 baht  ££ 1,000–4,000 baht  £££ over 4,000 baht

# Food and Drink

Thai cuisine, held by its many enthusiasts to be the best in the world, is incredibly diverse and sophisticated. It is generally very reasonably priced, too. Visitors will be pleasantly surprised how far their money goes in Thai restaurants, of which there are thousands. Bangkok, as well as most Thai cities, also offers a wide range of other cuisines, ranging from regional (Vietnamese, Cantonese, Filipino, Malay and Yunnanese – from Yunnan Province in southwest China) to international (Japanese, Korean, French, German, Italian and even Mexican). Thai cuisine may only have been popular in the West in the last 20 years, but now it shares pride of place with French, Italian and Chinese as one of the all-time great schools of cookery.

## Traditional Thai

- Thai cuisine, like that of neighbouring Southeast Asian countries, revolves around **rice**, although the national fondness for noodles shows the strength of Chinese influence.
- Thais eat two kinds of rice, the slightly fluffy, long-grain rice familiar in the west, eaten with a spoon and fork; and "sticky rice", usually served in the north and northeast, which is eaten with the fingers.
- **Noodles** are always eaten with chopsticks.

## Practical Tips

- Generally Thai restaurants serve all the **main dishes** at the same time.
- **Rice** plays a central role and is served in a large container.
- Diners are served with an individual portion of rice and then help themselves to small portions of curry, soup, fish, poultry and meat dishes.
- It is polite to **offer dishes** to guests, older people and women first.
- Thais are generally fastidiously clean and admire good manners. If you adhere to this, you will be considered a *pu-di angkrit*, an "English gentleman" (or lady)!
- Thais always eat rice and accompanying dishes using a **fork and spoon**. Knives are only used for European-style meals, as Thai food is generally served pre-cut into bite-sized pieces.
- There are no **fixed eating hours** in Thailand; Thais will eat at any time of the day or night. **Opening times** vary, but most restaurants are open seven days a week. Unlike many other countries there are no limitations on opening hours. Restaurants have very flexible hours, although they will probably be closed after 1 am. Some street food stalls might not open until as late as 10 pm and will continue serving until dawn.
- Thais eat when they are hungry, and also tend to eat less than Westerners, but more frequently. That said, restaurants catering to foreign visitors recognise the strange international habit of eating three fixed meals a day, and make allowances for it in their schedules. Hua Hin has a fine variety of Thai and international restaurants clustered in quite a small area. Ko Samui caters to just about every taste.

- Many of the top hotels around the country offer a great value **buffet lunch**. Check the local monthly listings magazines in Bangkok, Chiang Mai and Ko Phuket to see who's offering what.
- Bars and restaurants are banned from serving alcohol on royal birthdays, on holy days in the Buddhist calendar and during elections. In these cases, special allowances are generally made for foreign visitors.
- **Tipping** is not generally expected in Thailand, although many upmarket restaurants will add a 10 per cent service charge to a bill. Ordinary restaurants will not add any service charge, but like anywhere else in the world a small tip is usually much appreciated.

---

Bests...
...**floating restaurant:** Mae Nam (➤ 85)
...**Indian:** Ali Baba (➤ 145)
...**Isaan:** Vientiane Kitchen (➤ 60)
...**ocean view:** Old Siam (➤ 171)
...**seafood:** Captain's Choice (➤ 145)

...**Thai food:** Lemongrass (➤ 59), Spice Market (➤ 60)
...**traditional Thai surroundings:** Sala Thai (➤ 171)
...**unusual:** Cabbages & Condoms (➤ 58)
...**vegetarian:** Whole Earth (➤ 60)
...**view:** Border View (➤ 107)

---

Prices
Expect to pay per person for a meal, excluding drinks and service

£ under 200 baht  ££ 200–500 baht  £££ over 500 baht

---

# Shopping

Thailand offers some of the best shopping in Asia, also some of the most interesting and beautiful antiques and crafts anywhere in the world. The north, Chiang Mai in particular, is the centre for most local crafts, ranging from exquisite lacquerware plates and vases to colourful hill-tribe embroidered cloth bags, textiles and jewellery. Other crafts and items specific to Thailand include celadon (translucent Chinese porcelain, usually pale green), nielloware (vessels made of a mixture of silver, copper and sometimes lead decorated with incised patterns), rattan and pewter products.

## Markets

- Every village, town and city in Thailand has a **fresh produce** market.
- For Thais the fresh market is the **cornerstone** of their daily food shopping and therefore a fascinating place for the visitor to wander around.
- Many larger markets also incorporate a **dried goods** section, a good example of which is Warorot Market in Chiang Mai (➤ 92–94).
- Bangkok's enormous **Chatuchak Market** (➤ 51) sells everything from pets to opium pipes and pots to herbal remedies. You'll also find musical instruments, hill-tribe crafts, religious amulets, antiques, flowers, clothes imported from India and Nepal and camping gear.

- While each of Thailand's regions has its own specialities, crafts and produce from all over the country are available in Bangkok. You'll find the widest selection of goods and the best prices in Bangkok's markets and malls.

## How to Pay

- Street vendors will only accept **cash**.
- Many shops will take **credit cards** but some impose a 3–5 per cent surcharge for their use.
- Craft and antiques shops can usually arrange packing, shipping and documentation at reasonable prices.

## Antiquities and Buddha Images

- It is **illegal** to export valuable antiquities without a licence. Having said that, Thai artisans produce a range of authentic-looking reproduction antiquities.
- **A warning**: Buddha statues or amulets, whether old or new, should not be exported without a licence. This is because Thais do not wish Buddha images to be used as lampstands or for other non-religious purposes. They believe this demeans the Buddha.

## How to Bargain

- Thais generally like to bargain, so **expect to haggle** over prices, especially in small shops and from individual stalls, and particularly in Bangkok, Chiang Mai and Phuket.
- Bargaining doesn't apply in **fixed-price** establishments like supermarkets and department stores, but it *does* apply in markets and souvenir shops.
- The **general rule** is to offer half the price quoted and then slowly move towards a middle price that means you end up with a discount of between 25 and 30 per cent.
- The trick is to appear **friendly**, even jovial – but to bargain hard and to be prepared to walk away, still smiling. The chances are you'll be called back – probably also with a smile!

## Opening Hours

- Most **shops** open seven days a week from about 9 am to 5:30 pm.
- Many **convenience shops** stay open until 9 pm. In Bangkok, Chiang Mai and many resorts, 7-Eleven chain stores are open 24 hours.
- **Department stores** open from 10 am and close at either 9 or 10 pm.
- In the larger cities some **pharmacies** stay open 24 hours.
- **Markets** open as early as 3 am and many are finished by 8 am, others stay open until the early afternoon.

---

**Bests...**

...**crafts:** Baw Sang Village (► 108)

...**department store:** Central, Ploenchit (► 61)

...**fabrics:** Ban Boran Textiles (► 172)

...**hill-tribe crafts:** Hill Tribe Products Promotion Centre (► 108)

...**markets:** Chatuchak (► 51), Warorot (► 108), Night Market (► 108)

...**sarongs:** Sathorn Gold and Textile Museum (► 86)

...**silk:** Jim Thompson Silk Shop (► 61)

...**silver:** Thanon Wua Lai (► 108)

# Entertainment

## Information

- All major tourist destinations in Thailand have one or more **free listings magazines** readily available in bars, restaurants, cafés and travel agents.
- Bangkok has *Bangkok Metro Magazine* – not free, but an excellent listings magazine.
- Nearly every provincial capital has a Tourist Authority of Thailand office with a wide range of information.

## Festivals and Events

- Thailand offers a huge number of **festivals** and **temple fairs** during the year. Across the country there is always something going on, especially between late October and April (► 10–11). **Dates** can vary from year to year – check with the tourist office or what's on magazines.
- Among the most important nationwide festivals are **Songkran** (traditional Thai New Year, ► 10) and **Loy Krathong,** at November full moon (► 11).

## Nightlife

- Thailand's nightlife is legendary – and contrary to some western opinion it does not just revolve around the sex trade. Thais take their free time seriously, and love nothing better than eating, drinking and dancing.
- Most **bars** open late afternoon or early evening. Under current legislation, bars and discos have to close at 1 or 2 am, depending on their location.
- Bangkok is Thailand's main nightlife venue, but good **nightclubs** and **bars** can be found in Pattaya (► 124), on Ko Phuket (► 172), Ko Samui (► 148) and to a lesser extent in Chiang Mai (► 108).
- **Live music** is popular everywhere, although it will generally be Thai music or Thai versions of well-known western hits.

## Outdoor Activities

- Northern Thailand has great opportunities for **trekking** (► 95–97 and 108), with the added attraction of visiting various hill tribes.
- **Mountain biking, white-water rafting** and **rock climbing** (► 161) opportunities are also excellent throughout the country.
- Southern Thailand, especially the Andaman Coast, offers excellent possibilities for **diving and snorkelling**. The area around the **Similan Islands** (► 164) is considered one of the greatest dive sites in the world.
- The coastal destinations, Ko Phuket (► 164), Ko Samui (► 134–137), Hua Hin (► 130–131) and Pattaya (► 120), provide all kinds of **watersports**, including windsurfing, parasailing and yachting.

## Sport

- *Muay thai*, Thai kick-boxing, is Thailand's national sport. It's a tough activity where, in addition to gloved fists, elbows, knees, feet and indeed any part of the body (except the head) can be used to strike the opponent. It's skilled, fast-moving and can be very entertaining. The most popular venues are **Lumpini Boxing Stadium** (Thanon Rama IV, near Lumpini Park, Bangkok, tel: 02 251 4303), and **Ratchadamnoen Boxing Stadium** (1 Thanon Ratchadamnoen Nok, Bangkok, tel: 02 281 4205).
- Although *muay thai* is the national sport, **football** is the most popular spectator sport. There's big local support for the English teams Manchester United and Liverpool, while Everton's deal to carry a Thai brewery's logo on its team shirts has won that club a large following, too.

# Bangkok

Getting Your Bearings 40 – 41
In Three Days 42 – 43
Don't Miss 44 – 51
At Your Leisure 52 – 55
Where To 56 – 62

# Getting Your Bearings

Most visitors to Thailand arrive in Bangkok, the country's exciting metropolis. Thoroughly modern, and with a vibrant financial centre and shining skyscrapers, it is also an historic capital steeped in the traditions of its beloved royal family and the Buddhist religion. Bangkok is known the world over for the infamous red-light district of Patpong and the budget travellers who swarm to Khao San Road, but it is also the place Thais know as the "City of Angels", with glittering palaces, magnificent temples and giant golden Buddhas.

Crazy little three-wheeled *tuk-tuks* buzz around streets crammed with stalls tossing together exquisite dishes. You can find a serenity of sorts on the mighty Chao Phraya River with a ride on a traditional longtail boat or a luxurious teak barge that is the naval equivalent of the *Orient Express*. Or take the air-conditioned Skytrain railway system that whizzes high above the crowded streets. A single line underground metropolitan railway system, the MRT, opened in 2004 and runs from Bangkok's main railway station, Hua Lamphong, to Bang Sue, near the northern bus terminal. There are stops in all the main tourist and hotel zones: Rama IV Road, Silom, Sukhumvit and Asok Road, and at the Chatuchak Market.

Explore the canal network that gave Bangkok its nickname "Venice of the East" and the tiny alleyways of colourful Chinatown packed with gold shops and exotic produce. Follow in the footsteps of authors from Joseph Conrad to Graham Greene with tea in one of the best hotels in the world, the Oriental. Then enjoy endless shopping opportunities, from the mammoth weekend Chatuchak Market to the air-conditioned shopping malls, and visit the enormous treasure house of the National Museum, telling the story of Thailand's history and royal family.

Royal Barge Museum

PHRA PINKLAO BRIDGE

TH

THANON ARUN AMARIN

National Museum **5**

**6** Khao San Road

*Sanam Luang*

Grand Palace and Wat Phra Kaeo **1**

TH SANAM CHAI

THANON MAHARAT

TH

Wat Arun

**2** Wat Po

TH TRI PHET

THANON PRACHA THIPOK

Previous page: The Grand Palace, site of ceremonial occasions

Left: Chinese figures guard Bangkok's Wat Po

## ★ Don't Miss

1 Grand Palace and Wat Phra Kaeo ➤ 44
2 Wat Po ➤ 47
3 Chao Phraya River ➤ 49
4 Chatuchak Market ➤ 51

## At Your Leisure

5 National Museum ➤ 52
6 Khao San Road ➤ 52
7 Vimanmek Teak Palace ➤ 52
8 Jim Thompson's House ➤ 53
9 Patpong ➤ 54
10 The Oriental ➤ 54
11 Chinatown ➤ 55

THANON RATCHAWITHI

7 Vimanmek Teak Palace

Dusit Zoo

Chatuchak Market 4

SAMSEN

THANON

RAMA V

DUSIT

SRI AYUTTHAYA

THANON

SAWANKHALOK

Chitralada Palace

TH. WISUT KASAT

RATCHADAMNOEN

THANON

PHITSANULOK

THANON

THANON LAN LUANG

EXPRESSWAY

THANON PETCHABURI

BAMRUNG

THANON WORA CHAK

MUANG

KRUNG KASEM

YOMMARAT

Jim Thompson's House

8

THONG

BANTHAT

THANON

RAMA 1

PHAYATHAI

World Trade Centre

TH Chinatown

11

THANON YAOWARAT

CHAROEN

THANON

KRUNG

THANON

RAMA IV

PATHUM WAN

Chulalongkorn University

THANON RATCHADAMRI

3 Chao Phraya River

TH CHAROEN NAKHON

TH CHAROEN KRUNG

EXPRESSWAY

RAMA IV

Snake Farm

Lumphini Park

TH SI PHRAYA

THANON SURAWONG

9 Patpong

THANON

SILOM

10 Oriental Hotel

TAKSIN BRIDGE

THANON SATHON TAI

The enigmatic Chao Phraya River

0 — 1 km
0 — 1 mile

Take in Thailand's national treasures, the country's most magnificent palace, temple and museum, relax on Chao Phraya River and explore the streets of Chinatown.

# Bangkok in Three Days

## Day One

### Morning
Get up early to beat the crowds at the **❶ Grand Palace** (above and left, ➤ 44–46), which opens at 8:30 am. Have lunch at one of the cafés near the Grand Palace. Turn left at the palace entrance on to Thanon Na Phralan and walk past Silpakorn University for Fine Arts and over Thanon Mahathat to the Tha Chang Pier on the **❸ Chao Phraya River** (➤ 49–50).

### Afternoon
Take the River Express to Tha Tien for **❷ Wat Po** (➤ 47–48). Spend an hour exploring and end with an hour-long traditional Thai massage at the highly acclaimed massage school.

### Evening
Jump in a *tuk-tuk* to
**9 Patpong** (right, ► 54), the
legendary red-light district,
which also has a vibrant night
market and bar scene.

# Day Two

### Morning
Start the day at the **5 National
Museum** (► 52) where you will
need several hours to take it
all in. Its simple but pleasant
café is a good spot for a
coffee. Afterwards, you can
walk (or take a taxi) to the
river by turning right out of
the entrance on Thanon Na
Phra That and taking the first
right on to Thanon Phra Chan.
The River Express stop of the
same name is at the end of
this road, but if you continue
the short distance to the Tha
Maharat stop there are riverside restaurants that make a
pleasant stop for lunch.

### Afternoon
Take the River Express boat to **11 Chinatown** (► 55), getting off at the
Tha Rachawong stop, less than 10 minutes away. Wander around the
absorbing alleyways or follow the **walk** (► 174–176), which guides you
through the maze to hidden temples.

# Day Three

If you are here on a Saturday or Sunday spend a day at the weekend-only
**4 Chatuchak Market** (below, ► 51) either to shop or just marvel at the

weird and wonderful
goods on sale, from
traditional musical
instruments to Siamese
fighting fish. Have
lunch in one of the air-
conditioned restaurants
in the "Dream Section"
of the market. If a
weekend isn't included
in your trip, try out
**6 Khao San Road** instead
for street circus and a
lively atmosphere (► 52).

# ❶ Grand Palace and Wat Phra Kaeo

A combination of beautiful serenity and dazzling over-the-top royal splendour, the magnificent Grand Palace is the perfect first stop for any visitor to Bangkok. It offers a spectacular introduction to the twin themes that weave through almost every aspect of Thai life: Buddhism and royalty. Undoubtedly at the heart of the capital, this city within a city also contains the most sacred of all the country's many Buddha images.

Allow at least a couple of hours to see the highlights of this 24ha (59-acre) walled complex. A fair amount of walking is involved, queues can eat into your time and this is not a place to rush. Admission includes a brochure, which is hard to read and sadly lacking in detail, although the map covering the main buildings is useful for finding your way around.

More than 100 mansions, halls, pavilions and temples with **exquisite mosaic-encrusted spires** and pillars make up a fascinating combination of Victorian, Italian Renaissance and other styles, the oldest of which dates back 200 years.

Beautiful **murals** found inside the compound walls show the *Ramakien*, the Thai version of the Hindu epic, the *Ramayana*. Lovingly restored, they date from King Rama I (1782–1809).

Head first to the main attraction, the

**Wat Phra Kaeo is doubly sacred because of its royal associations**

**Emerald Buddha**, housed in **Wat Phra Kaeo**, a glitteringly decorative royal chapel. The Buddha is in fact made of jade, not emerald, and at only 60cm (1.5-feet) high is an almost invisible figure, perched high on a mountain of gold. It is the holiest Buddhist site in Thailand. It's unclear when the figure – Thailand's most revered Buddha image – was made, but historical records trace its origins back at least to the 15th century. It reached Bangkok at the end of an eventful journey from the north, and was once in its colourful history stolen by Laotian forces and then recovered in battle by the outraged Siamese.

In a row on the northern side of the temple are the Phra Si Ratana, a golden *chedi* (► 12 and 194), Phra Mondop, containing a Buddhist library not open to the public, and Prasad Phra Thep Bidom, the royal pantheon.

Outside the *wat* complex, to the south, is the surprisingly low-key **Amarindra Winichai Hall** (Audience Hall), where at one time the people petitioned the king. Every new king spends the first night after his coronation here, where coronation ceremonies still take place. King Bhumibol makes his birthday speech at the Winichai Hall.

The next structure along to the west is **Chakri-Mahasprasad Hall**, once the royal harem. Although British-designed, Siamese towers were added at the request of concerned court elders, who wanted the building to look traditional, and not too European. The tallest, central spire holds the ashes of the Chakri kings, the ones on either side contain those of the princes.

West again is the serene **Dusit Hall**. This funerary hall, modelled on the one at Ayutthaya (► 72–74), is still used for members of the royal family when they are lying in state.

At the end of your visit, make the **Wat Phra Kaeo Museum**, which houses a collection of gifts left for the Emerald Buddha, your final stop (► 46).

Grand Palace is only sometimes used for royal occasions

A detail of Kinnaree at the temple of Wat Phra Kaeo

## TAKING A BREAK

Sip a chilled coconut water on the usually uncrowded wooden
veranda of the **café** next to the Wat Phra Kaeo Museum.

🕂 200 B3  ✉ Naphralan Road  ☎ 02 623 500 and 02 222 0034,
www.palaces.thai.net  🕐 Daily 8:30–3:30  🚌 8, 12  💷 Expensive

---

### GRAND PALACE AND WAT PHRA KAEO: INSIDE INFO

**Top tips** The best time to visit is the **early morning**, when the heat and crowds
are at their most bearable.
- Do not wear **clothes** that reveal arms or legs, or even casual clothes or
footwear like vests, shorts, sarongs, mini-skirts, slip-on sandals or flip-flops. It is
considered disrespectful and you will be refused admittance. You may, however,
be able to borrow suitable attire from the office at the entrance.
- Consider taking one of the **English-language guided tours** (four times a
day between 10 am and 2 pm; 100 baht) to learn about the history of the many
buildings. A credit card or passport is required as deposit for the tape recorder
and headphones.
- The **entrance fee** includes entry to the Vimanmek Teak Palace (► 52–53), the
Royal Thai Decorations and Coins Pavilion in the palace grounds, and a
brochure which covers the main buildings.

**Hidden gem** Most visitors miss the **Wat Phra Kaeo Museum**, tucked away at
the opposite end of the complex. Although the exhibits are not of major interest, it offers an oasis of cool away from the Grand Palace crowds and is the
perfect antidote to all the glitz. Pad barefoot on polished wooden floors among
paraphernalia dedicated as offerings to the Emerald Buddha. This endearing
collection of gifts includes porcelain from Europe, an inlaid mother-of-pearl
royal couch and cabinets of brightly coloured Buddha images, as well as tools
and tweezers used in repairs.

# 2 Wat Po

This superlative royal monastery is not only the city's largest and oldest but also contains the country's longest reclining Buddha. Dotted with *chedis*, pagodas and *stupas* (➤ 12 and 194), this walled complex was built during the reigns of King Rama I and King Rama III by the best craftsmen in the land. Established as the country's first centre of education and Thai arts, it continues the role to this day as a living complex peopled with masseuses, astrologers and schoolchildren. At the same time, it is a peaceful oasis of beautifully landscaped areas with waterfalls, rock gardens, stone animals and tree-filled courtyards.

The most interesting sights are clustered around the northern section of the monastery. From the Thai Wang Road entrance, make the **Reclining Buddha** your first stop. The massive 46m-long (150 foot) Buddha looks as if it has been squeezed into the *viharn* (➤ 12 and 194). Gleaming gold leaf covers the stuccoed brick statue of the dying Buddha who is just about to enter Nirvana, and exquisite murals cover the walls. Make sure you walk all the way around the figure to see its feet, which are inlaid with mother-of-pearl, showing the 108 symbols of Enlightenment.

Leaving through the same door that you entered, walk past the waterfall on your right and between the two guarding "**rock giants**". There are fortune-tellers and a souvenir kiosk/snack bar on the left.

Turn right where **four towering pagodas** with glazed tiling and mosaics commemorate the first kings of the Chakri dynasty, founded in 1782.

On the left is the main **chapel of Phra Uposatha**, at the heart of the monastery, surrounded by a marble wall with eight sheltered gates and stone carvings of natural scenes. Balustrades with 152 reliefs of the Hindu epic the *Ramayana* (a Sanskrit poem regarded as sacred by the Hindus) were taken from the ruins at Ayutthaya; rubbings from the panels are sold at the temple and

Above: A revered Bodhi tree in the temple grounds

Above left: A detail from the medicine pavilion

Left: A stone carving detail

throughout Thailand. Walk a quarter of the way around the cloisters to the **Contorted Hermit Mount** to enter. It is covered with stone statues of exercising hermits, which were used to teach illiterate people about illnesses and massage methods. Inside is a seated Buddha in the position of meditation (► 14). Cloisters all the way around display hundreds of gold-leaf Buddha images in glass frames as well as Buddhist poems.

At the southern end of the monastery, a **massage school** functions as the national headquarters for Thai massage and medicine. If you only have one massage in Thailand, this is the place to have it. Traditional Thai massage is always applied with the recipient fully clothed, no appointment is necessary.

**TAKING A BREAK**

There is a small **snack bar** in the temple compound, which is fine for a cold drink.

The Reclining Buddha gleams with gold leaf

🕂 200 B2  ✉ Sanam Chai Road and Maharaj Road  ☎ 02 222 0933
🕐 Daily 9–5  🚌 6, 8, 12  💷 Inexpensive

## WAT PO: INSIDE INFO

**Top tips** Dress **respectfully** and cover up, although you can borrow a wrap to see the Reclining Buddha.
• Visitors are also requested to act **calmly and politely**.
• The **guidebook** for sale inside the Reclining Buddha chapel and at the entrance is beautifully produced, has a good map and unusually lively text.
• **No entrance** is permitted between noon and 1 pm.

**Ones to miss** The **crocodile pond and the belfry** are not worth seeking out.

# 3 Chao Phraya River

The majestic waters of the "River of Kings" which snakes its way through the city, provide both a fascinating perspective on the city and a peaceful thoroughfare. The river, as well as many smaller canals, or *khlong*, gave Bangkok the title "Venice of the East". Colourful floating markets cruise the waterway and luxury hotels and ancient temples line its banks. A concentration of major attractions from the National Museum and the Grand Palace down to Wat Po and Wat Arun form a "royal mile", all serviced by convenient pier stops.

Two river boat services ply up and down the Chao Phraya: the public commuter service, crowded but very cheap, and the Express Boat company's tourist line (► 50), which offers a day's 75 baht ticket allowing you to jump off or jump on at any point. A guide aboard every boat explains the sights en route. Industrial tugs, rice barges and longtail boats (narrow boats with high-powered engines attached by a pole or "tail") buzz along the waters, while slow river ferries zigzag from bank to bank.

**Below left: Traditional transport takes to the water**

An hour loop on a chartered longtail boat from **Tha Chang**, the pier near to the Grand Palace, costs around 400 baht. It passes the Royal Barge Museum and Wat Arun, but you will need to arrange in advance if you want to visit either of these attractions. Your boat driver may stop to buy a kebab from another vessel or even point out a stalking iguana, but these

**Below: The river is the heart of Bangkok**

tours are not officially guided. It is a great way to relax and catch a glimpse of waterside life, basic canalside homes and upmarket compounds, cruise past tree-lined banks and brightly coloured boats festooned with flowers, and catch glimpses into back gardens dotted with spirit houses (➤ 8–9).

When darkness falls, the river sparkles with the reflections of the many bankside illuminations. An **evening cruise** is the best way to see the lights of **Wat Arun**, (open 7:30–5:30), and **Rama IX Bridge**, the longest single-span suspension bridge in the world.

**Bangkok's backwaters can be explored by boat**

**River terrace of the Oriental**

## TAKING A BREAK

Both dinner and sunset cocktail cruises are offered by riverside hotels like the **Oriental** (tel: 02 659 9000, ➤ 54 and 57) and the **Marriott Resort and Spa** (tel: 02 476 0022).

200 C2

## CHAO PHRAYA RIVER: INSIDE INFO

**Top tips** Two river boat lines operate on the Chao Praya River. The cheaper of them is the regular public service.

- Boats are frequent (about every 15 minutes) but crowded.
- For a little more money (75 baht) you can buy a ticket that allows you to use the Chao Praya Express Boat company service (tel: 02 222 56179) from 9:30 am to 3 pm, jumping on and off at any of the stops en route. The boats have a guide aboard and the ticket includes a useful map of the river and its attractions.
- Longtail boat operators also ply for business, particularly at the Pra Athit pier, next to the Saphan Taksin Skytrain station. They demand sometimes ridiculously inflated prices, so bargain keenly.

# ④Chatuchak Market

This mammoth market, with more than 6,000 stalls, is a fascinating collection of everything from fighting cocks and poodle-grooming to towering plants and fake flowers. Thailand's best venue for a shopping spree makes for a weekend outing (it's only open on Saturday and Sunday) where you can wander among octagenarian violinists, young buskers and locals looking for the latest in interior decor.

*Colourful goods are in plentiful supply*

Arrive at around 9 am to beat the crowds. If you are a serious shopper, **Nancy Chandler's Map of Bangkok** (available from souvenir shops in tourist areas) shows all the stalls in detail. The clock tower in the centre is a good landmark and meeting point.

Types of goods for sale are grouped together in sections, each with their own distinct personality.

The "**Dream Section**" (indicated by a large sign) has toilets, restaurants, upmarket household goods, clothes stalls and cash dispensers. This is a good place to go if the noisy local flavour gets too much. Otherwise there are stalls selling cheaper household goods, second-hand trainers, traditional lacquerware, antiques and yoghurt fruitshakes. You will probably find an area you feel particularly at home in, whether you immerse yourself in the rattan goods and floating candles or gawp at the bizarre selection of pets which includes everything from beetles to iguanas (many imported illegally). Bargain, but politely.

### TAKING A BREAK

*Bright, young things hunt for the latest fashions*

The best area of the market to get something to eat is in the **Dream Section**, which has plenty of air-conditioned places.

✚ 200 F5  ✉ Thanon Phahonyothin  🕐 Weekends 8–6  🚌 2, 3, 9, 10, 13; Skytrain and MRT: Mo Chit, Chatuchak Park  🎟 Free

# At Your Leisure

### 5 National Museum

This delightful national institution, with its spacious lawns and separate buildings, was originally a palace. A good map with a brief guide is given free with the entrance fee. Don't miss the **Red House**, once the private living quarters of Queen Sri Suriye, sister of King Rama I, which contains her slippers. Other highlights are the Elephant Armoury and the royal chariot, articles from the Grand Palace theatre and the games room. A visit could be combined with the **National Gallery** near by, which has an interesting collection of Thai art. Guided tours in English on Wednesday and Thursday at 9:30 am focus on specific aspects of the museum and are very worthwhile.

➕ 200 B3  ✉ Thanon Naphrathat
☎ 02 224 1333  🕐 Wed–Sun 9–4
🚌 3, 6, 38  💷 Inexpensive

### 6 Khao San Road

The street circus that is Khao San Road attracts tourists from around the world. Squeezed into a strip of under a kilometre are stalls three-deep selling clothes, food and souvenirs, as well as a maze of streets with cramped, basic travellers' accommodation. Although it is very much youth and budget orientated and crawling with backpackers, Khao San Road is always lively and friendly and offers comforting international relief when Bangkok gets too much.

This is where to come for an English breakfast, restaurants showing American films and English- and other language books. The city's cheapest internet connections are found here and travel agents fight for attention. Towards the beginning of the evening the music cranks up and the street becomes a riot of neon. Tourists eat banana pancakes in the street pursued by a constant parade of *tuk-tuks* and vendors.

➕ 200 B3

### 7 Vimanmek Teak Palace

This sumptuous royal mansion is the largest golden teak building in the world, with just under 100 rooms. It was built by Rama V, King Chulalongkorn in 1868 as a summer retreat on Ko Si Chang

Buddhaisawan Chapel at the National Museum, Bangkok

**Vimanmek Teak Palace is splendid and serene inside and out, with extensive surrounding gardens**

island and then was moved here piece by piece in 1910. A guided tour (included in the entrance fee) takes you around the interior, with its European influences.

Also in the compound of this Dusit palace is a building housing a collection of crafts donated by Queen Sirikit, the present queen, and another displaying King Bhumibol's photography. Traditional **Thai dancing** is performed in the grounds daily at 10:30 am and 2 pm. The same dress rules apply here as at the Grand Palace (▶ 46).

⊞ 200 C4 ✉ Thanon Ratchawithi
☎ 02 281 1569; www.palacesthai.net
🕓 Daily 9:30–4 (guided tour only every 30 minutes, last tour 3:15 pm) 🚌 3 or 10 🎫 Inexpensive (free with a Grand Palace ticket)

## 🏠 Jim Thompson's House

Jim Thompson, an American architect, adventurer and entrepreneur, and Thailand's most famous expatriate, is credited with single-handedly reviving the country's ancient tradition of silk-weaving. His home is actually six teak houses (most over 200 years old), which he dismantled and reconstructed on this canalside site around a tropical garden and flower-filled courtyard, and then crammed with antiques.

The highly informative compulsory tour tells how he loyally followed traditional Thai building practices, even consulting an astrologer for an auspicious date to move in.

Jim Thompson disappeared in Malaysia's Cameron Highlands in 1967 under mysterious circumstances; several conspiracy theories are still alive today. One says he was eaten by a tiger, another that

**The elegant sitting room in the house of adventurer Jim Thompson**

American intelligence agents killed him. The latest theory is that he was run over by a truck and then buried by the frightened driver.

🚩 201 D3 ✉ 6 Soi Kasemsan 2, Thanon Rama I ☎ 02 216 7368 🕐 Daily 9–5 (tours every 45 minutes, last tour 4:30) 🚈 Skytrain: Siam Square 💷 Moderate

## City Sanctuaries

The secret to surviving hot and hectic Bangkok is to make regular escapes to oases of cool and calm.
• Chao Phraya River (➤ 49)
• High tea at the luxurious **Oriental Hotel** (➤ 54, 57)
• **Lumphini Park**'s lake and lawns, the city's lung and very popular with the locals. Go early at around 7 am to see Chinese practising *tai chi*, or take a boat or a picnic.
• The **Ice Skating Rink**, 8th floor of the World Trade Centre, where you can watch professionals and enjoy the cooling temperatures, or take to the ice yourself on rented skates.

## 🟎 Patpong

Crammed into four tiny streets, or *sois*, Patpong is Bangkok's notorious red-light district – a hotbed of go-go bars and sex shows that are sadly pathetic rather than erotic. If you are tempted to go into a bar, check the prices of drinks first – you may be charged an extortionate rate.

Patpong, however, is also a lively area where locals socialise and there's a popular **night market** frequented by tourists who are thrust menu cards detailing a variety of sex acts on offer. There are a handful of good restaurants (Barbican and Roma) and international designer stores. Food outlets such as KFC and Starbucks are here if you need to seek refuge in anonymous chains.

🚩 201 E1 ✉ Between Thanon Silom and Suriwong

## 🔟 The Oriental

This riverside hotel was set up by the founders of the Singapore Raffles Hotel in 1876. It is still considered one of the best hotels in the world, offering colonial-style luxury at a

The Oriental Hotel, dripping with elegance and luxury

## Bangkok for Kids
- Take a *tuk-tuk*, river boat or Skytrain.
- Visit **Dusit Zoo** (Thanon Ratwithi, open daily 8–6, inexpensive), with its playground and boats on a lake – avoid going on Sunday when it can get crowded.
- If you are going to the **Vimanmek Teak Palace** (➤ 52) call in at the small **Elephant Museum** in the palace grounds.
- Watch cobras being milked at the **Snake Farm** (Thanon Rama IV and Henri Dunant, tel: 02 252 0161, open Mon–Fri 8:30–4, Sat–Sun 8:30–noon, moderate).
- Go on a treasure hunt through **Chinatown** (➤ 174).

high price. It's a great place to go for tea or a drink. The **Authors' Lounge** is named after world-famous authors such as Somerset Maugham, Joseph Conrad and even Barbara Cartland, who made the hotel their temporary home. Traditional English high tea (sandwiches, cakes, biscuits and tea) is served in the lounge among potted palms and wicker furniture. Much more than just a hotel, it has a cultural programme, a Thai cookery course and its own floating restaurant.

➕ 200 C1 ✉ 48 Oriental Avenue, off Thanon Charoen Krung
☎ 02 659 9000,
www.mandarinoriental.com
🚃 Skytrain: Saphan Taksin; River Express: Oriental 💰 Expensive

## ⑪ Chinatown
This 200-year-old trading site with tiny, characterful streets crammed with exotic goods and dotted with temples is an atmospheric place for

wandering (➤ 174). Pedestrianised, stall-filled **Sampeng Lane** (Soi Wanit) is its focus, with the Indian Market, selling mostly fabrics, at the northern end. **Wat Leng Noi Yi** is the most interesting of the area's several temples, full of Chinese deities as well as a workshop making paper cars, fridges and other household representations for funerals – the Chinese burn these symbols of material wealth to ensure prosperity for their dead loved ones.

➕ 200 C2 🚃 River Express: Tha Ratchawong

# Where to... Stay

## Prices
Expect to pay per double room
£ under 1,000 baht  ££ 1,000–4,000 baht  £££ over 4,000 baht

## A-One Inn £
You've got the best of both worlds with this upmarket guest house. It's situated in a quiet lane, but in the heart of Bangkok's busiest shopping district. The rooms are comfortable, with air-conditioning and satellite TV. The café here is a good place to relax after a hot day on the busy streets. The friendly staff create a family atmosphere. A-One is within walking distance of Siam Square, the World Trade Centre complex and Jim Thompson's House (▶ 53–54).

**⊞ 201 E3 ⊠ 25/13 Soi Kasem San 1, Thanon Rama I, 30 ☎ 02 215 3029, fax: 02 216 4771, email: aoneinn@ thaimail.com, www.aoneinn.com ⊟ Siam**

## Asia Bangkok ££
This hotel is well located for the Siam Discovery Centre, Siam Square and the World Trade Centre. Excellent facilities include two large swimming pools, a sauna and health club. Rooms are tastefully decorated, with large marble bathrooms. What sets the Asia apart from other moderately priced hotels are its Vietnamese, Chinese and Brazilian restaurants. The Brazilian Rio Grill, a typical *churrascaria*, offering red and white meat grilled on skewers, is unique in Bangkok.

**⊞ 201 E3 ⊠ 296 Thanon Phayathai ☎ 02 215 0808, fax: 02 215 4660, email: info@asiahotel.co.th, www.asiahotel.co.th ⊟ Ratchathewi**

## Beaufort Sukhothai £££
The Beaufort Sukhothai is an exquisite luxury hotel, with much of its décor inspired by the arts and crafts of Thailand's one-time capital, Sukhothai (▶ 75–77). Although located on one of Bangkok's busiest roads, the hotel is set well back and provides a quiet oasis. All rooms and suites are decorated with beautiful Thai silks, teak furniture and artefacts you'd usually expect only to find in museums. The teak-floored bathrooms are enormous. Internet access is available from all rooms. The hotel's shopping arcade features outlets specialising in Thai paintings, sculptures and wood-carving. The Sukhothai has two of Bangkok's top restaurants, the sumptuous Celadon (▶ 58), and the Italian La Scala.

**⊞ 201 E1 ⊠ 13/3 Thanon Sathorn Tai ☎ 02 344 8888, fax: 02 344 8889, email: beaufort@ksc11.th.com, www.sukhothai.com ⊟ Saladaeng (the subway and Skytrain stations are some distance; a taxi is the best option)**

## Dusit Thani £££
The flagship of the Dusit hotel group, this was Bangkok's first high-rise hotel. It is in the heart of the Silom Road business district and close to the main nightlife area, Patpong (▶ 54). The rooms are sumptuous, with much use made of silk and other Thai fabrics, as well as teak furniture. The Dusit is famous for its restaurants, of which there are seven in all, and two bars. The rooftop D'Sens (French) restaurant has stunning views of the Bangkok skyline and overlooks the city's premier park, Lumphini. Other unusual facilities include an outdoor driving range, so don't forget your golf clubs.

**⊞ 200 E1 ⊠ 946 Thanon Rama IV ☎ 02 200 9000, fax: 02 236 6400, email: dusitbkk@dusit.com, www.dusit.com ⊟ Saladaeng**

## Swissotel Nai Lert Park £££
This luxury hotel, now part of the Raffles group, is set on 3.5ha (8.5 acres) of beautiful gardens. It has

its own fertility shrine, set up by a Thai businessman, who had it constructed to honour the female spirit that supposedly resides in the old banyan tree in the hotel grounds. Today people, mostly women, come to make offerings of carved wooden and stone phalluses to aid fertility. The grounds contain a large swimming pool, attractive Thai pavilions, or *sala*, and pretty ornamental bridges. All rooms have their own private balcony either overlooking the gardens or the Bangkok skyline. Other facilities include the excellent Amrita Fitness Club and Spa.

➕ 201 F3 ✉ 2 Thanon Witthayu ☎ 02 253 0123, fax: 02 253 6509, email: ash-usbangkok-nailertpark @swissotel.com, www.swissotel.com 🚉 Ploenchit

## The Oriental £££

Plenty of history is attached to this place, which has long been Bangkok's top hotel, and is regularly voted the best hotel in the world. Recently it has acquired many rivals in terms of luxury – but not character. Nowhere else boasts an Authors' Lounge, once frequented by Joseph Conrad, Somerset Maugham and Graham Greene. Suites are all named either after authors who have stayed here or ships that would have stood at anchor on the Chao Phraya River during Conrad's day. Every hotel facility is available and the standard of service is unsurpassed.

➕ 200 C1 ✉ 48 Oriental Avenue ☎ 02 659 9000, fax: 02 659 0000, email: orbkk-enquiry@mohg.com, www.mandarinoriental.com 🚉 Saphan Taksin

## Four Seasons £££

From the fabulous foyer to the picture-perfect rooms, the Four Seasons oozes class and an old-fashioned oriental charm. Afternoon tea is an experience not to be missed. Three of Bangkok's finest restaurants are within the hotel confines, the **Spice Market** (Thai, ▶ 60), **Biscotti** (Italian) and **Shintaro** (Japanese). Amenities include aerobics, ballroom dancing, yoga and an excellent spa. Its central location, facing the Royal Bangkok Sports Club, is perfect for shopping trips to the World Trade Centre and a visit to the Erawan Shrine, one of Bangkok's best-known religious symbols (▶ 8).

➕ 201 E2 ✉ 155 Thanon Ratchadamri ☎ 02 250 1000, fax: 02 253 9195, email: reservations.bkk@ fourseasons.co, www.fourseasons.com 🚉 Ratchadamri

## Royal ££

Having now undergone extensive renovations, the Royal, one of Bangkok's oldest and most venerable hotels, is an excellent bargain. It is situated on Ratanakosin Island, Bangkok's historical heart, close to the Grand Palace (▶ 44–46), the National Museum (▶ 52) and Wat Po (▶ 47–48). The rooms are comfortable. Restaurants are standard and there is a good swimming pool. What sets the place apart is its great location.

➕ 200 B3 ✉ 2 Thanon Ratchadamnoen Klang ☎ 02 222 9111, fax: 02 224 2083, email: reservation@ ratanakosin-hotel.com 🚉 No subway or Skytrain station near by; it is best to take a taxi

## Shangri-La £££

A huge, luxury, riverside property, and one of Bangkok's three best hotels, the Shangri-La is regularly voted on to the list of the world's finest hotels. It offers absolutely everything, including a helicopter transfer service to Don Muang International Airport. High tea (sandwiches, cakes, biscuits and tea) is served every afternoon in the foyer-lounge. Rooms are large, with great views of the busy river below. The beautifully landscaped gardens are a breath of fresh air after Bangkok's crowded streets.

➕ 200 C1 ✉ 89 Soi Wat Suan Plu, Thanon Charoen Krung ☎ 02 236 7777, fax: 02 236 8579, email: shangbg@ksc.th.com, www.shangri-la.com 🚉 Saphan Taksin

# Where to...
# Eat and Drink

### Prices

Expect to pay per person for a three-course meal, excluding drinks and service
£ under 200 baht  ££ 200–500 baht  £££ over 500 baht

## Bei Otto £££

Established in 1984, this German restaurant with a *bierhaus*, a delicatessen and its own bakery, is one of Bangkok's oldest international restaurants. Popular dishes include Bavarian grilled pork knuckle with potato dumplings and *sauerkraut*, the meat platter *wiener schnitzel* and a selection of cakes. Part of the pleasure of eating here is the knowledge that much of the food is home-made. As you would expect, Bei Otto carries a fine selection of German wines and beers.

Apart from the German restaurant, the premises also houses a good

European restaurant serving many international dishes such as pasta, steak and chips, roast beef and similar dishes.

✚ 201 off F2  ⊠ 1 Sukhumvit Soi 20
☎ 02 260 0869  ⊙ Daily 11 am–1 am, delicatessen 8 am–midnight  🚇 Asoke

## Bourbon Street ££

Bangkok ought to be one of the last cities in the world that you'd expect to find Cajun-Creole cooking, but Bourbon Street has been quietly turning out great dishes for more than 15 years. There's gumbo, blackened red fish, three different choices of jambalaya, barbecued baby back pork ribs and Cajun boiled crawfish, to name just a few. Split into two sections, the bar offers a variety of sports on TV, the restaurant a more relaxed atmosphere. On Tuesday nights there's an "all you can eat" Mexican buffet.

✚ 201 off F2  ⊠ 29 Sukhumvit Soi 22, Washington Square  ☎ 02 259 0328
⊙ Daily 7 am–1 am  🚇 Phrom Phong

## Cabbages and Condoms ££

A great value-for-money place with a serious underlying theme. This particular branch of the chain of Thai restaurants, owned by family-planning campaigner Mechai Viravaidya, was set up in 1986. Furnishings include flower arrangements made from condoms and a carpet embellished with a condom design. The food is generally excellent, with the family-planning theme extending to some of the names of dishes. Why not try the spicy condom salad? The beer garden outside is a great place to sit and drink *bier sot* (draught beer).

On leaving, instead of a dinner mint, you get a c

✚ 201 off F2  ⊠ 10 Sukh
12  ☎ 02 229 4610  🚇 Da
🚇 Asoke

## Celadon £££

Set amid a lotus-filled pond, Celadon is another classic Thai restaurant. Dine either in the *sala*, where the decor has a very contemporary Thai feel, or the beautiful garden. The surroundings are calm, quiet and elegant for busy downtown Sathorn. Specialities such as chicken in coconut and *galingal* (ginger) soup, deep-fried *garoupa* (a white fish popular in Southeast Asia) with dry curry, and chicken grilled in screwpine leaves (from the pandanus tree) prove the sophistication of Thai cuisine. Excellent Thai-style salads include banana blossom salad with shredded chicken and prawn. The wine list is extensive.

✚ 201 E1  ⊠ Sukhothai Hotel, 13/3 Thanon Sathorn Tai  ☎ 02 344 8888
⊙ Daily 11:30–2:30, 6:30–10:30

## Le Dalat ££

A Bangkok fixture, much copied, but never outdone, this is still the place for the best Vietnamese food in Thailand. Approached by a pretty tree-lined pathway, the restaurant is on two levels. The interior has a relaxed feel with some lovely bamboo touches. *Cha ca* (barbecued fish) is a favourite, and if you've never eaten Vietnamese food before, try the house dish, grilled meatballs with slivers of garlic, mango, chilli, ginger and starfruit. The staff are very friendly and they'll go out of their way to help you understand the menu.

➕ 201 off F2 ⊠ 47/1 Soi 23, Thanon Sukhumvit ☎ 02 261 7967 ⦿ Daily 11:30–2, 5–10 Ⓜ Asoke

## Gianni's £££

At Gianni's you can enjoy some of the finest Italian food in Bangkok, served in a quiet, modern environment. Proprietor Gianni Favri has managed to create a perfect little bit of Italy. The food is simple but excellent, with such delicacies as angel-hair pasta with lobster, goose liver salad and *osso bucco d'agnello* (braised lamb shank). Desserts are wonderful and include a delicious yoghurt and honey mousse and *tiramisù* of outstanding quality. The wine list is also Italian.

➕ 201 F2 ⊠ 51/5 Soi Tonson, Thanon Ploenchit ☎ 02 252 1619 ⦿ Mon–Sat 11–2:30, 6–11; closed Sun Ⓜ Ploenchit

## Himali Cha Cha and Son ££

There are a number of good-quality Indian restaurants in Bangkok, but few with such an interesting background as this. The original chef and proprietor, the late Cha Cha, worked for Lord Louis Mountbatten in the dog days of the British Raj and then for various Indian ambassadors around the world. His son has now assumed his mantle and Cha Cha's original restaurant can still be found just off Thanon Charoen Krung. All dishes are based on Cha Cha's recipes and are north Indian or Moghul in style. Traditional Indian drinks include Kingfisher Indian lager.

➕ 201 off F2 ⊠ 2 Sukhumvit Soi 35, Thanon Sukhumvit ☎ 02 235 1569 ⦿ Daily 11–3:30, 6–10:30 Ⓜ Saphan Taksin

## Lemongrass ££

This long-established and highly popular restaurant serves an excellent mix of well-known Thai regional dishes in an elegant old wooden house. The house itself is filled with antique furniture and various knick-knacks, all creating a rather eccentric mix. Look out for *kai yang phak panaeng* (sweet and spicy southern-style grilled chicken) and sun-dried salted fish. The wine list is a little limited, but they do have quite a good selection of French wines.

➕ 201 off F2 ⊠ 5/1 Sukhumvit Soi 24, Thanon Sukhumvit ☎ 02 258 8637 ⦿ Daily 11–2, 6–11 Ⓜ Phrom Phong

## Sala Rim Naam £££

An elegant Thai pavilion on the west bank of the Chao Phraya River, opposite the Oriental (▶ 54, 57), this is actually one of the Oriental's many excellent restaurants. Ferries run from the hotel on a regular basis, a great way to arrive at any restaurant. The teak pavilion, fitted out in bronze and marble, hosts some of Thailand's very best classical dancers from 8:30 pm every night. Food is uniformly top class, with such traditional Thai specialities as *yaam thalay* (seafood salad), *kaeng karii kai* (yellow curry with chicken) and *tom yam kung* (spicy prawn and lemongrass soup). As would befit a restaurant attached to one of the world's finest hotels, the wine list and service are both exemplary.

➕ 200 C1 ⊠ 597 Thanon Charoen Nakhon, Chao Phraya River, opposite the Oriental Hotel ☎ 02 437 9417 ⦿ Daily 11:30–2, 7–10:30 Ⓜ Saphan Taksin

## Spice Market £££

This superb Thai restaurant, decorated in the style of an old Thai spice shop, is one of Bangkok's finest. Rattan furniture and marble-topped tables add to the old-time ambience. Favourite dishes include a magnificent crispy catfish and green mango salad and crispy soft-shell crab in peppercorn.

🚇 201 E2 ⊠ Four Seasons Hotel, 155 Thanon Ratchadamri ☎ 02 251 6127 🕐 Daily 11:30–2:30, 6–11 🚉 Ratchadamri

## Supatra River House ££

This was originally the home of Khunying Supatra Singholaga, the founder of the Bangkok River Express boat service, which continues to ferry thousands of people up and down the Chao Phraya River every day (▶ 49). It is built in a classical Thai style and has a fabulous view of the Grand Palace (▶ 44–46). Upstairs is an interesting family museum. The menu is Thai, with dishes such as fried scallops with chilli, sun-dried freshwater fish and green mango salad. On Saturdays and Sundays traditional Thai dances are performed.

🚇 200 A3 ⊠ 266 Soi Wat Rakhang, Thanon Arun Amarin ☎ 02 411 0305 🕐 Daily 11:30–2:30, 6–11 🚉 No subway near by; it is best to take a taxi

## Vertigo £££

Perched on the sixtieth floor of the Banyan Tree hotel in central Bangkok, this spectacular restaurant certainly lives up to its name. It's so high and exposed that it has to close for much of the rainy season (June–September), but it is a magical place at any other time of the year, the finest vantage point to admire Bangkok's Manhattan-like cityscape. The prices are as high as the location, but the cuisine is suitably outstanding – the seafood platter for two is an exclusive array of the choicest and most exotic items (including Tasmanian oysters and Phuket lobster). The restaurant's Moon Bar – which claims to be the highest bar in the entire Asia-Pacific region – is a romantic place for a pre-dinner cocktail.

🚇 201 D1–E1 ⊠ Banyan Tree, 21/100 Thanon Sathorn Tai ☎ 02 679 1200, www.banyantree.com 🕐 Daily 5:00–midnight (weather permitting)

## Vientiane Kitchen £

For anyone wanting to try Isaan (northeastern Thai) and Lao food, it's hard to beat this place. Isaan food is generally simple and spicy. The most famous dishes on the Vientiane's menu include *somtam* (papaya salad with fish sauce, garlic, chilli peppers and peanuts) and *larb* (spiced minced meat) generally served with salad and a side plate of raw vegetables. This is often eaten with *kai yang* (grilled chicken). Another delicacy unlikely to appeal to any but the most adventurous visitor is *nam phrik mot som* (red ant egg dip). All these dishes are traditionally eaten with *khao niaw* (sticky rice), which is served in small woven bamboo baskets and eaten by hand. Tables surround a large tree and a traditional Isaan musical group does the entertaining.

🚇 200 off F2 ⊠ 8 Soi 36 Thanon Sukhumvit ☎ 02 258 6171 🕐 Daily noon–midnight 🚉 Thong Lo

## Whole Earth ££

Open for more than 20 years, the Whole Earth regards itself as Bangkok's finest and oldest vegetarian restaurant. In the upstairs section you eat cross-legged sitting on comfortable cushions at low tables. There are a few dishes for non-vegetarians, although the real treats are the mix of Indian and Thai vegetarian dishes. Specialities include Chinese soup with seaweed and black mushrooms, and roasted aubergine and vegetarian satay. Wine is available, but it's worth trying the various vegetable and herbal drinks on offer.

🚇 201 F2 ⊠ 93/3 Soi Lang Suan, Thanon Ploenchit ☎ 02 252 5574 🕐 Daily 11:30–2, 5:30–11 🚉 Chidlom

# Where to... Shop

Bangkok provides one of Asia's premier shopping experiences. Malls and individual shops offer a wide selection of specialities from Thailand's many and varied regions. Crafts, antiques, ceramics, clothes and fabrics, gems and *objets d'art* provide an unparalleled range of choice.

## TRADITIONAL CRAFTS

Although Bangkok is the main outlet for antiques and crafts, few are actually produced in the city.

**Elephant House** (67/12 Soi Phra Phinit, Thanon Sathorn Tai, tel: 02 266 5280) has Thai and Burmese antiques with an elephantine connection.

For Burmese wall hangings, Indian and Nepalese jewellery, Balinese woodcarvings and many local products try **Krishna's Asian Treasures** (corner Soill Thanon Sukhumvit, tel: 02 253 7693).

**Erawan Antiques** (148/9 Thanon Surawong) sells Buddhist and Hindu religious artefacts, and also some very beautiful antique furniture. The government-run craft store, **Narayana Phand** (127 Thanon Ratchadamri, opp. World Trade Centre), sells a vast range of goods.

A number of antiques and craft outlets are at **River City Shopping Complex** (23 Trok Rongnamkaeng, Thanon Yotha, near the Royal Orchid Sheraton Hotel), a huge Aladdin's Cave of treasures.

## SILK

The **Jim Thompson Silk Shop** (9 Thanon Surawong, tel: 02 234 4900) is perhaps the best place for silk in town, with high-quality clothing and household accessories.

**Shinawatra** (Thanon Sathorn Tai, near Soi Suan Plu, tel: 02 286 9991) offers a wide selection of silk and other textile products. It also has shops in Bangkok and Chiang Mai.

For silk produced using traditional methods and natural dyes try **Silk of Thailand** (77/165 Rajathevee Tower, Thanon Phayathai, tel: 02 653 7124).

## MARKETS

In the north of the city, **Chatuchak Market** (➤ 51, also known as the Weekend Market), at the southern end of Chatuchak Park, off Phahonyothin Road, is a delight to stroll around. It sells everything imaginable, from exotic fresh vegetables to Thai musical instruments.

If you're looking for clothes, including designer items, try **Pratunam Market** (at the junction of Phetburi Road and Ratchaprarop Road). For the archetypal Southeast Asian market head for **Pak Khlong Talaat** (Maharat Road, near the Memorial Bridge), where fresh flowers and vegetables are on sale 24 hours a day.

## MALLS/DEPARTMENT STORES

Thailand's leading department store chain, **Central**, has six outlets in Bangkok, the largest of which are in the main tourist areas of Silom and Thanon Ploenchit. They offer virtually everything a shopper seeks and have stylish bars, cafes and cinemas. The **Siam Discovery Centre** (Thanon Rama 1), attached to the rather older Siam Centre, offers floor upon floor of designer brand shops. Further along Ploenchit at the corner of Thanon Ratchadamri stands the huge **World Trade Centre** (Thanon Ratchadamri).

There's a duty free shop on its seventh floor, open from 10 am–9 pm. Opposite the World Trade Centre, **Gaysorn Plaza** (corner Thanon Ratchadamri and Ploenchit) has excellent household accessories shops, with unique contemporary Thai-style items.

# Where to...
# Be Entertained

## INFORMATION

Bangkok's main listings magazine is the excellent monthly *Metro Magazine*, available at most bookshops in the city.

## CINEMA

Many of the large shopping malls have multiplex screens, all air-conditioned and very comfortable. The **Major Cineplex World Trade Centre** (Floor 7, Thanon Ratchadamri, tel: 02 255 6565) is centrally located and shows a wide variety of films.

The annual **European Union Film Festival** takes place in May and June. Some of Europe's best contemporary films are shown at a number of locations, including the

**Alliance Française** (29 Thanon Sathorn Tai Tai, tel: 02 670 4200) and the **Goethe Institut** (181/1 Soi Goethe, tel: 02 287 0942).

## THEATRE

The **National Theatre** (2 Thanon Rachini Phra Nakhon, tel: 02 221 0174) has regular traditional performances of *khòn*, a formal masked dance drama, and *lakhon*, a more general form of dance.

## MUSIC

The **Saxophone Pub** (3/8 Victory Monument, Thanon Phayathai, tel: 02 246 5472), offering mainly jazz, is one of the oldest and most popular places, with different bands each night.

For Thai folk and country music, try **Ad Makers** (51/51 Soi Lang Suan, off Thanon Ploenchit, tel: 02 652 0168). For rock music, **Radio City** (76/1–3 Patpong Soi 1, tel: 02 266 4567) has excellent live bands. The occasional foreign band plays alongside some of Bangkok's finest at **Imageries By The Glass** (2 Sukhumvit Soi 24, tel: 02 261 0426).

North of Lumphini Park, **Soi Sarasin** and **Soi Lang Suan** provide a number of fun music venues; look out especially for **MCM Café** (106/12 Soi Lang Suan, Thanon Ploenchit) and **Brown Sugar** (231/20 Soi Sarasin).

## NIGHTLIFE

Bangkok's notorious nightlife is legendary, but it does not just revolve around go-go bars, massage parlours and escort agencies.

The city is packed with discos and nightclubs. **Concept CM2** (Novotel Siam, Siam Square Soi 6, tel: 02 255 6888) is one of the most

popular hang outs. **La Lunar** (Thanon Sukhunvit Soi 26, tel: 02 261 3991) attracts a lively crowd and some great DJs.

**Lucifer** (76/1–3 Patpong Soi 1, tel: 02 234 6902) creates a ghoulish atmosphere with techno music. **Icon: The Club** (formerly the famous Rome Club, 90/6 Thanon Silom, Soi 4, tel: 02 233 8836) has an excellent sound system, live singers and exotic male dancers. **Phuture** (Chao Phraya Park Hotel, 91/9 Thanon Ratchadapisek, tel: 02 693 8022), has a large, high-tech disco.

## CABARET

Bangkok's transvestite cabaret shows are slick and very professional. In Thailand, these shows are a popular form of entertainment and not in the least bit sleazy. **Calypso Cabaret** (Asia Hotel, 296 Thanon Phayathai, tel: 02 261 6355) plays host to a glittering array of Las Vegas-style starlets and is probably the best show in town.

# Central Plains

Getting Your Bearings 64 – 65
In Three Days 66 – 67
Don't Miss 68 – 77
At Your Leisure 78 – 81
Where To 82 – 86

# Getting Your Bearings

This landlocked area north and west of Bangkok is a fertile zone irrigated by rivers and waterfalls. Thailand's "rice bowl" and its wealthiest region is literally in the heart of the country. The pace of life here is generally slow.

The extraordinary ancient cities of Ayutthaya and Sukhothai are two historical jewels studding the flat plains at either end of the zone, with the historical towns of Kamphaeng Phet and Lop Buri in between. The landscape becomes more hilly in the west, with forests and wildlife protected in scenic national parks which offer walking and rafting.

**Above: Tourists on an elephant at Ayutthaya**

At the riverside town of Kanchanaburi is the iconic "Bridge over the River Kwai", along with many other powerful reminders of the prisoners of war who worked on the Death Railway.

**Previous page: Bathing in chocolate-coloured waters**

Burma flanks the western side with a border (Three Pagodas Pass) open only for locally resident Thais and Burmese .

Most people travel around this part of the country, seeing the major sights, which include traditional floating markets, on organised day trips from Bangkok, before heading north to the serene ancient kingdom capital of Sukhothai. If you want a more leisurely pace, you can visit them independently, with the freedom to linger.

**Below: Pavilions at Bang Pa-In Palace near Ayutthaya**

## ★ Don't Miss

1 **Kanchanaburi Town** ➤ 68
2 **Damnoen Saduak Floating Markets** ➤ 70
3 **Ayutthaya** ➤ 72
4 **Sukhothai** ➤ 75

## At Your Leisure

5 Kanchanaburi Province ➤ 78
6 Nakhon Pathom ➤ 79
7 Lop Buri ➤ 79
8 Kamphaeng Phet Historical Park ➤ 80
9 Umphang ➤ 81
10 Three Pagodas Pass/Burma ➤ 81
11 Sangkhla Buri ➤ 81

Sawankhalok

[101]

Sukhothai 4

Phrom Phiram

Kong Krailat

Phitsanulok

[12]

Wang Thong

Kamphaeng Phet Historical Park

8

Kamphaeng Phet

Sam Ngam

Sai Ngam

Phichit

[117]

Khlong Lan

Khlong Khlung

Pho Thale

Taphan Hin

Khanu Woralaksaburi

Nong Bua

[1]

Nakhon Sawan

Chumsaeng

Lat Yao

Phaisali

Krok Phra

Lan Sak

Tak Fa

1554m ▲ Khao Yai

Uthai Thani

Chai Nat

[1]

[32]

Ta Khli

Ban Mi

Khok Samrong

Ban Rai

Sanphaya

[311]

Sing Buri

[1]

Si Nakharin Reservoir

Dan Chang

Doem Bang Nang Buat

[340]

Lop Buri

7

Don Chedi

Phra Phutthabat

Erawan National Park

Suphan Buri

Ang Thong

[32]

Saraburi

[1]

Bo Phloi

U Thong

Sena

3 Ayutthaya

Bang Pa-in Palace

Kanchanaburi

1

Tha Muang

[340]

Kamphaeng Saen

Pathum Thani

Death Railway

[323]

Nakhon Pathom

6

Nonthaburi

Min Buri

Ratchaburi

Damnoen Saduak

BANGKOK

Floating Markets

2

Samut Songkhram

Samut Sakhon

Samut Prakan

[4]

*Bight of Bangkok*

0 ——— 100 km
0 ——— 60 miles

**The pristine waters of Erawan Falls, Kanchanaburi Province**

Zigzag across the tranquil plains, absorbing highlights that require a series of day trips. Paddle in a traditional floating market, cycle around staggering World Heritage Sites and journey to Kanchanaburi, a province both beautiful and haunted.

# Central Plains in Three Days

## Day One

### Morning

Day trips make an early start from Bangkok to combine visits to the town of **1 Kanchanaburi** (➤ 68–69), **2 Damnoen Saduak Floating Markets** (right, ➤ 70–71), and a quick tour of **6 Nakhon Pathom's** soaring *chedi* (➤ 79). Other organised tours visit the waterfalls and Hellfire Pass in **5 Kanchanaburi Province** (➤ 78–79) and miss out the floating markets. Tour buses usually stop at an unatmospheric roadside restaurant for lunch, despite the fact that it will probably be called Jungle View.

### Afternoon

You will have an hour or so to take in the cemetery in **Kanchanaburi** (➤ 69), the **JEATH War Museum** (➤ 69) and the **bridge over the River Kwai** (below, ➤ 68) before leaving to go back to Bangkok via Nakhon Pathom.

### Evening

A good way of having more time at the Kanchanaburi sights is to take a shared taxi back to Bangkok, for about 100 baht, rather than returning by tour bus. That way you can digest the day and get to sample seafood at the floating restaurants that have a real jungle view. Try those on Song Kwai Road where the ambience may take precedence over the food.

# Day Two

### Morning

Take an early morning train from Bangkok's Hualamphong station to ❸ **Ayutthaya** (right, ➤ 72–74) and rent a bicycle on arrival (or go for an organised tour). Enjoy an early, leisurely lunch to avoid the hottest part of the day at one of the floating restaurants on Mae Nam Pa Sak's west bank near the bridge of Saphan Pridi Damrong.

### Afternoon

Continue the tour of Ayutthaya's temples and, if you have time, venture out to the scenic western zone.

### Evening

Fill up at the Hua Raw night market next to the river near Chan Kasem Palace. From here you can follow the river back to the ferry point and train station to return to Bangkok on an early evening train.

# Day Three

Take a very reasonably priced flight to ❹ **Sukhothai** (left, ➤ 75–77). If the flights are full (it is best to reserve as far ahead as possible), consider taking the bus. The overnight train from Bangkok arrives inconveniently in the early hours of the morning at Phitsanulok. Rent a bicycle to explore the ruins and stay the night in Sukhothai.

# Kanchanaburi Town

Kanchanaburi Town is a relaxing destination, with riverside raft houses and guest houses in lush green surroundings. It is more famous, however, as the setting for a World War II POW camp, which was the base for workers on the Thailand–Burma Railway. Known as the "Death Railway", its construction cost thousands of lives. Most visitors fix their attention on the infamous River Kwai bridge, which featured in Pierre Boulle's book and, later, the 1957 Oscar-winning film, *Bridge on the River Kwai*.

## Bridge Over the River Kwai

There were actually two bridges over the River Kwai, a wooden structure which inspired the film, and a steel and concrete structure built by the Japanese forces when they realised the first bridge was too unstable. Both were destroyed by Allied bombing, but the second bridge was rebuilt and now carries the original Death Railway line.

Allied prisoners of war and conscripted Asian labourers worked on both bridges under brutal conditions. More than 16,000 of the 60,000 POWs building the bridges and the railway line to the Burmese border died. At least 80,000 Asian labourers also perished – a much less well-known figure. It's been estimated that a man died for every sleeper laid.

The story of the Death Railway is related in two Kanchanaburi museums.

The iconic Bridge over the River Kwai is a moving sight

## KANCHANABURI TOWN: INSIDE INFO

**Top tips** A **tourist train** goes from Bangkok to Kanchanaburi at weekends, leaving at 6:30 am and returning to Bangkok at 7:30 pm. A return ticket is 100 baht.
- **Read up** before you go if you don't know any of the history of the area, as the tours are perfunctory and, while the information in the JEATH War Museum is fascinating, there is rather too much to take in on one visit.
- If you are not on a tour, consider **renting a bicycle** as the town's sights are spread out over 5km (3 miles) along the river.
- Locals smile when visitors call their river the Kwai, as in "cry". The real pronunciation is "Kway", as in "sway". Pronounced the wrong way, Kwai can have a distinctly sexual meaning!

## The World War II Museum
This museum contains remains of one end of the original wooden bridge in a strangely eclectic exhibition. It is worth visiting for its collection of war-time mementoes and a display of Japanese and allied vehicles.

Paintings by POWs

## JEATH War Museum
The JEATH War Museum has moving displays including personal accounts and paintings by POWs, and replicas of the bamboo huts in which they lived. JEATH stand for Japan, England, Australia, America, Thailand and Holland – the countries which built the railway. The museum is on Pak Phreak Road, beside the Mae Khlong.

Right: Allied War Cemetery, last resting place of thousands of POWs

## The Cemeteries
Nearly 7,000 POWs are buried in the **Kanchanaburi War Cemetery**. The plaques and epitaphs are poignant reminders of how young these men were. It is immaculately kept, with plants and lawns.

The **Chung Kai Allied War Cemetery**, on the western bank of the river, receives far fewer tourists. Although it's a fair walk, you can cycle there.

### TAKING A BREAK
**Mae Nam floating restaurant** on the river opposite Thanon Song Khwae is a good place for a break. The atmosphere and setting are fantastic and the food is traditional Thai.

✚ 196 B1 TAT ✉ Saeng Chuto Road ☎ 03 457 7200

**JEATH War Museum**
🕐 Daily 8–6 💷 Inexpensive

**Kanchanaburi War Cemetery**
✉ Saeng Chuto Road 🕐 Daily 6–6
💷 Free

# ❷ Damnoen Saduak Floating Markets

The boats that paddle along the narrow canals (*khlongs*), are packed with produce grown in the agricultural surrounds of the region. One boat may be piled high with fresh coconuts, another packed with garlic; others sell a mix of vegetables and fruit. Mini floating restaurants dole out noodle soup to market workers. Women in traditional, bucket-like straw hats and navy blue outfits typically worn by Thai farmers, skilfully manoeuvre their boats, steering their produce along the canals.

**Away from the throng of the main *khlongs* (canals)**

## DAMNOEN SADUAK FLOATING MARKETS: INSIDE INFO

**Top tips** There is a **set price** for a boat (around 300 baht), irrespective of how many people are on board, so it makes sense to get a group together.
• The markets are **open** daily 6 to 11 am.
• If you want to **avoid the crowds**, one way is to stay overnight in Damnoen and visit the markets before the tour groups arrive at around 9 am.

**Hidden gem** Talat Khun Phitak canal is the quietest market. Take a water taxi from Khlong Thong Lang to get there, and maybe combine it with a trip to see the surrounding **coconut plantations**.

**Below: Fresh produce for sale at Damnoen Saduak market**

**Bottom: Local lunch break at a floating restaurant**

People have been hawking their wares here for more than 100 years. These markets, about 60km (37 miles) southwest of Bangkok, are the traditional way to shop, dating from when the canals were the major thoroughfares. Floating markets have all but died out in Bangkok – the ones that do exist are straggly, touristy affairs. Damnoen Saduak's distance from Bangkok and the fact that it is not accessible by train has in some ways saved it from over-commercialisation, although it is one of the most popular tours from the capital.

The main, and oldest, market is at **Ton Khem**, while the more touristy **Hia Kui canal** runs parallel to this. Lined with warehouses, it offers bird's-eye views from its bridges. The colourful scene is a frenzy of activity, with market traders peddling their wares. On shore, the stalls are lined with mostly souvenir-style goods, such as fans, hats and spices – but you will probably be over-charged.

Organised tours are convenient and a good way of combining the floating markets with Kanchanaburi Town or **Phetchaburi** (➤ 138–139). Be prepared to be herded and rushed. These trips can easily turn into a high-pressured shopping tour, with a "sugar factory" (just another market), the floating markets and a crafts centre crammed into the itinerary.

To go it alone, you can take a bus from Bangkok's southern bus terminal. The first air-conditioned bus leaves at 6 am and takes two hours, then you need to walk or take a *songthaew* (➤ 32) for 2km (1.2 miles) to the centre of the markets, **Talat Khlong Ton Khem**.

### TAKING A BREAK

Buy a **fresh coconut** full of juice from one of the boats on the river.

---

🚼 196 B1

TAT ✉ Phetchaburi ☎ 03 247 1005–6 ✉ 500/51 Phetkasem Road, Cha-am, Phetchaburi

# 3 Ayutthaya

This World Heritage Site was once the greatest city in Asia, and Thailand's capital for more than 400 years. Founded in 1350, Ayutthaya was an incredibly advanced civilisation – in fact, it was so powerful that it conquered mighty Angkor, in present-day Cambodia, and took on Khmer traditions. It had one million inhabitants in the 17th century – twice that of London during the same period. Visiting merchants from China, Japan, Holland, England and France are said to have declared it the most beautiful city they had ever seen.

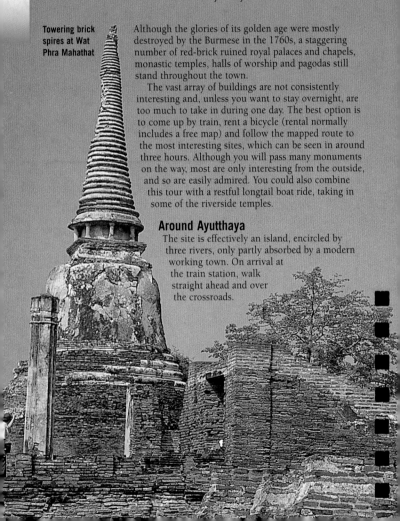

**Towering brick spires at Wat Phra Mahathat**

Although the glories of its golden age were mostly destroyed by the Burmese in the 1760s, a staggering number of red-brick ruined royal palaces and chapels, monastic temples, halls of worship and pagodas still stand throughout the town.

The vast array of buildings are not consistently interesting and, unless you want to stay overnight, are too much to take in during one day. The best option is to come up by train, rent a bicycle (rental normally includes a free map) and follow the mapped route to the most interesting sites, which can be seen in around three hours. Although you will pass many monuments on the way, most are only interesting from the outside, and so are easily admired. You could also combine this tour with a restful longtail boat ride, taking in some of the riverside temples.

### Around Ayutthaya

The site is effectively an island, encircled by three rivers, only partly absorbed by a modern working town. On arrival at the train station, walk straight ahead and over the crossroads.

Take the ferry for the short river crossing, and then the second left along Thanon Naresuan to the 14th-century **Wat Mahathat**. This is the biggest and most significant temple complex, which includes the royal monastery. Buddha images found in the ruins here as recently as 1956 are now in the Chao Sam Phraya National Museum (► 74). Make sure you find the much-photographed Buddha head entangled in a frame of vines. Opposite, **Wat Ratchaburana** was built on the site of a cremation of two kings, and their ashes are contained here in *chedis*. Follow the stairs down to the crypt to see its faded murals.

About 1km (0.6 miles) along this road, **Phra Mongkonbophit** contains a huge, gilded Buddha almost 13m (43 feet) high. The gleaming statue was re-covered in gold leaf in 1992. As a present-day centre of worship, the temple bustles with Thais making offerings of lotus flowers, incense candles and gold plate.

Opposite is **Wat Phra Si San Phet**, built as a royal palace when Ayutthaya was established. Although partly restored, it is still essentially in ruins. A royal temple was built

*Above: A Buddha head is caught in the roots of a banyan tree at Wat Phra Mahathat*

*Right: A young girl sells Benjarong-ware at Ayutthaya*

*Right: Riding like royalty, tourists take a tour of the park*

A buddha at
Wat Phra
Mahathat in
Ayutthaya

here in 1448, with later additions, such as *chedis*, to contain royal remains and royal halls of worship.

The **Chao Sam Phraya National Museum** (Si Sanphet Road, open Wed–Sun 9–4, inexpensive) is two blocks south of here, crammed full of gold treasures, including an elephant weighed down with jewels, and the original relic casket from Wat Mahathat.

At the end of the road to the right, **Wat Lokayasutharam** has a huge Buddha (37m/ 121-feet long) reclining in the open air, his head cushioned by a lotus.

### TAKING A BREAK

Try one of the several floating restaurants on the river either side of Pridi Damrong Bridge, such as **Phae Krung Kao** (► 85), south of the bridge, for some excellent seafood. Alternatively there's **Chainam** (► 85), for Thai breakfast, coffee and inexpensive Thai specialities served throughout the day.

➕ 196 C2 **TAT** ✉ Si Sanphet Road, Ayutthaya ☎ 03 524 6076

## AYUTTHAYA: INSIDE INFO

**Top tips** The booklet *Interesting Temples and Ruins in Ayutthaya* is worth buying for background information, but the map is almost illegible. It is available all over the town and at the Chao Sam Phraya National Museum.

• Tours from Bangkok to the **Bang-Pa-In Palace** (open daily 8:30–5, moderate) in a longtail boat include a couple of hours in Ayutthaya. Although it's an interesting way to travel, you won't have too much time in the historical city itself.

• Whether bicycling or walking, **avoid the heat of the day** (11–3) by starting early and taking a long break for lunch. Temperatures in Ayutthaya tend to be even higher than in Bangkok.

• Wait to **rent a bicycle** until the other side of the ferry crossing, where prices are lower.

**Hidden gem** Visit the impressive **Wat Chaiwatthanaram**. In a peaceful grassy riverside spot on the edge of town, it tends to receive few visitors. From Wat Lokayasutharam, turn left down Thanon Khlong Thaw, then first right, over the river and then turn left. This monastery, where royal cremations took place, was built by King Prasatthon in 1630 on the site of his old home to honour his mother. It was built in the Cambodian Khmer style, with similarities to Angkor Wat in Cambodia, and one theory suggests it was constructed to celebrate the king's victory over Cambodia. Its large, central *prang* stands in the middle of four smaller ones and eight smaller still, symbolising the centre of the universe.

**One to miss** Chan Kasem Palace, on Uthong Road, is a museum with a rather jumbled selection of exhibits. The palace, once home to the heir to the throne, was razed by the Burmese. It was rebuilt and now contains a collection of minor royal objects.

# ④ Sukhothai

The name of Thailand's original capital (1238–1376) means "rising of happiness" and it is still seen as a symbol of a golden age. Founded in 1238 when two Thai generals took control from the Khmer Empire, Sukhothai became a centre of artistic greatness, where harmony reigned and justice prevailed. Its lawns, lily ponds and buildings, restored with assistance by UNESCO and surrounded by orchards and rice fields, now form one of Thailand's most visited spots.

Sukhothai's decline came in the 15th century when Ayutthaya (▶ 72–74) gained political dominance. Houses at that time were mostly built of wood and haven't survived, so what remains are the crumbling brick religious buildings. However, unlike Ayutthaya, the old and new cities are separate, which makes a visit here much more enjoyable. Most people stay in the new city, with its better range of accommodation and long-distance bus connections, and travel the 12km (7.5 miles) to the old city by *songthaew* (similar to a *tuk-tuk*: noisy, with two benches facing one another in the back). The best way for visitors to get round Sukhothai is by bicycle which can be rented at the main entrance. Each of the sights mentioned here takes about 20 minutes to visit, with about 5–10 minutes travelling time in between.

The original walled city is now covered by **Sukhothai Historical Park** (Muang Kao Sukhothai), which is divided into five zones, each charging a separate entrance fee. Most of the interesting temples are in the central zone, although even here you need to be selective. Rent a bicycle (and ask for a free map) opposite the **Ramkhamhaeng Museum**, a

**Bottom: Wat Mahathat's** *chedis*

**Below inset: The Great Buddha at Wat Mahathat**

### Rama the Strong

King Ramkhamhaeng (Rama the Strong), was the most important of the royal city's kings. He established a forerunner of modern Thai script, promoted Theravada Buddhism (the school taught by the Buddha, meaning "doctrine of the elders" and following the Hindu theory of reincarnation) and pushed the boundaries of the kingdom to almost the size of present-day Thailand. His much-quoted stone inscription of 1292 describes a bell in front of the palace gate that could be rung by any subject who wanted to air a grievance.

short walk from where *songth-aews* drop passengers and just outside the entrance to the central zone. A copy of King Ramkhamhaeng's inscription and bell, an armoury and intriguing items such as gambling chips and bullets are on display in the museum.

Next to the museum, **Wat Trapang Thong** is a still functioning monastery on an island surrounded by lotus-filled ponds. Here monks weed the stone Ceylonese-style *chedi* trees which have words of wisdom attached to them. The *mondop* (a square-shaped spired construction) contains a 14th-century giant Buddha footprint.

Take the first left inside the entrance to the central zone to **Wat Mahathat**. The largest and most important temple in Sukhothai was at the heart of the kingdom both politically and spiritually. The complex, surrounded by a moat and brick wall, contains 200 (mostly ruined) brick *chedis* in the Ceylonese and Khmer style. Two blocks southwest is **Sri Sawai**, built as a Hindu shrine with three Khmer-style *prangs* (central tower). Due north is **Wat Trapang Ngoen**, which features a classic lotus-bud *chedi* and an ordination hall, and **Wat Sra Sri**, with its circular *chedi*.

Leaving the central zone via the Northern Gate, turn left into **Wat Phra Pai Luang**, which shows a variety of building styles. The *prangs* were built by the Khmers and the *viharn* (temple assembly hall) and *chedis* are later Buddhist additions. At its northeast corner is

Right: A spectacular 15m (49 foot) Buddha in Wat Si Chum

➕ 196 B3
**Sukhothai Historical Park**
🕐 Daily 8–6 💵 Separate entrance inexpensive; central entrance moderate

**Ramkhamhaeng Museum**
🕐 Daily 8:30–4:30
💵 Inexpensive

Wat Sra Sri, at the very centre of the complex

**Thuriang Kiln**. Although there is not much to see, it is a reminder that ceramics were an important revenue for Thailand, and exported as far afield as the Philippines and Japan.

Continue south and take the second road on the right to visit a string of temples in the western zone. First stop is **Wat Si Thon**, where a monk is said to have lived surrounded by mango fields. **Wat Saphan Hin** is the fourth temple, reached by a short, steep climb to a standing Buddha with an outstretched palm and views of the surrounding countryside.

## TAKING A BREAK

The **café in the Ramkhamhaeng Museum** is a pleasant place for a cup of tea next to the water. The restaurant opposite is a good spot for lunch. In New Sukothai, try the **Dream Café and Antique House** (➤ 85) for Thai, Chinese or Western food and its speciality, herbal liquors.

### SUKHOTHAI: INSIDE INFO

**Top tips** The **single ticket**, which includes entry to all five zones, doesn't save you money, although it is valid for a month.
• From the end of October to mid-November the festival of **Loy Krathong** gives thanks to the goddess of water. Lighted candles, incense and lotus buds are set sail in banana-leaf boats. The festival is celebrated all over Thailand but it is more of a spectacle here, with illuminations of the ruins and fireworks.
• If you go to the ruins of Sukothai's sister city, Si Satchanalai, join an organised tour. The Si Satchanalai Historical Park is worth a visit, but very difficult to locate.

**Hidden gem** The north and west zones where **buffalo, cows and farm workers** dot the lush green landscape where once stood a mighty city.

# At Your Leisure

**Just one of Erawan Falls' seven tiers, Kanchanaburi Province**

## 🐘 Kanchanaburi Province

The spectacular waterfall in **Erawan National Park** in Kanchanaburi Province is something of a national symbol. Each of the seven tiers has its own clear water pool which invites swimming. The park's 2km (1.2-mile) trail leads to the triple cascade at the top and requires suitable footwear. This very attractive park, just 65km (40 miles) from Kanchanaburi Town, is popular with Thais, especially at weekends and holidays. It is worth avoiding these times if you want to enjoy the peace of the landscape. Trekking trips in Kanchanaburi Province can include elephant safaris, visits to waterfalls and river-rafting, rather than hiking.

The two-hour train journey along the section of the Death Railway from Kanchanaburi to Nam Tok starts by crossing the bridge over the River Kwai (➤ 68). This highly scenic and very popular trip grimly illustrates the horror experienced in building the railway. **Hellfire Pass**, 18km (11 miles) northwest of Nam

## For Kids
• Longtail boat rides through the **Damnoen Saduak Floating Markets** (➤ 70–71)
• The **monkeys of Lop Buri** that animate the towns's historic buildings (➤ below)
• River-rafting, waterfalls and elephant rides in **Kanchanaburi Province**
• Boat and bicycle trips around the ruins of **Ayutthaya** (➤ 72–74)

Tok, is the highest of a series of mountain passes and one of the most treacherous parts of the Death Railway. The prisoners of war who were forced to cut through the rock gave it the name "Hellfire" because of the nightmarish scene created by the fires, torches and lamps when they worked through the night. Three-quarters of those who worked on this stretch died, and they are sensitively remembered at the **Hellfire Memorial Museum**, with accounts from survivors. A 90-minute memorial trail passes the site of the Pack of Cards Bridge, so called by the prisoners because it collapsed three times.

**Sai Yok National Park**, 10km (6.2 miles) further up the road, lays claim to two large waterfalls, limestone caves, teak forests and natural springs. Wildlife here includes gibbons, barking deer and the world's smallest mammal – the hog-nosed (bumblebee) bat. It was, however, also the venue for disturbing scenes in the film *The Deerhunter*.

➕ 196 B1
**Erawan National Park**
➕ 196 B2 🕐 Daily 8–4 💷 Expensive

**Hellfire Memorial Museum**
➕ 196 B2 ✉ At the start of the memorial trail ☎ 01 210 3306 🕐 Daily 9–4 💷 Free (donations gratefully accepted)

**Sai Yok National Park**
➕ 196 B2 ✉ TAT in Kanchanaburi ☎ 03 451 6163 🕐 Daily 8–4 💷 Expensive

## ❻ Nakhon Pathom
**Phra Pathom Chedi** is the main attraction in Nakhon Pathom (56km/35 miles west of Bangkok), and is said to be the tallest Buddhist monument in the world. It dominates the skyline all around. A whistle-stop visit to the *chedi* is usually squeezed in to a tour from Bangkok on the way back from the Damnoen Saduak Floating Markets (➤ 70–71) and Kanchanaburi Town (➤ 68–69).

Although there is not much here to see for visitors, Nakhon Pathom is thought to be Thailand's oldest town, and the place where Buddhism first entered the country. There are two museums in the town, both confusingly called **Phra Pathom Museum**. The newer one has 6th- to 11th-century local artefacts and the other, a small room, is crowded with amulets, Chinese ceramics, Thai musical instruments and gems.
➕ 196 C1
**Phra Pathom Museums**
➕ 196 C1 ✉ Phra Pathom Chedi compound 🕐 Wed–Sun 8–4 💷 Inexpensive

## ❼ Lop Buri
The **monkeys** that have overrun Lop Buri, one of Thailand's oldest inhabited towns, are almost a tourist attraction in their own right. Lop Buri was a Khmer provincial capital in the 11th century and Thailand's second capital from the 17th to 19th centuries. The **Narai National Museum**, in a 17th-century palace complex, displays plenty of Buddhas. **Wat Phra Si Ratana Mahathat** has a 12th-century Khmer central *prang*.

## Scenic Journeys
• Walking to the waterfall in **Erawan National Park** (➤ 78)
• Day-long rail route to **Three Pagodas Pass** from Kanchanaburi (➤ 81)
• Three-day trek from **Umphang** (➤ 81), offered by guest houses, including trekking, rafting and an elephant ride.

Monkeys have made their homes at Phra Prang Sam Yod, Lop Buri

Both are worth a look and are within easy walking distance of the train station. A frequent bus service runs to **Wat Phra Phutthabat**, the Temple of the Buddha's Footprint, 17km (10.5 miles) southeast of town.

✚ 196 C2

**TAT**

✉ Ropwat Phrathat Road
☎ 03 642 2768-9

**Narai National Museum**
🕑 Wed–Sun 8:30–4:30 💰 Inexpensive

**Wat Phra Si Ratana Mahathat**
🕑 Daily 8–6 💰 Inexpensive

## 8 Kamphaeng Phet Historical Park

In the 13th century this ancient riverside city was part of the Kingdom of Sukhothai. Even before this, it was an important centre in the Khmer Empire. Today it is a provincial town whose partly restored old buildings form a historical park and a World Heritage Site. The star attraction is **Wat Phra Kaeo**, with its weather-sculpted Buddha statues. The Emerald Buddha, Thailand's most important Buddha image, was once held here, but is now kept in Wat Phra Kaeo in Bangkok (➤ 45).

The monastery of **Wat Phrathat** and **San Phra Isuan Shrine** are also worth a look. The **National Museum** has archaeological finds from all over Thailand as well as from excavations in Kamphaeng Phet. Next door is the **Provincial Museum**, displaying collections introducing the history and traditions of Kamphaeng Phet province. A group of forest (*arunyik*) temples to the north of the walled city were built by meditating monks.

### Border Country

Around seven million Mon people live in Thailand and Burma. Originally thought to have hailed from India or Mongolia, they established a kingdom in south Burma before even the Burmese arrived. They have suffered oppression for centuries from the Burmese, who continue to oppress them. Use of the Mon language has been banned since the mid-18th century, but forced labour, rape and illnesses associated with underprivilege are more disturbing modern atrocities, and the reason for the large number of refugee camps in the area around Sangkhla Buri.

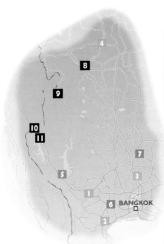

✚ 196 B3
**TAT**
☎ 05 551 4341

**Kamphaeng Phet Historical Park**
⏰ Daily 8–4:30　💵 Inexpensive

**National Museum**
⏰ Wed–Sun 8–4　💵 Inexpensive

**Provincial Museum**
⏰ Wed–Sun 8–4　💵 Inexpensive

## 9 Umphang

This riverside village surrounded by spectacular scenery doesn't get too many visitors. On the border with Burma and in the middle of nowhere, it is reached by a roller-coaster road or "Sky Highway" that zooms past pretty hill-tribe villages. This is trekking country, with trips to Mae Sot and the Tee Lor Su Waterfall as well as river-rafting expeditions.
✚ 196 B3

## 10 Three Pagodas Pass/ Burma

Three Pagodas Pass is an outpost on the Burma/Thailand border where there is really nothing much to see apart from the trio of pagodas on a roundabout from which it takes its name.

It is said that they were built in the 18th century as a demonstration of peace between Thailand and Burma (modern Myanmar).

Thailand traditionally prevented foreigners crossing into Burma from the Three Pagodas Pass as a sensible precaution due to border fighting between the Burmese military and Mon and Karen rebels.

Things are generally peaceful now and if the border is open you can visit the Burmese village of **Payathonzu** for the day, although it's a good idea to check the current situation first.

The market in Payathonzu has exotic goods from neighbouring countries. On both sides of the border you can find hand-embroidered textiles from India, precious gems from Cambodia and intricate Indonesian woodcarvings. Hard bargaining is expected.
✚ 196 A2

## 11 Sangkhla Buri

Around 20km (12.4 miles) from the Three Pagodas Pass, Sangkhla Buri is a nicer place to stay the night if you are intending to visit the Pass.

Populated with mostly Mon and Karen people, it is more Burmese than Thai and very little English is spoken. Its focus is a reservoir that was created by the damming of the Khwae Noi River. You can still see parts of the drowned villages and trees. A daily morning market at **Wat Wangwiwekaram** sells crafts from Burma, China and India. There are canoeing trips on the **Kheuan Khao Laem Reservoir** and a long wooden bridge leads over the body of water to a welcoming Mon settlement.
✚ 196 A2

A Karen tribesman carries teak leaves to make a house roof

# Where to... Stay

**Prices**

Expect to pay per double room

£ under 1,000 baht  ££ 1,000–4,000 baht  £££ over 4,000 baht

The central plains have a broad range of accommodation, from the jungle resorts of Kanchanaburi Province to the comfortable hotels of Thailand's former ancient capital, Ayutthaya. The country's other ancient capital, Sukhothai and nearby Phitsanulok also have a wide range of accommodation, including some of the region's top hotels.

Many of the resorts and tour companies in Kanchanaburi Town offer overnight rafting trips along the River Kwai to see the famous bridge.

## AYUTTHAYA

### Ayutthaya Grand ££

The Ayutthaya Grand is one of only a handful of good hotels to be found in the main city area. A large, comfortable place, it's situated a little to the east of the main town, beyond the Pa Sak River. The well-appointed rooms offer a haven from the busy town centre and include all modern amenities. The Grand's nightclub is one of the most popular in town, with an attached coffee shop. There is also a large swimming pool.

🚇 196 C2  ✉ 55/5 Thanon Rotchana

☎ 03 533 5483, fax: 03 533 5492,

email: aygrand@ksc.th.com

### Krungsri River ££

Situated at the eastern end of the Pridi Damrong Bridge and overlooking the busy Pa Sak River, this is the best hotel in Ayutthaya. The imposing foyer sets the tone and the beautifully decorated rooms will not disappoint. All rooms have satellite TV and mini-bar. There is an attractive pool, fitness centre, sauna, bowling alley, snooker tables and pub. It also houses the excellent Gu Cheung Chinese restaurant.

🚇 196 C2  ✉ 27/2 Moo 11, Thanon Rotchana  ☎ 03 524 4333, fax: 03 524 3777, email: hotel@krungsiriver.com, www.krungsiriver.com

### U-Thong Inn £

Don't confuse the U-Thong Inn to the east of Ayutthaya, beyond the Pa Sak River, with the more downmarket U-Thong Hotel. It is well positioned for all the main historical sights and regularly used for conferences, so it is often quite full. The new wing has proved to be the better value of the old and new wings. All rooms are clean and airy with satellite TV and mini-bar. Breakfast is included in the price of the room. Other facilities are a pool and sauna.

🚇 196 C2  ✉ 210 Thanon Rotchana  ☎ 03-5212531, fax: 03 524 2236, email: uthong@ksc.th.com, www.uthonginn.com

## KANCHANABURI

### Felix River Kwai £££

On the west bank of the River Kwai and in landscaped tropical gardens, the Felix is within walking distance of the famous bridge (▶ 68). This luxurious resort offers every facility including a fitness centre, tennis courts, two large swimming pools and a number of restaurants. The Good Earth serves fine Chinese cuisine. Rooms are spacious with satellite TV and a personal safe.

🚇 196 B1  ✉ 9/1 Moo 3 Thamakhan  ☎ 03 4515061, fax: 03 451 5095, email: felix@ksc.th.com, www.felixriverkwai.co.th

## Jolly Frog Backpackers £

For a completely different experience, this backpackers' favourite offers bamboo huts next to the river and floating rafts. Accommodation is quite basic, but if you are prepared to rough it for a day or so the Jolly Frog has a unique warmth and friendliness. It's well located for Kanchanaburi's major sights (► 68–69). Guests are encouraged to swim in the river at the end of the attractive garden. The restaurant is popular with guests from many of the surrounding hotels.

🚼 196 B1 ⊠ 28 Soi China, Thanon Mae Nam Khwae ☎ 03 451 4579, fax: 03 462 4329, www.jollyfrog.fsnet.co.uk

## Kasem Island Resort £

This resort is in a wonderful location on its own island in the middle of the Mae Klong River, south of the main town. Pretty thatched cottages and houseboats sit peacefully away from the busy town. Rooms are clean and tastefully decorated. The resort offers river-rafting and fishing trips, as well as a pleasant bar. The free ferry from the Chulkadon Pier slightly to the north of the island stops after 10 pm, so be careful not to be caught out too late.

🚼 196 B1 ⊠ Kasem Island, 27 Thanon Chaichumphon ☎ 03 451 3359, email: kasemisland@yahoo.com, www.geocities.com/kasemisland2003

## River Kwai Hotel ££

The River Kwai Hotel is an old favourite, centrally located and a little way from the river. The advantage of its position is that you miss the whine of longtail boats during the day, and the noisy disco boats on the river into the early hours of the morning. All rooms are air-conditioned. It is well situated for visiting the JEATH War Museum (► 69) and the Allied War Cemetery (► 69). There's a coffee shop, a disco and a swimming pool.

🚼 196 B1 ⊠ 284/3-16 Thanon Saengchuto ☎ 03 451 3348, fax: 03 451 1269, email: rkhk@riverkwai.co.th, www.riverkwai.co.th

(► 68–69)
(► 69)
(► 69)

## LOP BURI

## Lop Buri Resort ££

Few visitors to the ancient town of Lop Buri take the time to stay the night, which is a pity as it's one of the most interesting places in central Thailand. The Lop Buri Resort, slightly out of the old town to the west, is the newest and best hotel. The rooms are all decorated using a variety of Thai textiles and crafts. Each is dedicated to one of Thailand's 76 provinces. The facilities include a sauna and fitness centre and a large swimming pool. The hotel's Kongjeen Chinese restaurant is very good.

🚼 196 C2 ⊠ 144 Thanon Phahonyothin (opposite Lop Buri Inn Plaza) ☎ 03 642 0777, fax: 03 661 4795

## PHITSANULOK

## La Paloma ££

La Paloma is one of a number of fine hotels offering remarkably good value considering the excellent facilities. It's geared towards Thai families, and the staff are very friendly. Comfortable air-conditioned rooms with satellite TV are very reasonable if the hotel is empty, although you will have to bargain for this rate. Expect to pay double this in the high season. Other facilities include a swimming pool and a good restaurant with traditional Thai food.

🚼 196 C3 ⊠ 103/8 Thanon Sithamatraipidok ☎ 05 521 7930–6, fax: 05 521 7937, email: lapaloma@hotmail.com, www.phitsanulok.com/lapalomahotel

## Phitsanulok Thani Hotel ££

Situated a little way from the interesting riverfront, this large, quiet, comfortable hotel is well located for the Phitsanulok Folklore Museum and the Buranathai Buddha Casting Foundry on Thanon Wisut Kasat. The large, attractive foyer/lounge regularly has live music. As with some of the other good hotels in the town, you can get discounts on rooms at certain times of the year. The large, pleasant rooms all have a fridge, mini-bar and cable TV.

➕ **196 C3** ✉ **39 Thanon Sanam Bin**
☎ **05 521 1065, fax: 05 521 1071,**
**email: sale@phitsanulokthani.com,**
**www.phitsanulokthani.com**

## Sappraiwan Grand Hotel and Resort £££

Nestled in the hills 50km (31 miles) northeast of Phitsanulok, this is the perfect place to relax. There are mountains, waterfalls, rivers and jungle in the surrounding countryside. The Kaeng Sopha Waterfall is particularly beautiful and not far away. All rooms in the main building have either river or tropical garden views, satellite TV and wooden furniture. Dotted around the 150ha (370-acre) site are private one- and two-bedroom chalets. There's also a fitness centre, swimming pool and the excellent Wang Thong restaurant.

➕ **196 C3** ✉ **79 Moo 2, Tambon Kaeng Sopha** ☎ **05 529 3293,**
fax: 05 529 3293, email:
service@sappraiwanresort.co.th,
www.sappraiwanresort.co.th

## Topland ££

A large, modern hotel, Topland is set in the heart of the city. There are beautifully appointed rooms and suites with all the facilities associated with a first-class hotel. The large marble bathrooms are the perfect place to relax after a day in the sun. The hotel is connected to the Topland Plaza Shopping Complex, which has a department store and several smaller shops. Along with Topland's own restaurants, the Plaza has a number of good places to eat.

➕ **196 C3** ✉ **68/33 Thanon Ekathotsarot** ☎ **05 524 7800,**
fax: 05 524 7815, email: phsoffice@
topland.com, www.toplandhotel.com

## Lotus Village ££

A French-Thai couple run this enchanting resort-style hotel near

Sukothai's central market. Accommodation is in cosy timber-built bungalows nestled in shady gardens near the Yom River. The main house, where breakfast is served, is strewn with interesting antiques and bric-a-brac, collected during the wide travels of the owners, who have an encyclopaedic knowledge of the area – "Tourist office?" responds Kun Daen, "We're it."

➕ **196 B3** ✉ **170 Thanon Ratchathanee** ☎ **05 562 1484, fax: 05 562 1463, www.lotus-village.com**

## Pailyn Sukhothai ££

Located just 4km (2.5 miles) from Sukhothai Historical Park (➤ 75), the Pailyn is the closest luxury hotel to the ruins. The modern main building, with a hint of traditional central Thai architecture, looks out towards the beautiful Khao Luang Mountain. The large, well-equipped rooms are decorated with Thai fabrics and offer views of either the mountain or the rice fields, which can look stunning just

before harvest. The hotel has its own disco and pub and a restaurant serving a variety of Thai, Chinese and Western dishes.

➕ **196 B3** ✉ **10/2 Thanon Charodwithong** ☎ **05 563 3334, fax: 05 561 3317,**
**email: pailynshotel@hotmail.com**

## Central Mae Sot Hill Hotel ££

This is a good place to recover from the rigours of a trip to Umphang (➤ 81). It's a large, comfortable hotel with tennis courts, a swimming pool and fitness centre. It's well located for the Friendship Bridge marking the border between Thailand and Burma. The bridge crosses the Moei River and trips to the Burmese border town of Myawaddy are possible, ask at reception for the latest information.

➕ **196 B3** ✉ **100 Asia Road**
☎ **05 553 2601-8, fax: 05 553 2600,**
**email: www.centralhotelresorts.com,**
**www.centralhotelsresorts.com**

# Where to...
## Eat and Drink

**Prices**

Expect to pay per person for a three-course meal, excluding drinks and service
**£** under 200 baht **££** 200–500 baht **£££** over 500 baht

## AYUTTHAYA

### Chainam £

Chainam serves excellent Thai coffee accompanied by a good Western breakfast. For the rest of the day reasonable Thai and some average Western dishes are available.

➕ 196 C2 ✉ Thanon U-Thong Kalahom, opposite Chan Kasem Palace ☎ 03 525 2013 🕐 Daily 8 am–9 pm

### Phae Krung Kao ££

This attractive floating restaurant on the Pa Sak River is a great place to sit and relax and watch the activity on the rivers surrounding the town. The restaurant specialises in seafood and also offers a wide range of Thai chicken and pork dishes.

➕ 196 C2 ✉ South of Pridi Damrong Bridge, Moo 2 Thanon U-Thong ☎ 03 524 1555 🕐 Daily 10 am–9 pm

## KANCHANABURI

### Mae Nam ££

A number of floating restaurants vie for business south of the centrally located Rattanakarn Bridge. Mae Nam, one of the largest, offers freshwater fish and seafood. Particularly good is the *pla nung khing* (steamed fish with ginger, chilli and mushrooms). There are also meat and vegetarian dishes. In the evenings there is live music.

➕ 196 B1 ✉ On the river at the end of Lak Muang Road ☎ 03 451 2811 🕐 Daily 8:30 am–midnight

## PHITSANULOK

### Rim Nam Food Market £

This group of food stalls next to the Nan River is famous for *phak bung loi faa* (flash-fried morning glory vine). Once the morning glory has been flash-fried, it's thrown from the wok through the air onto a waiting plate. Sometimes the throw can be made over a considerable distance.

➕ 196 C3 ✉ Thanon Phuttha Bucha 🕐 Daily 5–11 pm

### Rim Nan ££

Rim Nan is a floating restaurant with a superb house speciality, *neua yang* (barbecued beef). Moored by the west bank of the Nan River, the restaurant feels more like a brightly lit pleasure cruiser than a floating platform. The river catches the cool breezes during the hot season, so it's a great place to sit and relax any time during the day or night.

➕ 196 C3 ✉ 63/2 Thanon Wang Chan ☎ 05 525 1446 🕐 Daily noon–2:30, 7:30–10:30

## SUKHOTHAI

### Dream Café/Antique House ££

Full of Thai old-world character, the Dream Café is decorated with 19th- and early 20th-century curios and antiques. The menu offers Thai, Chinese and Western dishes and also a long list of *lao yaa dawng* (herbal liquors) that are purportedly good for the health, consisting of a variety of herbs, roots, fruits and seeds, mixed with *lao khao* (white liquor), an alcoholic drink made from sticky rice. Ice creams and sundaes complete the menu.

➕ 196 B3 ✉ 86/1 Thanon Singhawat ☎ 05 561 2081 🕐 Daily 10 am–11 pm

# Where to... Shop

All the main towns in the central plains – Ayutthaya, Kanchanaburi, Lop Buri and Phitsanulok – have large and well-stocked malls.

## AYUTTHAYA

**Bang Sai Arts and Crafts Centre** (Tambon Chang Yai, Bang Sai; tel: 03 536 6092) trains local people in the production of traditional arts and crafts and has a well-stocked sales outlet. It's 24km (14.8 miles) southwest of Ayutthaya, but worth the journey.

At the **Ayutthaya Park Complex** (126 Thanon Asia, Klong Suan Plu District), which is slightly out of the main town, has an indoor floating market offering a range of interesting souvenirs.

## SUKHOTHAI

Due to the excellent clay found in the Si Satchanalai and Sawankhalok area north of Sukhothai, an ancient **ceramics** tradition still thrives and is sold in shops in Si Satchanalai and Sukhothai.

Kilns in Si Satchanalai and Sawankhalok have been producing **celadon** for centuries. Little finds its way to local shops, but you can buy from **Sawankhalok's principal factory**, opposite the PTP petrol station on the Phitsanulok highway (open Mon–Fri, 9–6). Sukhothai gold and silver jewellery is highly prized for its flamboyant decorative style and use of coloured enamel. The Sawankhalok road 3km (2 miles) north of Sukhothai has gold and silver merchants. **Lumchad Ancient Silver** (340/5 Sawankhalok Road) is recommended. The **Sathorn Gold and Textile Museum** and shop (Highway 101, Si Satchanalai) sells fine gold, silver and superb local textiles.

# Where to... Be Entertained

## FESTIVALS

Big annual events to look out for include **Kanchanaburi's River Kwai Bridge Festival** (end November/beginning December, ▶ 11). The famous bridge (▶ 68) becomes the venue for a number of events that culminate each evening with a spectacular sound-and-light show.

The **Loy Krathong Festival** (full moon between late October and mid-November, ▶ 11) takes place within the Sukhothai Historical Park, with the ancient monuments lit up in dramatic fashion (▶ 75).

## AYUTTHAYA

**Ayutthaya Park** (126 Thanon Asia) has a bowling alley, cinemas and an artificial sea world.

## OUTDOOR ENTERTAINMENT

**Safarine** (tel: 03 462 7140, www.safarine.com) offers customised jungle tours and river trips for all ages. **AS Mixed Travel** (293 Thanon Mae Nam Khwae, tel: 03 451 2017), offers one- and two-day mountain-bike tours.

## NIGHTLIFE

**Kanchanaburi** has live music at the **Apache Saloon** (Thanon Saengchuto) and floating discos. **Phitsanulok** Plaza has a range of pubs and dance clubs. The **Tree House** restaurant (Airport Road, tel: 05 521 2587) and **Sukothai's Rajthanee Hotel** (229 Charodvitheetong Road) have live music nightly.

# The North

Getting Your Bearings 88 – 89
In Six Days 90 – 91
Don't Miss 92 – 99
At Your Leisure 100 – 103
Where To 104 – 108

# Getting Your Bearings

Most visitors to Thailand make the pilgrimage to the scenic north to relax in the cool green mountains, to shop for some of the best crafts in the country and to trek to hill-tribe villages. The ancient and modern city of Chiang Mai is the capital of the area and, with its rich collection of temples, its moated old city, night market and night bazaar, is a place where people linger. This is the ideal place to learn the art of Thai cooking, or even study the Thai language or Buddhist meditation.

The ancient kingdom of the north was known as Lanna, the "land of a million rice fields", a fertile region watered by chocolate-coloured rivers and plunging waterfalls. It is easy to spend a few weeks enjoying the unhurried pace of life and exploring the surrounding scattered villages in the lush mountains where the clean air is perhaps envied by the people who live in Bangkok.

**Hill-tribe head-dresses are still often worn**

The distinct region in the very north that borders Burma and Laos, known as The Golden Triangle, was the legendary zone of drug smuggling in the 1960s and 1970s, and offers the chance to travel to these neighbouring countries. It's bordered by mountain ranges, including the highest peak in the country, Doi Inthanon (2,565m/8,413 feet), which is part of a national park of the same name and great for walking and trekking.

## At Your Leisure

**4** The Golden Triangle ➤ 100
**5** Chiang Saen ➤ 101
**6** Chiang Rai ➤ 101
**7** Chiang Mai Courses ➤ 102
**8** Lamphun ➤ 103
**9** Doi Khun Tan National Park ➤ 103

## ★ Don't Miss

**1** Chiang Mai ➤ 92
**2** Trekking ➤ 95
**3** Mae Hong Son ➤ 98

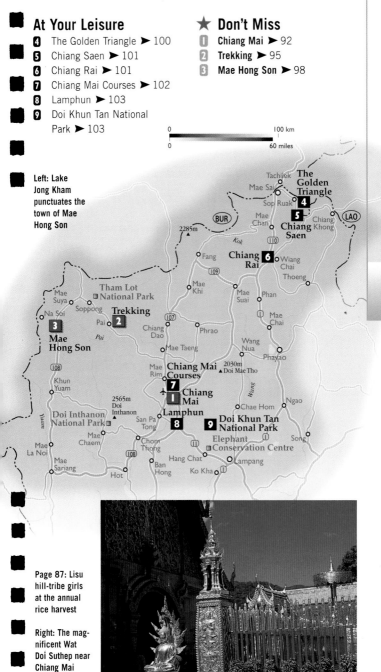

Left: Lake Jong Kham punctuates the town of **Mae Hong Son**

Page 87: Lisu hill-tribe girls at the annual rice harvest

Right: The magnificent Wat Doi Suthep near Chiang Mai

Visit the temple-studded city of Chaing Mai, set against a stunning mountain backdrop. Trek in the nearby hill-tribe villages or take a jeep tour through the scenic landscape.

# The North in Six Days

## Day One

### Morning
The most comfortable way to get from Bangkok to ⓘ **Chiang Mai** (right, ► 92–94) is to fly, or catch the overnight sleeper train. On arrival, spend a few hours exploring the old city with its moat and *wats* by bike or on foot. Take a *tuk-tuk* to the **Hill-Tribe Museum** (► 94) on the outskirts of town.

### Lunch
Take a *songthaew* to have lunch at Galae (► 106) on the lower slopes of Doi Suthep (the mountain that overlooks Chiang Mai), and check out their central and northern Thai dishes.

### Afternoon
Take another *songthaew* further up the mountain to visit the temple **Wat Doi Suthep** (left, ► 92), the north's most important temple, and enjoy the spectacular views of the surrounding countryside.

### Evening
Enjoy the spectacle that is **Chiang Mai's night bazaar** (► 93), shopping for crafts and souvenirs, or just wandering around the many stalls. Have dinner at the Brasserie (► 106). There is live music every night and cocktails are served until the early hours. It can get busy at weekends, so arrive early.

# Days Two to Four

Go on a **2** **three-day trek from Chiang Mai** (➤ 95). Most involve several hours' walking every day. Elephant-riding (left) and river-rafting are optional extras. Hill-tribe communities (below) are the main attraction and accommodation is in village huts. Return to Chiang Mai.

# Days Five and Six

Complete the jeep tour (➤ 177) of the villages on the road to **3** **Mae Hong Son** (below, ➤ 98–99) starting from Chiang Mai. If you arrive back in Chiang Mai in time, you can go to a traditional show with a northern-style dinner at the Old Chiang Mai Cultural Centre (➤ 106) between 7 and 10 pm.

# ▯Chiang Mai

Chiang Mai, capital of the north and Thailand's second-largest city, has more than a hundred temples. With its cooler climate, visible expatriate community and sophisticated atmosphere, it's a relaxing place to spend a few days before setting off on a trek. The moat-enclosed, partly walled old town invites wandering, as does the biggest night market in the country, which is a treasure trove of crafts.

## Wat Doi Suthep

The mountain-top temple of Wat Doi Suthep, 16km (10 miles) west of town, is easily reached by *songthaew*. It is said that the location was decided by a sacred white elephant who picked this spot by trumpeting and then circling here three times before lying down to die. Wat Doi Suthep is the north's most important temple, where candlelit processions are made on major religious occasions. It is also part of a national park, rich in birdlife.

Above: An intricate roof detail from Wat Chiang Man

## Other Temples

It would take several days to visit all the temples in town, so start with the top three, which can be visited on a half-hour walking route.

Right: The ancient temple complex of Wat Chiang Man

**Wat Phra Singh**, at the western end of Thanon Ratchdamnoen, is an impressive complex with a 14th-century *chedi* containing the ashes of King Kam Fu. The carved wooden **Viharn Lai Kam** is a classic example of Lanna-style architecture. Inside is one of three **Phra Singh Buddha** images, a highly revered statue believed to have been magically created in the 2nd century. This one is in bronze and is surrounded by exquisite 18th-century murals depicting life in this part of Thailand.

*Below: The famous Viharn Lai Kam, Wat Phra Singh*

**Wat Chedi Luang**, on Phra Pok Klao Road (off Ratchdamnoen), has a giant 60m (197-foot) ruined brick *chedi* that once sheltered the Emerald Buddha, now in Wat Phra Kaeo in Bangkok (➤ 45) and still contains the city's *lak muang*, or spiritual pillar.

**Wat Chiang Man**, near Thanon Wiang Kaeo, is Chiang Mai's oldest temple. Enter the *viharn* on the right of the main entrance to see two important Buddha images in stone and crystal.

## Night Bazaar

The night bazaar is a shopping haven full of fake perfumes, designer copies and tourist junk, as well as lacquerware, woodcarvings, silverwork, antiques and spices. Watch out for labels saying "100 per cent silk" – very often the fabric is in fact viscose or even polyester. Stalls are set up along **Chang Khlan** between Thanon Tha Phae and Si Don Chai at around 6 pm and are not taken down until around 11 pm.

➕ 196 B4
**TAT**
✉ 105 Thanon Chiang Mai–Lamphun, opposite Lek Bridge
☎ 05 324 8604　🕐 Daily 8:30–4:30

### Hill-Tribe Museum
✉ Ratchamangkhala Park　🕐 Daily 9–4　💷 Free

*Right: Beautifully illuminated Wat Chedi Luang*

## A Hard Bargain

Goods on sale in Chiang Mai's shops and markets are often sold at over-inflated prices. Knowing the system – which applies to shopping anywhere in Thailand – is essential. Buying where there are no fixed prices is a ritualised game, with figures punched out on a calculator. The seller will quote you a much higher price than they expect to get. It is up to you to work out how much higher and to bargain hard, but politely. The rule is to offer half the demanded price and to settle for something in-between.

During the day, **Warorot Market** sells more local goods and produce.

## Hill-Tribe Museum

Almost half of the 750,000 hill-tribe people of northern Thailand are **Karen**. The last 20 years have seen an influx of around a million refugees from Laos, Burma and Cambodia, three-quarters of whom are Karen from Burma, fleeing the military regime there. Some 100 or so of these are **long-necked women** (➤ 99) living in tourist villages, which charge an entrance fee and display the women, as if in a zoo, for tourists to gawk at.

The Hill-Tribe Museum has fascinating and well-presented displays about the hill tribes. Information is given about the various communities, each with their distinct beliefs, dress and farming practices.

Housed in a three-storey pavilion in the middle of a lake in Ratchamangkhala Park on the city's northern outskirts, it is worth visiting for its lovely location alone. The easy-to-miss **crafts centre** on the ground floor is also worth a visit.

### TAKING A BREAK

Try **Heuan Phen** (➤ 106) on Thanon Ratchamankha, for good northern Thai food, or **Khao Soi Islam**, a Muslim restaurant on Thanon Charoen Prathet Soi 1.

---

## CHIANG MAI: INSIDE INFO

**Top tips** Rent a **bicycle** for in town, but avoid the Superhighway around the city.
• **Nancy Chandler's Map of Chiang Map** (available from newsagents and tourist souvenir shops) has detailed plans of the night bazaar and Warorot Market as well as sightseeing tips, out-of-town trips and information about getting around.
• As it can get hot in the city from April to June, it is worth considering booking into a hotel with a **swimming pool** or seeking out one of the **public baths**.
• Chiang Mai Land Sports Club (off Chang Klan Road) is open to visitors, and has a 30m (98.5-foot) pool, tennis courts and an airy restaurant.

**Hidden gem** Examples of the different **styles of house** built by the various **hill tribes** can be found in the Hill-Tribe Museum grounds next to the lake.

# 2 Trekking

Much of the lure of northern Thailand comes from its trekking opportunities. Just about everyone who makes it to this region jumps at the chance to journey on foot through jungle and mountains, visiting unique hill-tribe villages and staying in the headman's house for the night. These treks do not normally involve strenuous hiking.

Right: Elephant trekking at Baan Meung Phen

Below: Trekking on foot in the forest

Although the 750,000 hill-tribe people are usually referred to collectively, these "mountain people" – a more accurate translation of the Thai term – form distinct communities (➤ 20–22). They originate from countries as diverse as Burma (Karen people), Tibet (Lisu, Lahu and Akha) and China (Mien and Hmong). Belief systems, dress and agricultural practices all vary from tribe to tribe.

## Tribal Etiquette
• **Ask before taking photographs**. Many villagers are uncomfortable about having their picture taken; this especially applies to pregnant women and babies.
• Though it is tempting to **take gifts** with you for the tribes, they can have a negative impact. Showing family photographs or postcards of home is a better idea.
• **Dress modestly** (shirt or T-shirt, long trousers or a skirt).
• **Do not show public displays of affection**. These are offensive to villagers as well as to Thai people in general.
• **Respect the villagers' beliefs**. Do not touch or sit beneath the entrance gate or giant swing in an Akha village (Akha are the poorest of the hill-tribes; the gates and swing at the entrance to their villages are sacred). Do not photograph or touch shrines in houses.

### Choosing a Trek

There is an overwhelming number of agents trying to sell treks. The first step is to decide on your requirements.

- **How many days** do you want to go for? It could be anything from two to fourteen – although three-day trips are by far the most common and enough for most people.
- Are you willing to **pay extra** for transport costs to a more remote area? It is worth confirming whether private vehicles – rather than public buses, which can mean long waits – are used.
- Do you want extras such as **river-rafting** and **elephant-riding**? These can be fun and are very popular.
- Try to **speak to the guide**, rather than just the person selling you the trek, before you commit yourself. That way you can check out his/her level of English and general approach. Most guides should speak some English and know about how to behave with the hill tribes.
- **Ask other travellers** who have just returned from a trip or get the list of licensed companies from TAT.
- **Establish in writing** what exactly is included in the trek cost (for example, what kind of food and what kind of bedding might be provided if it turns cold).
- **Establish exact departure and return times**.
- If you go on a trek organised by the place where you are staying, **make sure that there will still be a room** for you when you return; sometimes rooms can be booked out to other parties while you are on your trek.
- **Check who else is going on the trip with you** (eight is the maximum total).
- Ask about the **level of fitness** required. Although most are not as strenuous as trekking in other countries, a certain standard might be required. Survival Partnership (►opposite) offers the full range of treks, including treks for the "couch potato".
- Make sure that the trek has **two guides** – someone at the front and someone bringing up the rear.

## RESPONSIBLE TOURISM: INSIDE INFO

**Top tips** Be aware of the impact your tourism will have on the communities you visit. Tours that are sensitive to the local people and environment can be rewarding for tourists and locals alike. The **Responsible Ecological Social Tours Project** (REST) works with local communities in Thailand to develop community based tourism (www.rest.or.th). Another good point of reference for responsible tourism is the **Tourism Concern** website, www.tourismconcern.co.uk

**Below right:** An Akha tribes-woman at the Doi Mae Salong morning market

**Bottom right:** Bamboo rafting on the Pai River

**Below:** Trekkers in Pa Mon Nok village

**Inset:** An Akha house, San Charoen Mai village

To get the most out of a trek, first visit the **Hill-Tribe Museum** (➤ 94) in Chiang Mai to learn something about the various tribes.

Most treks are organised from **Chiang Mai**, where around 200 agencies offer organised treks covering nearly everywhere that can be trekked in the north. **Chiang Rai**, **Pai** and **Mae Hong Son** also have tour agencies, but these tend to offer more local treks. A tour from somewhere other than these four will probably be cheaper, but more informally arranged and with less regulation. There is a constant search by both tour operators and tourists alike for the next new and exotic villages. Ten years ago Pai was billed as the "untouristed zone", although now it has plenty.

A rising awareness about the impact of tourism on the environment and local communities in recent years has brought about an increased number of eco-friendly and ethically-orientated tours in these areas (see panel above).

### TAKING A BREAK

Food is always provided on any organised trek, but check what it is likely to be. Village food can be very basic and it usually pays to pack your own "survival kit". Include plenty of fruit.

# 3 Mae Hong Son

Mae Hong Son, more poetically known as the "City of Three Mists", is in fact a town of just 6,000 people. It was isolated until a paved road was built in the 1960s, and despite the airport bringing in people from Chiang Mai every day, it still has a remote atmosphere. The lush paddy fields, scenic waterfalls and mountains, and dense forest that surrounds it are home to many Burmese and hill-tribe people.

## The Town
Most people come to Mae Hong Son to explore the surrounding area on treks, and it has more than its fair share of backpacker guest houses. Visit **Wat Doi Kong Mu** to the west, with memorable views over the town and valley. From the summit you can also see the mountains in Burma to the west.

**Right: Queen Sirikit's *chedi* at Doi Inthanon National Park**

## The Loop
A 600km (372-mile) twisting and steep route, much of it built by the Japanese during World War II, forms a **scenic loop** (► 177) from Chiang Mai, and halfway round is Mae Hong Son. Starting in Mae Hong Son, **Highway 108** goes from Mae

**Below: The scenic mountain town of Mae Hong Son encircles Jong Kham Lake**

## Long-Necked Women

One of the most disturbing tourist attractions here is the "long-necked" women of the Paduang tribe who have left Myamnar (Burma) to escape its repressive regime. The women wear brass coils up to 30cm (12 inches) high on their necks, increasing them in number from a young age. The coils force the collarbone and ribs down rather than stretching the neck, which is the visual effect. These women are put on show to those who pay the entrance fee to the village – predominantly at Nai Soi, 35km (22 miles) northwest of Mae Hong Son. Many tourists have reported feeling sickened at the sight, and there is some argument that visitors encourage the continuation of a practice that is outlawed in Myanmar as barbaric and would otherwise die out.

Hong Son to Chiang Mai and **Route 1095** goes from Chiang Mai to Mae Hong Son. You can do the loop in either direction.

Highway 108 winds south from Mae Hong Son to the well-maintained and much-visited **Doi Inthanon National Park**, home to hundreds of species of birds. Paved roads lead to Doi Inthanon, the highest mountain in Thailand, although at only 2,565m (8,413 feet) it is rather disappointing.

Two royal *chedis*, built to honour the 60th birthdays of the king and queen of Thailand, are where Thais come to pay their respects to the much-loved royal couple (► 15–17). Nearby, the **Kew Mae Pan Trail** follows a two-hour circular walk through the forest.

The first main stop on Route 1095 on the Chiang Mai to Mae Hong Son loop is **Pai**, 100km (62 miles) east of Mae Hong Son. It has a laid-back atmosphere, hot springs and some tourist facilities, including internet cafés and international cuisine.

The small, friendly market town of **Soppong**, strung along the Pai River, has the most important cave in the whole area, **Tham Lot**.

### TAKING A BREAK

The **Golden Teak** terrace restaurant at the Imperial Tara Hotel (► 107) overlooks the large garden, or try **Bai Fern** (► 107) for Chinese and Thai dishes.

---

➕ 196 A5
**Doi Inthanon National Park**
☎ 05 335 5728, www.dnp.go.th 🕐 Always open 🚌 From Chiang Mai or Mae Sariang to Chom Thong, bus to Mae Klang, then Songthaew 💷 Expensive

---

### MAE HONG SON: INSIDE INFO

**Top tip** The **ideal time** to visit the area is between November and March although nights can be cold. Between June and October heavy rains can make travel difficult.

**One to miss** Despite the coachloads of tourists that flood **Fish Cave**, north of Mae Hong Son, it is relatively uninteresting and worth avoiding.

# At Your Leisure

## 4 The Golden Triangle

Much less magical than its name suggests, this is the area where the borders of Thailand, Burma and Laos meet, and the Ruak and Mekhong rivers converge. You know you have arrived by the large signs that tell you so.

Coachloads of tourists stream in every day to the village of **Sop Ruak**, with its souvenir stalls and two large, chic hotels. Once a thriving centre of the opium trade, Sop Ruak has two excellent museums on the subject of narcotics: the **Opium Museum** is in the centre of the village; the grand **Hall of Opium** is just outside on the road to **Mae Sai**. If you're in a hurry, visit the Opium Museum, if you have the time the Hall of Opium is a must.

A climb to the hilltop temple of **Wat Phra That Phu Khao** above Sop Ruak is rewarded with panoramic views, from the confluence of the Mekong and Ruak rivers to Burmese mountains as far as the eye can see.

Take a **longtail boat trip** (a group of four can share the cost) on the Mekong River. You will get a look at Laos (and a chance to step briefly on its soil) as well as the mammoth casino and hotel on Burmese land, the Golden Triangle Paradise Resort, set up by Khun Sa, a Thai drug warlord.

✚ 196 C5

**Opium Museum**
✉ 30km marker, southeast edge of Sop Ruak ⏰ Daily 7–6 💰 Inexpensive

**Hall of Opium**
✉ Sop Ruak ⏰ Thu–Sun 10–3:30 💰 Expensive

Looking across the Mekong River to Laos on the opposite bank

### Opium

Illicit opium-growing and trading is firmly associated with The Golden Triangle in most people's imagination. Although it has been illegal to grow opium since 1959, it is only in recent years that there has been significant success in reducing crops with the help of government initiatives. However, rates of addiction still run high among the hill-tribes, opium is still grown in the north of Thailand and remaining production of heroin (a refined form of opium) has been pushed across the borders to Laos and Burma.

## 5 Chiang Saen

This ruined riverside settlement on the northern reaches of the country stands at an historic trading cross-roads with Laos and China. Although it has some ancient **wats** and a **national museum**, its appeal lies in its uncommercial, likeable atmosphere. There is activity along the Mekhong River where boats from China and Laos call in. Possibly once the capital of an ancient kingdom, the town was founded in the 14th century, destroyed by the Burmese in 1804 and has only existed in its present form for 100 years or so. The National Museum has some interesting artefacts and Buddha images.

🚹 196 C5
**National Museum**
🕒 Wed–Sun 9–4 💲 Inexpensive

## 6 Chiang Rai

Situated on the Kok River, Chiang Rai was once the capital of northern Thailand. It has grown quickly over recent years to become a commercial tourist centre, offering upmarket accommodation and package tours. During the day you might want to take a look at **Wat Phra That Doi**

Temperate Flower Gardens at Doi Tung, Chiang Rai

**Tong**, with its wooden *lak muang* (the city pillar, home of the city's guardian spirit), and **Wat Phra Kaeo** where the Emerald Buddha (➤ 45) was first discovered. Craft shops, the **Hill-Tribe Museum** and the night bazaar are other diversions, but the town is most popularly used as a base for treks and tours in the area.

🚹 196 B5
**TAT**
✉ 448/16 Thanon Singhaklai
☎ 05 371 7433 🕒 Daily 8:30–4:30

**Hill-Tribe Museum**
✉ 620 Thanon Tanalai ☎ 05 374 0088
🕒 Daily 9–7 💲 Inexpensive

## For Kids
• The **Elephant Conservation Centre**, 30km (18.5 miles) northwest of Lampang, has authentic training displays, daily shows (9:30 am and 11 am, plus Sat and Sun 2 pm) and rides. Call 05 422 8034 for information.

• The **visitor centre at Doi Inthanon National Park** has interactive displays about the wildlife aimed at younger visitors.

• **Boat trips** on the Pai River from Huai Deua, near Nai Soi near the Burmese border.

• **Chiang Mai Zoo**, on the outskirts of the city (8–7, last entry 5 pm, inexpensive), has masses of Asian birds as well as Thai elephants and other animals.

## 7 Chiang Mai Courses
Cookery courses are a popular pursuit in Chiang Mai. They can teach you how to find your way around a Thai market, the art of pineapple-cutting, and delicious recipes using fresh coconut milk, fiery chillies and sweet basil.

An impressive *chedi* at Wat Phrathat Haripunchai, Lamphun

The **Chiang Mai Thai Cookery School** was the first of its kind, and so popular that the city is now packed with similar operations offering courses ranging from one to several days.

If you are not interested in things culinary, **Thai language**, **traditional massage** and **meditation** (Vipassana, Hindu and Buddhist) **courses** can keep you busy for anything up to a month.

The following are some of the well-established schools.

🚩 196 B4

**Chiang Mai Thai Cookery School**
✉ 47/2 Thanon Moon Muang
☎ 05 320 6388  💷 Expensive

**AUA Language School**
✉ 73 Thanon Ratchdamnoen
☎ 05 321 1377  💷 Expensive

**Old Medicine Hospital (massage)**
✉ Soi Siwaka Komarat, opposite Old Chiang Mai Cultural Centre
☎ 05 327 5085  💷 Expensive

**Northern Insight Meditation Centre**
✉ Wat Ram Poeng, Thanon Canal
☎ 05 327 8620  🕐 Month-long Vipassana courses only
💷 Expensive

The small **National Museum** has a collection of religious artefacts, including some Buddha images. **Wat Kukut** (or Wat Chama Thewi), on the other side of town, has possibly the two oldest *chedis* in the country.

🔹 196 B4
**National Museum**
🕐 Wed–Sun 9–noon, 1–4
💰 Inexpensive

The flower shop at the entrance to Doi Khun Tan National Park
Below: a moth orchid

### 🛈 Lamphun

This quiet town, surrounded by rice fields on the banks of the Kuang River, is best seen as a day trip from Chiang Mai, 26km (16 miles) away. Lamphun was the capital of the Haripunchai principality between 750 and 1281. It has many ancient temples, which are still in use today.

**Wat Phra That Haripunchai** is a temple complex thought to have been founded in the 11th century. It features the 46m (151-foot), 15th-century *chedi* **Suwan**, with a pure gold tiered umbrella.

#### Mae Sai to Burma

From Mae Sai in the far north of Thailand you can cross into Burma for a day's shopping in the Burmese border town of Tachilek. The local market there is packed with traders selling local gems and uncut stones. Prices are low, but be wary when offered "rubies" or "sapphires" at knock-down rates – not everything that sparkles in this market is genuine. The Burmese authorities levy a US$5 fee for spending a day in Tachilek, while for US$10 you can buy a two-week visa allowing you to travel as far as the Chinese border at Kengtung. Local taxis will take you there for around US$25 return. Visiting Tachilek is also a useful way of extending your Thai tourist visa – many expatriates use this route regularly to stay legally in Thailand.

### 🛈 Doi Khun Tan National Park

This 225sq km (88-square-mile) former hill station is made up of bamboo, tropical forests and pine trees. It lies at the 1,363m (4,470-foot) summit of **Doi Khun Tan**, famous for orchids and other wildflowers. It is possibly Thailand's least visited national park, yet easily reached from Chiang Mai, with trains from Chiang Mai to the park's station, 1.5km (1 mile) from the headquarters. The **tunnel** on the train journey – at 1,362m (4,467 feet), the longest tunnel in Thailand – cuts right though the mountain.

**Self-guided** (easy) **trails** run through the park and to the summit. Bungalow and camping accommodations are available. At weekends and holidays there tend to be more visitors.

🔹 196 B4   ☎ 05 331 1608   💰 Expensive

# Where to... Stay

**Prices**

Expect to pay per double room

£ under 1,000 baht   ££ 1,000–4,000 baht   £££ over 4,000 baht

## CHIANG MAI

### Amari Rincome ££

One of the older hotels in town, the Amari Rincome is tastefully decorated throughout with beautiful local crafts and artefacts. It's a good place for families with children, with one of the best swimming pools in Chiang Mai. The hotel is renowned for its reasonably priced lunchtime buffets, while regular food fairs promote a wide range of international cuisines.

➕ 202 A3 ☒ 1 Thanon Nimmanhaemin ☎ 05 389 4884-93, fax: 05 322 1915, email: rincome@amari.com, www.amari.com

### Chiang Mai Gate £

This quiet guest house in an unusual location in the heart of the old silversmith area of Wualai has beautiful rooms decorated in traditional northern Thai style. The bar and restaurant are relaxed and the pool secluded. Although a little away from the usual tourist areas, it's only a short walk north to the old city's southern gate and from there to some of the more important historical temples. The bars and restaurants of the Moon Muang and Thanon Thapae areas are a few minutes' walk to the northeast.

➕ 202 C1 ☒ 11/10 Thanon Suriwong ☎ 05 320 3895, fax: 05 327 9085, email: cmgate@chiangmai-online.com

### Lai Thai Guesthouse £

If you're planning to visit Chiang Mai during the annual water-throwing festival in April (▶ 10), and you don't mind getting wet for three days, then this is the place to stay. Located by the moat surrounding Chiang Mai's old city, Lai Thai offers good-value, no-frills accommodation and a relaxing pool.

➕ 202 C2 ☒ 111/4–5 Thanon Kotchasan ☎ 05 327 1725, fax: 05 327 2724

### Four Seasons £££

This resort tucked away in the spectacular Mae Sa Valley, with 8ha (20 acres) of gardens, is one of the north's best-kept secrets. There are two small lakes and terraced rice fields with their own water buffalo in the grounds. Large pavilions and 13 palatial Residence Suites housed in three- or four-storey villas dot the landscape. Each of the pavilions is roomy and decorated with rich Thai fabrics. Each Residence Suite offers master, guest and children's rooms with private plunge pools or rooftop penthouse and a live-in house-keeper. Other attributes include world-class spa facilities.

➕ 196 B4 ☒ Mae Rim-Samoeng Old Road ☎ 05 329 8181, fax: 05 329 8190, email: rcm.reservation@fourseasons.com, www.fourseasons.com

### River View Lodge £

Overlooking the River Ping, this large, almost Swiss-style, chalet is secluded and yet close to the heart of Chiang Mai. It offers comfortable rooms decorated with traditional northern Lanna furnishings (wall-hangings made from woven Lanna cloth, low rattan tables, wooden and paper lanterns). Try to get one of the rooms with a river balcony. You'll find the River View at the end of a quiet little lane, not too far from the famous night bazaar (▶ 93). Facilities include a swimming pool.

➕ 202 D2 ☒ 25 Thanon Charoen Prathet, Soi 2 ☎ 05 327 1110, fax: 05 327 9019

## Tamarind Village £££

Chiang Mai has experienced a boom in traditional Lanna-style "boutique" hotels in recent years, and this is one of the most attractive of them. Tucked away in the centre of the old city, shielded from the traffic by shrubbery and towering bamboo, it's a tasteful oasis of calm. Whitewashed corridors, embracing a secluded pool area, give it an almost monastic atmosphere, but the rooms are opulent, furnished in teak woods and featuring selected antiques.

➕ 202 C2 ⬜ 50–1 Ratchadamnoen Road ☎ 05 341 8888, fax: 05 341 8890, www.tamarindvillage.com

## MAE HONG SON

## Imperial Tara ££

Set amid extensive tropical gardens, this beautifully situated resort slightly to the south of the main town offers genuine peace and tranquility. Mae Hong Son is a slow and easy-going town and the

Tara mirrors this feeling perfectly. The rooms are designed in the northern Thai style, with a hint of Burmese influence and they blend with the surrounding teak forest. The terrace restaurant overlooks the large garden and the small stream that intersects the hotel.

➕ 196 A5 ⬜ 149 Moo 8, Tambon Pang Moo ☎ 05 361 1272, fax: 05 361 1252, email: taramaehongson@imperialhotels.com www.imperialhotels.com

## GOLDEN TRIANGLE/SOP RUAK

## Anantara Golden Triangle £££

It's difficult to think of a more romantic location than this fabulous luxury resort combining classic northern Thai and contemporary design, overlooking the junction of two rivers (Mekhong and Ruak) and three countries (Thailand, Laos and Myanmar-Burma). In the heart of the fabled Golden Triangle (▶ 100), the hotel is surrounded

by 160ha (395 acres) of lush gardens and bamboo forests. All the rooms offer unparalleled views of either Laos or Myanmar. Facilities offered include mountain biking, elephant rides and longtail boat cruises on the Mekong River.

➕ 196 C5 ⬜ The Golden Triangle, Chiang Saen district, Chiang Rai province ☎ 05 378 4084, fax: 05 378 4090

## CHIANG RAI

## Dusit Island Resort ££

Although a large and somewhat impersonal place, this is nevertheless the best of the hotels in Chiang Rai. The Dusit occupies its own island in the middle of the River Kok. All rooms have wonderful views of the surrounding valley and the hotel's beautiful gardens. There are a number of good restaurants within the hotel, but the pick of the crop is undoubtedly Chinatown, their excellent Chinese restaurant.

➕ 196 B5 ⬜ 1129 Thanon Kraisorasit ☎ 05 371 5777, fax: 05 371 5801, email: chiangrai@dusit.com, www.dusit.com

## Golden Triangle Inn £

Within easy walking distance of downtown Chiang Rai, this attractive low-rise hotel has cleverly blended the modern with the traditional. All rooms are large and have air-conditioning and an American breakfast is included in the rate. The attractive landscaped grounds have a painstakingly cultivated Japanese/Thai garden. At weekends the attached café showcases traditional Lanna music, a quiet and relaxing affair using string and xylophone-like instruments. Also on the same site are a helpful travel agency and a car-rental office.

➕ 196 B5 ⬜ 590 Thanon Phahonyothin ☎ 05 371 6996, fax: 05 371 3963, www.goldenchiangrai.com

# Where to...
# Eat and Drink

## Prices

Expect to pay per person for a three-course meal, excluding drinks and service
£ under 200 baht  ££ 200–500 baht  £££ over 500 baht

Northern Thailand has inherited the culinary, more spicy, legacy of the once-powerful Lanna Kingdom, with ties to Burma and the Chinese province of Yunnan. Naturally, Chiang Mai, as the largest city in the north, has the largest and best selection of restaurants.

## CHIANG MAI

### The Antique House £

If you fancy the table you dine at in this century-old mansion you can buy the table, or any of the other antiques scattered around. The best value, however, is the food, northern Thai cuisine at its best. A string duo plays classical Thai music as you eat.

➕ 202 D2  ✉ Charoen Prathet (next to the Diamond Hotel)  ☎ 05 327 6810  🕐 Daily 11–midnight

### Brasserie ££

Perfectly situated on the east bank of the River Ping near the Nawarat Bridge, the Brasserie is perfect for an evening meal. This stretch of the river has many good restaurants, but the extensive Thai and European menu coupled with the live music sets the Brasserie apart.

➕ 202 D2  ✉ 37 Thanon Charoen Rat  ☎ 05 324 1665  🕐 Daily 10 am–1 am

### Galae ££

For atmosphere, especially in the early evening, Galae is hard to beat. Situated on the lower slopes of Doi Suthep (the mountain that overlooks Chiang Mai) and at the edge of a small lake, it offers great views of the city itself. The menu consists mainly of central and northern Thai dishes. The house dishes include *kai galae* (roast chicken with herbs).

➕ 202 A2  ✉ 65 Thanon Suthep  ☎ 05 327 8655  🕐 Daily 10–9

### Heuan Phen £

Excellent northern Thai food is served in the main building during the day and in an old wooden house to the back of the main restaurant at night. Specialities include *nam prhik ong* (minced pork with tomatoes and chillies, almost like a Thai bolognese sauce), and *kaeng hang lay* (curried pork with fresh ginger and peanuts).

➕ 202 C2  ✉ 112 Thanon Ratchamankha  ☎ 05 327 7103  🕐 Daily 8 am–3, 5–9:30

### Huan Huay Kaew ££

This rustic restaurant, built almost entirely of bamboo, sits on several levels at the edge of the Doi Suthep National Park, with many of the tables overlooking the park's most beautiful waterfall. The Thai cuisine is outstanding, offering rare regional specialities like Gaeng Som, a fragrant fish soup laced with orange. A string trio performs every night.

➕ 196 B4  ✉ 31/2 Moo 2, Thanon Suthep  ☎ 05 389 2698  🕐 Daily 11–11

### Old Chiang Mai Cultural Centre ££

At the Cultural Centre, traditional northern-style *khantoke* meals are accompanied by Thai classical dance and music. The Cultural Centre is set in a series of old teak houses and the meal is served on a low, tray-like table called a *khantoke*. Central dishes include *nam prik ong* (minced pork and tomatoes), *kaeng hang lay* (curried pork with fresh ginger and peanuts), *khaep mu* (crispy fried pork rinds), and *tam makhua* (an aubergine and garlic dip with hard-boiled eggs and fresh mint).

➕ 202 B1 ✉ 185/3 Thanon Wualai ☎ 05 320 2993-5 🕐 Daily 7 am–10 pm

### Salungkham £

From the tree-shaded outside dining area of this traditional northern Thai restaurant you can watch your meal being prepared at the open kitchen/grill. Non-smokers are catered for in the inside restaurant. Try the mixed grilled beef and northern Thai sausage (*yang ruam*) or the steamed Thai-style whipped eggs (*khai tun*).

➕ 196 B4 ✉ 834/3 Phaholyyotin Road ☎ 05 371 7192 🕐 Daily 10.30–10.30

## LAMPANG

### Riverside Bar/Restaurant ££

On the banks of the Yom River, this very popular place serves excellent Thai food. Much of the atmosphere derives from the proximity of the Yom River, with its houseboats and floating restaurants. The house speciality is fish, prawns and seafood, but the usual regulars are available too. The fried chicken and cashew nut is recommended. There is live Thai folk music most nights.

➕ 196 B4 ✉ 328 Thanon Tipchang ☎ 05 431 5286 🕐 11 am–midnight

## MAE HONG SON

### Bai Fern ££

An excellent mix of Thai and Chinese dishes is served in this attractive old restaurant. The friendly atmosphere and the ambience is enhanced by many local decorative items on the walls. One of the best places in town, with a candlelit terrace. There are also some Western dishes on the menu.

➕ 196 A5 ✉ Thanon Khunlum Praphat ☎ 05 361 1374 🕐 Daily 7 am–10 pm

### Golden Teak Restaurant ££

This restaurant is part of the upmarket Imperial Tara hotel complex (▶ 105). Thai food is available, but if you crave good Western food – this is the place. In Mae Hong Son – which is rare in Mae Hong Son – this is the place. The Western breakfasts are particularly good.

➕ 196 A5 ✉ 149 Moo 8, Tambon Pang Moo ☎ 05 361 1021–5 🕐 Daily 7 am–midnight

## GOLDEN TRIANGLE/SOP RUAK

### Border View ££

Thai and Chinese food are served on a beautiful terrace of the Imperial Hotel overlooking the Mekong River in the heart of The Golden Triangle. The steaks are tender and the cooks know how to produce a satisfying Western breakfast, as well as other Western dishes.

➕ 196 C5 ✉ 222 Golden Triangle ☎ 05 378 4001 🕐 Daily 7 am–midnight

## CHIANG RAI

### Mae Ui Khiaw ££

Not far from the town centre, this is the best place for northern Thai cuisine. On offer are all the classic dishes such as spicy tomato and pork curry, pork and ginger curry and various chilli dips. There's a pleasant local atmosphere, friendly service and authentic local cooking.

➕ 196 B5 ✉ 1064/1 Thanon Sanambin ☎ 05 375 3173 🕐 Daily 7 am–9 pm

### Haw Naliga £

Located near the Chiang Rai clock tower, after which it is named, this restaurant is always popular, especially late into the night as it's one of the last places in town to close. Recommended dishes include *khao kua moo* (pork with pickled cabbage and boiled eggs), which is very good on a cold northern night. There's also an extensive range of noodle dishes.

➕ 196 B5 ✉ 402/1-2 Thanon Banprakhan 🕐 Daily 7 am–early am

# Where to...
# Shop

The north's finest shopping prospects are found in Chiang Mai, one of the best places to shop in Southeast Asia.

## CHIANG MAI

The **Night Market** (Thanon Chang Khlan, daily 6–11 pm; ▶ 93) provides a shopping mecca.

Out-of-town shopping trips include **Baw Sang Village** and **Thanon Sankhampaeng**, where there are dozens of high-quality showrooms, workshops and export centres offering every sort of local product, including Baw Sang's famous umbrellas and parasols.

Just to the south of Chiang Mai on Route 108, **Hang Dong** is the main centre for woodcarvings and rattan furniture.

**Thanon Wua Lai**, just south of Chiang Mai Gate, is the heart of the old silverworkers' district, and is lined with shops selling finely crafted silverware.

**Warorot Market**, in the centre of the city's busy commercial district, is the main local market. Here you can find every kind of northern Thai food, exotic fruits, and imported clothing and other goods from nearby Burma, Laos and South China.

The **Hill Tribe Products Promotion Centre** (217 Thanon Suthep, Wat Suan Dok, tel: 05 327 7743), under the patronage of King Bhumibol, sells a wide variety of hill-tribe paraphernalia such as hats, bags, jackets, jewellery, blankets and baskets.

The best department stores in town are the **Central Airport Plaza**, at the corner of Mahidol and Hang Dong Roads and **Central** (99/4 Moo 2, Thanon Huay Kaew, tel: 05 322 4999), both with a wide variety of goods at very reasonable prices.

# Where to...
# Be Entertained

## CHIANG MAI NIGHTLIFE

For an early drink in a British-style pub, try **The Pub** (189 Thanon Huay Kaew, tel: 05 321 1550). Young Thais favour art deco pubs like **Fine Thanks Pub** (119 Thanon Nimmanhaemin, tel: 05 321 3605), where local bands play Thai and Western favourites. A must for those seeking live music with a jazzy feel is **The Good View** (13 Thanon Charoenrat, tel: 05 324 1866) by the river, both popular and highly recommended.

**The Peak** (Thanon Chang Khlan, tel: 05 382 0776) offers a different form of entertainment. A man-made cliff towers over the area giving the intrepid a go at rock climbing. Bars and restaurants surround the cliff.

**Bubbles Disco** (46–48 Thanon Charoen Prathet, tel: 05 327 0099)

fills with Thais and visitors every night. If you enjoy a show, reserve tickets for the **Simon Cabaret** (next to the Rim Ping supermarket, Chang Puak Road, tel: 05 341 0321-3), a Las Vegas-style spectacular with a cast of stunning transvestites.

## TREKKING

A **trek** to a hill-tribe village is one reason why people travel to the far north. Trekkers usually walk for three to five hours a day. Thanon Charoen Prathet, between the river and the Night Market, has many companies offering trekking tours. Among the best are the **Wild Planet Adventure Centre** (73 Thanon Charoen Prathet, tel 05 327 7178), and **Somboon Tour** (25 Thanon Charoen Prathet, tel 05 381 8067).

# East Coast

Getting Your Bearings 110 – 111
In Five Days 112 – 113
Don't Miss 114 – 119
At Your Leisure 120 – 121
Where To 122 – 124

# Getting Your Bearings

This corner of the country juts out into the Gulf of Thailand and is flanked by Cambodia on its eastern side. Its charms are varied and idiosyncratic and the islands off the rugged coast are less developed than the more polished resorts of the south. But the region is within much easier reach of Bangkok if you are short of time, with blinding white beaches on the islands, limited traffic and an altogether more peaceful atmosphere.

Choose from the rocky fishing island of Ko Si Chang and the thickly forested national park islands of Ko Chang and Ko Samet. The beaches on the mainland coast have little to recommend them, having been blighted by oil industry developments. If you are really short of time, you can take a train journey that hugs the coast, stopping off at Ko Si Chang and Pattaya.

The theme here is essentially relaxation, but for the energetic, there is also diving, rainforest trekking and watersports at the brash international resort of Pattaya. The interior features the gem capital of Chanthaburi, with a large Vietnamese population, and Khao Yai National Park, which links with two other national parks (Thap Lan and Pang Sida). The park has hiking trails that follow animal tracks.

Left: Fishing boats at Bang Bao village, Ko Chang

# ★ Don't Miss
1 Ko Chang ➤ 114
2 Ko Samet ➤ 117

# At Your Leisure
3 Chanthaburi ➤ 120
4 Pattaya ➤ 120
5 Ko Si Chang ➤ 121
6 Khao Yai National Park ➤ 121

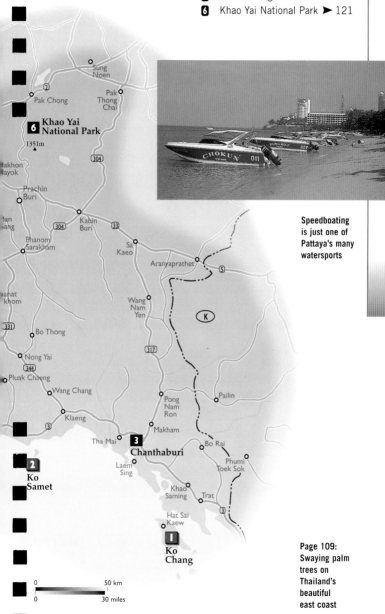

Sung
Noen

(2) Pak Chong    Pak
Thong
Chai

**Khao Yai**
6 **National Park**

1351m

Makhon
Nayok

Prachin
Buri

Ban
Sang    (304)    Kabin
Buri    (33)

Phanom
Sarakham    Sa
Kaeo

Aranyaprathet    (5)

anat
khom

Wang
Nam
Yen    K

(331) Bo Thong

Nong Yai    (317)

(344)
Pluak Chaeng

Wang Chang    Pong
Nam
Ron    Pailin

Klaeng    Makham

Tha Mai    3    Bo Rai
**Chanthaburi**
2    Laem    Phumi
**Ko**    Sing    Toek Sok
**Samet**    Khao
Saming    Trat

(3) Hat Sai
Kaew

1
**Ko**
**Chang**

Speedboating
is just one of
Pattaya's many
watersports

Page 109:
Swaying palm
trees on
Thailand's
beautiful
east coast

0    50 km
0    30 miles

Relax on the twin national park islands of Ko Chang and Ko Samet. Take it easy on the beach, go for a scenic walk or set sail to tiny islets. Then visit Chanthaburi to fill up with world-renowned noodles and witness its frantic gem-trading.

# East Coast in Five Days

## Day One

### Morning

Start on the island of ❶ **Ko Chang** (below, ➤ 114–116). Take a walk through dense rainforest to the **waterfall of Khlong Phu** from Hat Sai Kaew, making an early start to avoid the heat of the day. The clear pool of water is a great place for a scenic dip. Return to Hat Sai Kaew beach and tuck into a fresh crab salad at one of the many beachside restaurants.

### Afternoon and Evening

Stroll along the white sands of **Hat Sai Kaew** and through the freshwater streams. Then relax in a hammock on the beach or have a massage under the trees. Mac Bungalows on Hat Sai Kaew is a good place for a beach barbecue (on Saturday nights they have dancing on the beach). Choose your fresh catch – maybe a barracuda or tiger prawns – from a bed of ice. Order the marinade of your choice, such as lemon, chilli and garlic and accompany it with a cocktail, perhaps a fresh banana daiquiri.

## Day Two

Go on a guided jungle walk into the interior of **Ko Chang** (➤ 114–116). You can cross the island on foot in a day. Alternatively, take a snorkelling or diving trip to one of the many other islands in the archipelago.

# Day Three

### Morning

Catch the ferry to the mainland. From the pier it's a short *songthaew* ride to **3 Chanthaburi** (► 120). Take a look at the cathedral (right) and the haggling sapphire and ruby dealers around Thanon Si Chan and Trok Kachang before a lunch of famous Chanthaburi noodles.

### Afternoon

Catch a bus, then a ferrry to the island of **2 Ko Samet** (► 117–119), a tiny island of white-sand beaches.

# Day Four

### Morning

Relax on one of Ko Samet's **beaches** along the east coast. Generally the further south you go, the quieter they are. The beach at Ao Nuan has a restaurant of the same name. It is less commercial than the other beaches and serves Thai and good vegetarian food.

### Afternoon

Walk along the rocky coastline visiting a series of pretty beaches on the way. Cross over to the **west coast**, away from the crowds (the island is only a couple of kilometres wide) and watch the sun dip into the sea from a clifftop viewpoint. Take care here, as in most places it is not safe to go down to sea-level.

# Day Five

### Morning and Afternoon

Take a **fishing or snorkelling trip** (above, ► 119) to the islands of Ko Mak, Ko Kham and Ko Kut. Have lunch on one of the islands' beaches.

### Evening

Watch a film while eating dinner in one of the many restaurants on **Hat Sai Kaew** (► 117) that show videos.

# Ko Chang

Brightly painted fishing boats ferry passengers across the water from the mainland to Ko Chang, where wooden *song-thaews* chug up the steep winding road from the pier. This island of jungle-covered mountains has plunging waterfalls, trees filled with birds and rivers rushing down to the sea. Fishing hamlets and long, white-sand beaches fringe the coast and walking trails explore the untouched interior.

### Beach Activities
• Succumb to a **Thai massage** on the sand.
• Enjoy a **candlelit dinner** on the beach with waves lapping at your feet.
• **Sip a cocktail** under a fairy-lit tree on a Moroccan rug.
• Swing in a **hammock** on the balcony of your beach bungalow.
• Take a **snorkelling** trip to one of the nearby islands.

**Seafood restaurants at Bang Bao fishing village**

Ko Chang, named because it is thought to look like a sleeping elephant (*chang* is Thai for elephant), is the largest of 52 islands that make up the National Marine Park.

It measures 30km (19 miles) long and 8km (5 miles) wide. Despite being Thailand's second largest island after Ko Phuket (► 164–165), it remains relatively unspoiled. The island has only had a paved road (which runs all the way round it) and electricity for a few years and is at a happy stage of development. Most of the accommodation is low key and rustic and although some small resorts have sprung up in recent years, development is restricted to the west coast – where you'll find the best beaches.

**Ko Chang means "Elephant Island" in Thai**

Pretty beach bungalows at Hat Sai Kaew

## Hat Sai Kaew

Hat Sai Kaew, which means "White Sand Beach", is a wide 5km (3-mile) stretch of fine white sand backed by trees and palms and cut through with rivers. This is the busiest and most attractive beach, where accommodation ranges from rustic shacks with hammocks slung on balconies to more upmarket places with swimming pools that cater to package tourists. Although there are pancake stalls, cappuccinos on some menus and internet cafés along the road, the feel is essentially local. Be careful when you are swimming off the coast here, the currents are strong.

You can take guided interior jungle walks from **Rock Sand Bungalows** at Hat Sai Kaew that include a walk through jungle, past streams and mangrove forests.

## Other Sights

**Hat Khlong Phrao**, 15 minutes south by *songthaew* from Hat Sai Kaew, is another beach. There is less infrastructure here, and it is nearly always empty. There is not much traffic, and thick vegetation and rainforest borders the route from Hat Sai Kaew.

Head inland to **Khlong Phu waterfall**, about 2km (1.2 miles) along the main road. The clear pool is good for swimming and you can sunbathe on the rocks.

### How To Get There

Boats run from Laem Ngop, on the mainland, to Ko Chang every hour (every two hours in low season). *Songthaews* are timed in relation to boat arrivals. At Hat Sai Kaew, they pick up passengers around 15 minutes after the boat docks. There are no particular stops, just flag the *songthaew* down on the main road.

Continuing south for 2km (1.2 miles) is the beach of **Hat Kai Bae**, with some bungalow accommodation. The beach here is narrow and tends to disappear at high tide.

The other islands that make up the archipelago include **Ko Mak** (population 400), **Ko Kham** and **Ko Kut**, each with limited accommodation. Few of these islands can be reached during the rainy season from May to October, but from November to April daily boats are available from Laem Ngop (ask at the ticket office near the pier for details). To go on snorkelling or diving trips to these islands contact either **Eco Dive** (tel: 01 983 646) or **Sattha Tour** (tel: 06 898 6565 or 07 135 3611).

Top: Bang Bao is a busy fishing village

Above: Prawns drying on a wooden jetty

### TAKING A BREAK

Most of the **bungalows** at **Hat Sai Kaew** have restaurants offering European or Thai dishes. Many also offer evening beach barbecues. In the day there are restaurants and bars on the **beaches** around the island where you can fill up with seafood, pizzas, Thai food, cocktails, beer and soft drinks.

➕ 199 D3  **TAT**  ☎ 03 955 5135

## KO CHANG: INSIDE INFO

**Top tips** The island is one of the few places in Thailand where **mosquitoes are malarial**, so take anti-malaria tablets before you arrive and bring repellent.

• Don't buy a **return boat ticket**. You won't save much money, and it means you are restricted to the return times of the same operator.

• Take money with you. There are **no banks** on the island and travellers' cheques are cashed at very poor rates.

• In **high season, at weekends and on public holidays** the island can get crowded and the more expensive accommodation gets booked up. Either avoid these times or make reservations well in advance.

# ② Ko Samet

White-sand beaches, low, forested hills and a wonderful dry
climate characterise Ko Samet. This tiny island is less than 6km
(3.7 miles) long and its rugged west coast and beach-fringed
east coast are connected by rough walking
tracks that cross the jungle interior.

**Butterflies the
size of birds
are a common
sight on Ko
Samet**

Although tourism has been established here for 20 years and there is
a ferry from **Ban Phe** on the mainland (30–40 minutes; every hour 8–5
from November to February, every
two hours rest of the year), there is
still very little traffic. The island was
made a national park in 1981, but it is not
as protected as it could be and there are some unattractive
areas. A national park entrance fee (moderate) is payable at
the visitor information centre on arrival.

### Hat Sai Kaew

The main beach, Hat Sai Kaew (Diamond Beach), on the
northeast of the island, is 30m (33 yards) wide and awash
with striped deckchairs, parasols, palm trees and bamboo
tables and chairs from the many restaurants. Development is
solid here and bungalows have been built back from the
beach on stilts in the trees. Food-sellers balance baskets of
fruit and other produce and hawkers lug boards of beaded
jewellery across the sand. Masseuses manipulate bodies on

**The diamond-
white sands of
Hat Sai Kaew**

cotton sheets in the shade. At night there are barbecues, fairy
lights and fire-eaters on the sand, and videos are shown in the
restaurants behind the beach.

## Other Beaches

The long bay of Hat Sai Kaew has a rocky outcrop that separates it from the smaller and more attractive beach at **Ao Hin Kok** further south. Here is a statue of the *Prince and the Mermaid* – the subjects of an epic love poem by the country's most famous poet, Sunthorn Phu (1786–1856).

The *Prince and the Mermaid* statue at Ao Hin Kok

Several smaller and less crowded beaches continue along the east coast south of Ao Hin Kok – all excellent places to relax and enjoy some home-cooked Thai food.

The next main beach, in the horseshoe bay of **Ao Wong Duan**, tends to be a frenzy of hair-braiding, henna-tattooing and jet-skiing, with holiday-makers keen to take in every experience.

The furthest beach to the south, with a feeling of real isolation and peace, is **Ao Kiu**, which is reached through forest.

The only beach on the west coast is **Ao Phrao**, also known as Paradise Bay (*ao* means "bay" in Thai). In fact the rest of the west coast is more or less inaccessible. With a handful of bungalows and restaurants, Ao Phrao doesn't get as many visitors as the east coast beaches, but is well worth a look.

## From Top to Toe

From the northeastern tip of Hat Sai Kaew, where most people stay, take a walk along the coast. Clamber over craggy headlands, follow sandy paths through woodland and walk along white-sand beaches and quiet coves. It's around 3km (2 miles) from Hat Sai Kaew to **Ao Thian** (Candlelight Beach), with its spindly wooden pier. Secluded and quiet, it is a beautiful spot.

You can afford to explore, as it is difficult to get lost, and sooner or later you will reach the sea. If you take one of the tracks to the western side of the island from Ao Thian or Ao

Ko Samet has plenty of delightful beaches to choose from

➕ 199 D3
**TAT**
✉ Rayong ☎ 03 865 5420

## KO SAMET: INSIDE INFO

**Top tips** Don't buy a **return boat ticket** from the mainland. You won't save much money, and it means you are restricted to the return times of the same operator.
● You can take **snorkelling and fishing trips** to the islands of Ko Kudi, Ko Mum and Ko Thalu, arranged through the various bungalow operations. Day trips include equipment.
● When you arrive on the island, *songthaew* **fares** to the beaches are displayed on a board. Drivers will try everything, including ignoring you and taking other passengers, to get you to pay the charter rate. It is a good idea to gather a group together before approaching them.
● In **high season**, **at weekends and on public holidays**, the island can get crowded and the more expensive accommodation gets booked up, so try and avoid these times or book in advance.
● **Camping** is allowed on the beaches.
● **Water** is brought in from the mainland, so use it sparingly.

Wong Duan you will come across a windswept coast. Take the inland track back to the east coast for a change of scene, some shade and the chance to see dancing butterflies the size of small birds.

### TAKING A BREAK

**Seafood** plays a big part in the menus of most of the restaurants. There are restaurants on all the **beaches** and the bungalows often have restaurants attached providing good Thai food and Western dishes.

# At Your Leisure

## 3 Chanthaburi

This pleasant town is the focus for a major gem-mining area. Since the 15th century, prospectors hopeful for plunder of sapphires and rubies have flocked in from Burma, Cambodia and China. But its main ethnic population is made up of Vietnamese Catholics who came here between the 18th century and the 1970s trying to escape various periods of persecution.

Chanthaburi has no obvious sights, but it is a pleasant place to wander around for a few hours. From the bus station, walk along Thanon Saritidet to the banks of the Chanthaburi River and turn right. Pass the wooden shop houses here until you reach the foot-bridge to the **Catholic cathedral**. The cathedral was built in 1880 by the French, who occupied the town during the latter part of the 19th century.

Back on the river's western bank is the **gem-trading area**. Just north of here is a

**market** selling exotic fruits such as *durian* and *rambutan* which are grown in the surrounding orchards. Every year in May or June, the province (along with Trat and Rayong) hosts a fruit festival with pageants, parades and competitions.

➕ 199 D3
**TAT**
✉ Rayong ☎ 03 865 5420

## 4 Pattaya

It's hard to ignore this large, loud, international resort which welcomes no fewer than one third of all overseas visitors to Thailand. Although many are here for the brash nightlife, you'll also see a number of families and couples on package deals. Pattaya is Thailand's notorious centre for selling sex, a hangover from its days as an R&R destination for American troops during the Vietnam War. It has the largest gay scene in Thailand.

However, it has an international airport with good domestic connections, world-class hotels and excellent watersports facilities. A riot of neon blazes along the palm-lined promenade of **Pattaya Beach** and down "Walking Street" next to shopping plazas, fast-food outlets and girlie bars at the South Pattaya end. **Jomtien Beach**, further south, is a nicer beach than Pattaya and good for windsurfing.

➕ 198 C4
**TAT**
✉ 382/1 Thanon Mu 10 Chaihat, Pattaya
☎ 03 842 7667

Floral offerings at King Taksin the Great Memorial, Chanthaburi

Brash and brightly lit Pattaya

## 5 Ko Si Chang

This rocky fishing island is two hours by bus and boat from Bangkok. Ferries go from Si Racha every hour from 6 am to 8 pm. The rugged coastline and the cargo ships that plough the nearby shipping lanes mean it is not a lazy beach retreat (it gets crowded at weekends and on public holidays), but it is a peaceful break away from some of the other more commercial resorts. Don't buy a return boat ticket as it's not much cheaper and you'll be restricted to the return times of the operator.

Rama V's summer palace, built here in the 1890s, was moved in 1910 to create Bangkok's **Vimanmek Teak Palace** (► 52–53). The remaining buildings were left as ruins after occupation by the French in 1893, although they are being restored.

**Hat Sai Kaew** has sand and is the best place to swim; most of the other beaches are too rocky.

On the central western side of the island, the Buddhist temple of **Tham Chakraprong** offers good views if you can make the steep climb to the top of the cliff it is perched upon.

Nearby **Hat Khao Khat** is an obvious vantage point for watching the sun set.

➕ 198 C4

### Cambodia

The crossing to Cambodia from Ban Hat Lek is long and involved. It means several changes of transport and takes a full day. The route has only been open to foreigners since 1998 and as the situation can change at any point, you are advised to check with the Cambodian Embassy in Bangkok (185 Thanon Ratchadamri Lumphini, tel: 02 254 6630) and with other travellers as to whether it is possible and if a visa is needed.

## 6 Khao Yai National Park

Thailand's first national park is also its most highly esteemed and most popular. Mountains and five types of forest make up the varied landscape. Hundreds of elephants, a few endangered tigers and a number of white-handed gibbons live here, along with many species of birds, while fast-flowing waterfalls and rivers are breeding grounds for kingfishers and orchids.

In order to get the most out of a visit it is best to spend at least one night in the park and to hire a guide (ask at the TAT office). You can camp and there is basic accommodation.

The park may be closed for periods in the monsoon season (► 188).

➕ 199 D5
**TAT**
✉ 2102 Thanon Mitaphap, Khorat
☎ 04 421 3666 ℹ Information and accommodation: www.thaiparks.com

# Where to... Stay

**Prices**

Expect to pay per double room

£ under 1,000 baht  ££ 1,000–4,000 baht  £££ over 4,000 baht

## KO CHANG

### Cookie Hotel and Bungalows £

The bungalows here have verandas and most have individual views. They also have en suite bathrooms. The huts are set in three rows, with those nearest the sea being the most expensive. There are a few rooms with air-conditioning, but most have fans. There's also a restaurant serving Thai and Western food.

🞧 199 D3  🖂 Hat Sai Kaew

☎ 01 861 4227, 01 863 5563

### Khlong Phrao Resort ££

With 80 comfortable cabins and cottages built around a lagoon, this is a good place to relax. Some rooms are air-conditioned, but the more expensive cottages all have air-conditioning, satellite TV and hot water. The resort can arrange scuba-diving and snorkelling trips to the nearby coral reefs.

🞧 199 D3  🖂 Hat Khlong Phrao

☎ 03 955 1115, fax: 03 959 7106,

www.khlongphraoresort.com

### Mac Resort Hotel £

The Mac Resort Hotel has thatched huts, most with fans, but some with air-conditioning. There are verandas with sea views. This is a good place to watch the sun set and moon rise over a fresh seafood beach barbecue.

🞧 199 D3  🖂 Hat Sai Kaew

☎ 03 955 1124, fax 03 955 1125

## KO SAMET

### Samet Ville Resort ££

All the bungalows at this private resort overlook pretty Ao Wai. Both fan-cooled and air-conditioned bungalows are available. The ferry from Ban Phe on the mainland will take you to Ao Wai if requested.

🞧 199 D3  🖂 Ao Wai

☎ 03 865 1681, fax: 02 246 3196,

www.sametvilleresort.com

### Vongdeuan Resort £

This hotel in beautiful Ao Wong Duan has air-conditioned bungalows with large balconies. There are also cheaper rooms with fans.

🞧 199 D3  🖂 Ao Wong Duan

☎ 03 865 1777, fax: 03 865 1819,

www.vongdeuan.com

## PATTAYA

### Grand Jomtien Palace ££

Most accommodation in Pattaya is big and brash, and the Grand Jomtien is large, but more friendly. It's in the middle of Jomtien Beach, some way from Pattaya's raunchy nightlife, so good for families. It has some of the best restaurants the Jomtien area has to offer.

🞧 198 C4  🖂 356/1 Thanon Jomtien Beach  ☎ 03 823 1405, fax: 03 823 1404, email: rsvn_ptty@ grandjomtienpalacehotel.com, www.grandjomtienpalacehotel.com

### Royal Cliff Beach Resort £££

One of Pattaya's oldest and best hotels, this resort is really four hotels. The 545-room Royal Cliff Beach Hotel caters mainly for package tours, the low-rise Royal Cliff Terrace has a more personal atmosphere, the Royal Cliff Grand looks after the business market and the Royal Wing offers luxury. There are eight excellent restaurants, three swimming pools, six floodlit tennis courts and other sports facilities.

🞧 198 C4  🖂 353 Thanon Phra Tamnuk  ☎ 03 825 0421, fax: 03 825 0511, www.royalcliff.com

# Where to...
## Eat and Drink

### Prices

Expect to pay per person for a three-course meal, excluding drinks and service
**£** under 200 baht **££** 200–500 baht **£££** over 500 baht

Most of the bungalow operations on Ko Chang have their own restaurants. Food is generally fine, with many offering international dishes as well as Thai cuisine. The main beach on Ko Samet, Hat Sai Kaew, has some large seafood restaurants. Pattaya has restaurants with cuisine from every corner of the globe. The resort is divided into three areas – north Pattaya for quality hotel restaurants, central Pattaya for small, friendly bars and eateries, and south Pattaya for seafood.

### PATTAYA

#### Lobster Pot £££

One of Pattaya's longest surviving seafood restaurants, Lobster Pot, sitting on a pier overlooking Pattaya Bay, serves the best seafood in town. There's a friendly atmosphere, and an extensive menu that includes superb king lobster thermidor. Apart from seafood there are tender steaks, baked potatoes and a range of Thai favourites, which are highly recommended.

➕ 198 C4 ✉ 288 Walking Street, South Pattaya ☎ 03 842 6083 🕐 Daily noon–1 am

ask for your meal *mai phet* ("not spicy"), then it won't be. There are more than 200 Thai and European dishes. The ambience is sophisticated and relaxed and there's a separate air-conditioned section.

➕ 198 C4 ✉ Soi 5, Pattaya Beach Road ☎ 03 842 8387 🕐 Daily 11–3, 5:30–midnight

#### Pan Pan San Domenico £££

This restaurant offers Italian food of the very highest order. Although a little out of town, approximately halfway between South Pattaya and Jomtien, it's well worth the small effort required to get there. An extraordinary range of pasta, served with various seafood, chicken and meat sauces, is complemented by tasty desserts – try the *tiramisu* – and fragrant, freshly brewed coffees. The wine list is extensive.

➕ 198 C4 ✉ Thanon Thappraya, South Pattaya ☎ 03 825 1874 🕐 Daily 9.30–11

#### PIC Kitchen ££

Located on a quiet street in central Pattaya, this establishment has become something of an institution over the years. Fine Thai cuisine is served in a series of elegant teak houses set amid lush tropical gardens. The food is served in traditional style at low wooden tables, but with the taste buds of foreign visitors very much in mind – if you

#### Ruen Thai ££

Located in central-south Pattaya, this large restaurant is set in a series of wooden pavilions surrounded by fountains, waterfalls and fishponds. Popular with visitors, it has nightly classical Thai dancing (8–midnight) and high-quality Thai food, including everything from chicken with cashew nuts and dried peppers to *tom yam gung* (spicy prawn soup) and *tom kha gai* (chicken in coconut and ginger). The restaurant has its own children's facilities, including a playground.

➕ 198 C4 ✉ 485/3 Thanon Pattaya 2nd ☎ 03 842 5911 🕐 Daily 11–midnight

# Where to...
## Shop

Pattaya has a variety of shopping opportunities, but the best can be found in the large air-conditioned malls. The stalls along Pattaya Beach Road mostly offer overpriced fake goods. Ko Chang and Ko Samet have only small local stores.

### NORTH PATTAYA

**Central Festival Centre** (Pattaya 2 Road) has some attractive shops, including several very good craft outlets. The largest mall in Pattaya, **The Royal Garden Shopping Plaza** (adjoining Pattaya Marriott Hotel), has a Boots chemist and, on the top floor, a branch of the American Ripley's Believe It Or Not! Museum (► this page). On the ground floor look for the dancing fountain.

### SOUTH PATTAYA

South Pattaya is the main shopping area, with many shops selling crafts, silk, jewellery and gems. One of the woodcarving outlets, **Luukmai Gallery** (234/4 Walking Street, tel: 01 864 8393), sells exquisite carved panels and large wooden elephants. **Tom's Gems** (239/2 South Pattaya, opp. Diamond Hotel, tel: 03 842 2811) has been in business since 1975 and makes fine jewellery to order. For excellent leather goods, try the **Pattaya Shoes Department Store** (109/19 M10 Thanon Phatunmak, tel: 03 842 3919), which sells much more than only well-made shoes. It has a "walking street" section stocked ceiling-high with everything from suitcases to leather belts.

Pattaya has its fair share of **portrait painters**. One of the better galleries for this is **NL Gallery** (593 South Pattaya Road, tel: 03 871 0975). Their reproductions from photographs are very good.

# Where to...
## Be Entertained

### NIGHTLIFE

**Ko Chang** and **Ko Samet** nightlife is limited, **Pattaya**, with more than 400 beer bars, is the place to go. Once you look beyond the fact that it is a town selling sex, it does have other entertainment options.

The **Pattaya Palladium** (78/33 Pattaya 2 Road, tel: 03 842 4933) is a large entertainment complex with the largest disco in Thailand. If you're a Hammond organ enthusiast, **The Blues Factory** (Soi Lucky Star, off Pattaya's Walking Street, www.thebluesfactorypattaya.com) has the only functioning instrument in Thailand. It also has one of the country's leading showbands – and a happy hour that starts (not ends) at 9 pm! For the ultimate transvestite cabaret club, **Alcazar** (78/14 Pattaya 2 Road, tel: 03 842 8746) puts on elaborate shows.

### FAMILY ENTERTAINMENT

The **Pattaya Kart Speedway** (248/2 Thanon Thepprasit, tel: 03 842 7383) is a fun place for an afternoon, with vehicles for adults and children.

The **Elephant Village** (east of Pattaya, off Thanon Sukhumvit, tel: 03 824 9818) has daily shows including log-rolling and football.

**Ripley's Believe It Or Not! Museum** (Pattaya 2 Road, tel: 03 871 0294) has some curious displays.

Northeast of Pattaya, the **Si Racha Tiger Farm** (341 Moo 3, Nongkham, Si Racha, Chonburi Province, tel: 03 829 6556) has the world's largest collection of tigers, and plenty of other animals.

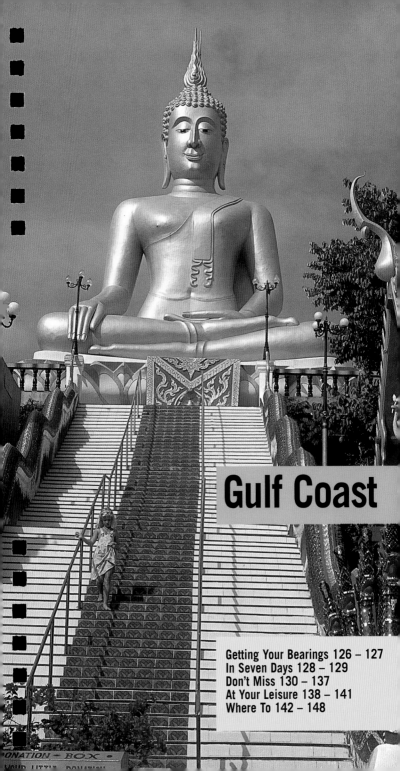

# Gulf Coast

Getting Your Bearings 126 – 127
In Seven Days 128 – 129
Don't Miss 130 – 137
At Your Leisure 138 – 141
Where To 142 – 148

# Getting Your Bearings

Weaving its way down the east side of Thailand's peninsula is the 750km (465-mile) Gulf coastline. Dip into its delights, or do as many visitors do and follow the train line that hugs the coast until Surat Thani, the jumping-off point for the Ko Samui archipelago. From here the train traces an inland and less well-trodden route all the way to Malaysia. A Muslim influence becomes noticeable in the mosques and curries as you approach Malaysia.

**Above: A hotel on the head-land, Chaweng Noi, Ko Samui**

**Previous page: Big Buddha on Ko Samui is a local landmark**

**Right: Flutes for sale, Lamai Beach, Ko Samui**

It is the beaches and islands that are the major magnets in this part of Thailand. Only a few hours from Bangkok is the royal resort of Hua Hin and King Bhumibol's chosen retreat.

The international hotels soon give way to a very different kind of hideaway: Khao Sam Roi Yot National Park. This sleepy backwater has subtle charms of bird life, marshlands, deserted sands and local rural life.

The internationally known idyllic islands of the Ko Samui archipelago attract both package tourists and budget travellers. While by no means undiscovered, these islands remain enchanting, with a reputation for excellent seafood and watersports. Many visitors arrive by plane; others board ferries from the mainland which spirit them across the turquoise waters to enjoy white-sand beaches fringed with towering palms.

For those who want something other than just glorious beach retreats, Phetchaburi offers an historic alternative in its temples, and the city of Nakhon Si Thammarat provides a cultural stop-off, with a host of Hindu shrines, Buddhist temples, mosques and churches.

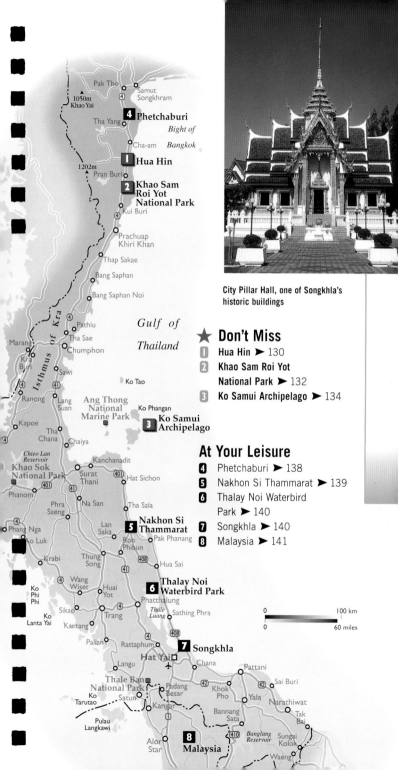

City Pillar Hall, one of Songkhla's historic buildings

★ **Don't Miss**

1 **Hua Hin** ➤ 130
2 **Khao Sam Roi Yot National Park** ➤ 132
3 **Ko Samui Archipelago** ➤ 134

## At Your Leisure

4 Phetchaburi ➤ 138
5 Nakhon Si Thammarat ➤ 139
6 Thalay Noi Waterbird Park ➤ 140
7 Songkhla ➤ 140
8 Malaysia ➤ 141

This coast is Thailand's holiday strip – even King Bhumibol has his summer palace here. Start with a luxurious hotel, take in some wildlife on an exciting tour and round off the trip with gleaming white-sand beaches.

# The Gulf Coast in Seven Days

## Day One

### Morning
Take an early train or bus from Bangkok to **4 Phetchaburi** (left, ➤ 138–139). The journey takes two and half hours from the southern bus station, or three hours by train from Hualamphong station.

### Afternoon
Spend several hours exploring the temples on foot before taking a bus (an hour-and-a-half journey) to **1 Hua Hin** (➤ 130–131). Travelling by rail is less practical as trains arrive in Hua Hin either in late evening or early morning. Check into the beautifully restored 1920s, colonial-style Sofitel Central Hotel, formerly the historic Railway Hotel (below, ➤ 142).

### Evening
Sip a cocktail in the Elephant Bar of the Sofitel Central. Wander through the gardens, with their giant animal topiary, maze and life-size chess set, to the beach. Walk along the sand to the Seaside Restaurant (31–4 Thanon Naretdamri). This atmospheric, family-run place overlooking the water serves seafood – try the local cottonfish in white wine sauce – as well as international dishes.

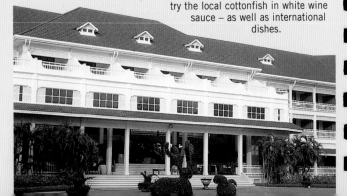

# Day Two

### Morning/Afternoon
Hire a jeep early to increase the chance of seeing wildlife (it tends to appear at sunrise or sunset) and drive an hour south to **2** **Khao Sam Roi Yot National Park** (above, ➤ 132–133) and follow the tour, ➤ 184.

### Evening
Return to **Hua Hin**. Walk along the beach for a Singha beer in a deckchair at sunset and then wander around the night market. It is compact, with a good mix of merchandise and friendly traders. Even bargaining can be relaxing here. If you want something more substantial than a seafood snack at a food stall, there's the Brasserie de Paris (➤ 144), an excellent French restaurant on Thanon Naretdamri, or the Railway Restaurant (➤ 144) in the Sofitel Central for Thai and international dishes.

# Days Three to Seven

Take the train or fly from Bangkok to the **3** **Ko Samui archipelago**. The overnight sleeper train arrives at Surat Thani, from where you need to take a short bus ride to catch the ferry. Flights take one hour and twenty minutes and there are lots of flights daily. Each of the three islands – **Ko Samui** (➤ 134), **Ko Phangan** (➤ 134) and **Ko Tao** (➤ 136) – has a distinct personality, so choose one that suits you. If you have time, do an island hop. Spend the days relaxing on the white-sand beaches and the nights enjoying the seafood for which the islands are famous. Or try some of the many water-sports on offer. From Ko Samui, try to make time for a day trip to **Ang Thong National Marine Park** (➤ 134). Boats leave daily at 8:30 am, returning at 5 pm.

# ☐ Hua Hin

At night the illuminations of the naval ships protecting the royal family and the neon green fishing lights in the bay blaze out the twin attributes of this town – a charming mix of ramshackle fishing village and a royal resort. It's Thailand's oldest beach resort – check out the pastel parasols, striped deckchairs and horse rides on the huge, open expanse of sand.

Hua Hin is a good place for a splurge – either as an introduction to the country or as a final fling before you leave. You will get much more for your money in an upmarket hotel here than in Bangkok, but try to avoid weekends when they can get busy.

Hua Hin became fashionable as a beach resort in the 1920s when the Bangkok–Malaysia rail line, the **royal Klai Klangwon Palace** (► 131) and the Railway Hotel (now the Sofitel Central, ► 142) were built.

Above: The old Railway Hotel, now the Sofitel Central, is an architectural gem

The 5km (3 mile) **beach** is not as pretty as Ko Samui, Krabi and Ko Samet, but the shoreline, with a traditional pier and "**monkey island**", an outcrop covered with monkeys and topped with a temple, has an undeniable charm. The resort's more recent success as a **weekend resort** for Bangkok resi-

Below: Have a Thai massage at Hua Hin

dents has led to some high-rise hotels and a few girlie bars. There are also six **golf courses** in the area (► 148).

### TAKING A BREAK
For fresh seafood, go to **Saeng Thai** (► 145) near the pier, or **Suan Guang** (► 145) for a great green Thai curry.

✚ 198 B3
**TAT**
✉ Thanon Damnern Kasem/ Highway 4 ☎ 03 253 2433

## The Royal Palace

In 1926 the Klai Klangwon Palace (not open to the public) was completed on the seafront 2km (1.2 miles) north of Hua Hin. This is where King Bhumibol and Queen Sirikit stay when they are in town. Locals know when the much-loved royal family are in residence by subtle changes in security and traffic regulations. The name Klai Klangwon means "far from worries". It could be considered a bit of a misnomer when you consider that in 1868 King Rama IV caught malaria on a visit to Khao Sam Roi Yot National Park near here and died almost as soon as he returned to Bangkok. It was also when staying here in 1932 that King Rama VII heard news of a *coup d'état* that resulted in the beginning of the constitutional monarchy.

Horses and hawkers on the beach at Hua Hin

## HUA HIN: INSIDE INFO

**Top tips** Don't be tempted to order food from the **stalls on the beach** if you are not prepared to wait an hour or so. When it does come, it will invariably be delicious, but the stallholder has to order it by mobile phone from someone who cooks it at home and then delivers it!

• In the early morning and evening **fishermen** unload their catches by the pier. Wander down to watch the scene, and locals bargaining for the latest catch.

# ② Khao Sam Roi Yot National Park

This peaceful national park on the coast is a sleepy backwater of marshland, mangroves and mudflats and is a breeding ground for birds. There are empty beaches of golden sand backed by pine trees and communities of shrimp farmers and fishing families. Its name means "mountain of three hundred peaks", which refers to its dramatic limestone outcrops of up to 650m (2,132 feet). There are several hundred species of birds here, including waterbirds such as purple herons and spotted eagles in winter, as well as animals such as dusky langurs (a type of monkey), long-tailed macaques, barking deer, mongooses and lizards. Take a pair of binoculars.

Only 60km (37 miles) south of Hua Hin (► 130–131), the park is an easy day trip. Don't take a taxi or public transport, because you will need transport to get around the park as the attractions are widely spread out. You can take an organised tour, but the best option is to hire a car and follow the circular guided tour of the park that starts from Hua Hin and links the park's highlights (► 184).

**Hat Laem Sala** is a small beach with a visitor's centre, bungalows and campsites. It can only be reached by boat from the sands east of the village of Bang Pu (to which there

✚ 198 B3

A leaf monkey surveys the scene in the park

Mountains and marshland complement each other in this tranquil haven

is no entry), or a 20-minute walk over the steep headland.

From Hat Laem Sala it is a half-hour walk to **Tham Phraya Nakhon**, a secluded royal pavilion built by Rama V (► below).

To the south of the park is the **headquarters**, which are not worth a visit unless you need to buy water. The displays and some short trails starting from here are all rather decrepit and the staff speak little English, but you will probably see lots of monkeys by the road.

You will be rewarded with great views if you climb up **Khao Daeng** – the access point is about 50m (164 feet) before you reach the park headquarters.

**Above: Craggy karst outcrops form distinctive features**

**Right: Khao Daeng provides sweeping views**

## TAKING A BREAK

Have lunch at **Hat Sam Phraya**, in a pretty beachside spot set in pine trees. The restaurant has mostly seafood dishes.

## KHAO SAM ROI YOT NATIONAL PARK: INSIDE INFO

**Top tips** At lunchtime you might be lucky enough to see the locals in their fishing boats lined up on shore near **Bang Pu** disentangling their small fish catches from their nets.

• The best time for spotting **birds and wildlife** is early morning or early evening.

• Although the leaflet you are given at the entrance checkpoint is in Thai, it has a useful, if basic, **map** in English.

• Although the chances of catching **malaria** are slight, it's worth taking insect repellent with you.

**Hidden gem** Tham Phraya Nakhon is a beautiful royal pavilion built in 1890 and named after two lords who were both called Nakon. Rama V visited in 1890 and signed his name in the cave. Rama VII continued the tradition in 1926 and Rama IX made the trip twice. Although it is popular with Thais, it is in a very remote location, reached by boat and a 30-minute walk.

# 3 Ko Samui Archipelago

This eighty-island archipelago includes a trio with global reputations – Ko Samui as an international resort, Ko Phangan for the biggest beach party in the world and Ko Tao for diving. Turquoise waters edged with dense palms and white beaches provide the ultimate image of a tropical paradise. From the sea, the islands rise above the horizon like desert islands waiting to be discovered: palm trees border bays and beaches of gleaming white sand, backed by jungle-clad hills. If these islands seem familiar, you may have seen them in the film *The Beach*. But any visitor arriving by sea is still guaranteed a frisson of initial discovery.

## Ko Samui

The story goes that Ko Samui has more **coconuts** per square metre than anywhere else in the world. But it is world famous for its international **beach scene**.

The large, sweeping, scenic beaches of Chaweng and Lamai are justifiably the most popular. **Ban Chaweng**, patrolled by hawkers, has a cosmopolitan atmosphere, with Mexican restaurants, Irish pubs and large hotels. It is bigger, busier and altogether more urban than neighbouring **Hat Lamai**.

The 12m (40-foot) **Big Buddha** statue on the north coast is an immaculate golden surreal image which looks inland. The beach of the same name, dotted with ramshackle piers made of tree trunks, is where boats leave for the island of Ko Phangan.

## Ko Phangan

Ko Samui's younger, wilder sibling has dirt roads, rustic accommodation and a lively nightlife. Young backpackers flock here throughout the year and during its world-famous

Left: Giant demon or Yak at Big Budda

Below: Hat Lamai on Ko Samui has a lively beach scene

### Ang Thong National Marine Park

Day trips run from Ko Samui to Ang Thong National Marine Park, a group of 41 small islands which makes up half of the islands in the Ko Samui archipelago. There are limestone caves and coral reefs, and you may be lucky enough to see dolphins, wild pigs, lizards, dusky langurs and even leopard cats. **Ko Wua Talub** (Sleeping Cow) is the largest island and the site of the national park headquarters. A climb to its peak offers panoramic views. Ang Thong gets its name, which means "golden bowl", from a volcanic lake on the island of **Ko Mae Ko**, which features in the best-selling novel and Hollywood film *The Beach*.

**full moon parties** it is overrun with people in a hedonistic party mood.

The pretty, tiny crescent of beach of **Hat Rin Nok**, known as **Sunrise Beach**, is the focus for the activity, but still manages to be friendly and intimate. The eastern side of the little tail of land in the south of the island has crooked alleyways packed with tourist facilities and shops selling Nepalese goods. **Paradise Bungalows** provides a barbecue on the sand and is the prettiest spot on the beach. A selection of freshly caught seafood and a glass of wine is inexpensive meal, and a cocktail beach bar is attached to the restaurant. At night the beach fills up with eager party animals who sit on Moroccan cushions on the sand and dance to techno music in the bars and clubs.

On the less scenic, but quieter western side of the island, **Hat Rin Nai**, or **Sunset Beach**, acts as a kind of overflow, with cheaper and more basic accommodation. Predictably, it is a good sunset spot – **Coral Bungalows** is the place to go for cocktails as the sun disappears into the water.

Above: Big Buddha in the village of Ban Plai Laem, Ko Samui

Right: Luxury resorts are everywhere at Chaweng Beach, Ko Samui

If you want to find more upmarket accommodation, try **Ao Chaloaklam** on the north coast, which tends to be popular with Thai visitors.

It is possible to walk along the beach from Hat Rin to Ban Tai. At the village of **Ban Tai** – like others on the island – locals can be seen playing football, shooting pool and repairing motorbikes as if the first longtails bringing tourists had never arrived. You can continue all the way to the port of **Thong Sala** and the **Pang Waterfall National Park**, a few kilometres inland. Climb the 250m (273-yard) trail to the top of the falls for a fabulous view over the south and west of Ko Phangan.

## Ko Tao

This tiny, turtle-shaped island (*tao* means "turtle" in Thai) offers some of the cheapest and best **diving** in the world and a peaceful alternative to the sophisticated delights of its sister islands.

The village of **Mae Hat** is the base for most of the dive operations, as well as tourist facilities. Accommodation north and south of here is reached in a 10-minute walk.

**Hat Sai Ree** to the north of Mae Hat is the longest stretch of sand and the centre for accommodation. **Ao Chaloke Ban Kao** on the south coast has become popular with several dive companies, but development is sadly out of keeping with the character of the rest of the island.

Most of the dive companies here are of a very high standard, with English-speaking instructors and well-organised trips. **Big Blue** and **Buddha View** are recommended. Although diving in the exceptionally clear waters around

*Above left:
Ko Phangan
attracts a
young, active
crowd*

➕ 198 C2
**TAT**
✉ Na Thon, Ko Samui ☎ 07 742 0504

### Big Blue Company
✉ Big Blue Resort, Hat Sai Ree
☎ 07 745 6179 🏠 Accommodation
free if you dive (although you won't
be able to stay if you don't!)

### Buddha View Dive Company
✉ Buddha View Dive Resort, Ao
Chalok Ban Kao ☎ 07 745 6074/5,
email: buddha@samart.co.th

### Ko Tao's Top Five Dive Sites
Of the 25 or so dive sites around Ko Tao, the following are the best:
- **White Rock** (Hin Khao) – amazing coral and plenty of fish
- **Ko Nang Yuan** – good for beginners
- **Shark Island** – coral, angelfish and parrotfish
- **Sail Rock** – underwater chimney, colourful fish
- **Southwest Pinnacle** – the top site for scenery, visibility and variety of fish

**The fascinating underwater world of Ko Tao's waters**

Ko Tao is possible all year round, visibility can be affected by heavy rain.

### TAKING A BREAK

On **Ko Samui**, Ban Chaweng offers Indian dishes at **Ali Baba** (▶ 145) and a trendy Thai and Californian menu and good wines are available at **Betelnut** (▶ 145), On **Ko Phangan** you could try **Sala-Thai** (▶ 146) on Lamai Beach for Thai and international food and a lively atmosphere.

## KO SAMUI ARCHIPELAGO: INSIDE INFO

**Top tips** Hat Rin Beach on Ko Phangan is the venue for the **full moon parties**, which attract thousands of young revellers. If they don't appeal, stay away as the whole island gets completely taken over and the music and crowds can be overwhelming.

- Post-parties, the island of **Ko Tao** receives a mass exodus from Ko Phangan when it can be difficult to find accommodation and the atmosphere changes.
- December to March is **peak season** for all of the islands. During this time prices shoot up and accommodation can be scarce.
- June to October is the time of the **southwestern monsoon**.
- **Car and motorbike rental** is not recommended on either Ko Samui or Ko Phangan. Vehicles race around Ko Samui's main road as if it were a motorway, resulting in around 20 tourist deaths a year. Ko Phangan's road is a hair-raising roller-coaster.

**Hidden gem** Visitors tend to ignore the **interiors** of all three islands, where there are deer, pigs, orchids and jungle treks.

# At Your Leisure

## ❹ Phetchaburi

This compact town, dissected by the River Phet, is full of temples dating from several different periods. The town began life in the 11th century when the Khmers ruled the area, and it took off as a trading post in the 17th century.

Rama IV had a palace built here in the mid-19th century and today it is a centre for sweet-making, using sugar from the sweet-sapped palms in the area.

Half a day is enough time to spend here. The best option is to visit as a day trip from Hua Hin (► 130–131) or Bangkok (often combined with Damnoen Saduak Floating Markets, ► 70–71), or as a stop-off going south.

Focus on the five most significant temples, which can be seen on a walk of a couple of hours. **Wat Yai Suwannaram**, **Wat Borom** and **Wat Trailok** form a cluster on the northeastern edge of town. The restored, 17th-century **Wat Yai Suwannaram**

King Rama IV's Palace on a hilltop high above Phetchaburi

has various Buddha images, a *bot* (main sanctuary) with interesting murals and a library built on stilts to prevent insects from nibbling at the books.

A short walk south is **Wat Kamphaeng Laeng**. Built in the 13th century in the Khmer style to house Hindu deities, it has since been adopted for Buddhist worship.

Due west and across the river is **Wat Mahathat**; though much destroyed by the Burmese, it's the most significant temple of all, with Buddhist relics donated by the king. If you have time you can take a cable-car up to Rama IV's palace, **Khao Wang**, on the western outskirts and visit the museum of **Phra Nakhon Khiri**, which was once the king's summer house.

There are also two cave **wats** (temples) on this side of town –

Khmer-style *prangs* at Wat Mahathat, Phetchaburi's most important temple

**Four Royal Retreats**
• **Klai Klangwon Palace** in Hua Hin (► 131) is used by the present King Bhumibol
• **Tham Phraya Nakon**, in Khao Sam Roi Yot National Park (► 133), is an elegant hidden royal pavilion built by Rama V
• **Khao Wang** in Phetchaburi (► 138) was Rama IV's hilltop palace
• **Khao Tung Kuan** in Songkhla (► 141) is a hilltop royal pavilion built by Rama V

**Khao Banda-it**, and **Khao Luang**, which has long been a favourite picnic spot for the King Bhumibol and Queen Sirikit and their family.

🔲 198 B4

**TAT**

✉ Cha-am ☎ 03 247 1005

**Phra Nakhon Khiri**
🕐 Wed–Sun 9–4 ✋ Inexpensive

**Cable-car to Khao Wang**
🕐 Daily 8–4 ✋ Inexpensive

## 🖪 Nakhon Si Thammarat

Many people are so dazzled by the lure of Ko Samui and its islands that they fail to see this town altogether. Strung out along the Khlong Na Wang River, this religious centre has a collection of Hindu shrines, Buddhist temples, mosques and churches that testify to its role as a major missionary centre.

**Wat Mahathat** – the most sacred shrine in the south – includes the **Viharn Kien Museum**, with an eclectic collection of around 50,000 artefacts donated by worshippers at the shrine. The **National Museum** has an unmissable 9th-century statue of Vishnu and two rare Vietnamese bronze drums.

**Shadow puppets** (*nang thalung*) are found throughout Southeast Asia, but life-size puppets, *nang yai*, are unique to Thailand and are used in the epic *Ramayana*. At the **Suchart House**, watch Suchart Subsin making

Row of gilded Buddha images, Wat Phra Mahathat, Nakhon Si Thammarat

the puppets from water buffalo or cowhide and then projecting them on to a giant screen. You can even buy them as souvenirs. There are set characters such as a wizard called Yogi and a furious fat man wielding a sword, but performances are rare these days and limited to special occasions.

➕ 198 B1

**TAT**
✉ Sanam Na Muang ☎ 07 534 6515–6

**National Museum**
✉ Thanon Ratchadamnoen
☎ 07 532 4480 🕐 Wed–Sun 9–4
💲 Inexpensive

**Suchart House**
✉ 110/18 Thanon Si Thammasok Soi 3
☎ 07 534 6394 💲 Inexpensive

**Viharn Kien Museum**
✉ Thanon Ratchadamnoen 🕐 Daily
8:30 am–noon, 1–4

## 6 Thalay Noi Waterbird Park

The name *thalay noi*, meaning "little sea", describes this area of marsh, lagoon and sea where hundreds of bird species breed. You may see white egret, purple heron and brown teal. The best variety of the mostly migratory birds are seen in March and April.

Even if you are not much of a bird-lover, it's an atmospheric spot where you can take longtail boat trips (two hours from Phatthalung) that

*The sun setting on the Thalay Noi Waterbird Park*

**For Kids**
• The **seaside attractions** of Hua Hin (▶ 130–131).
• The **gardens of the Sofitel Central Hotel** in Hua Hin (▶ 142), with topiary dancing elephants, a life-size chess set and maze, have an Alice in Wonderland appeal.
• **Wading through the mud** to a boat bound for the royal pavilion of Tham Phraya Nakhon (▶ 133).
• Spotting **monkeys** and other wildlife in Khao Sam Roi Yot National Park (▶ 132–133).
• Ko Samui's **go-karting track** just west of the village of Bophut (Samui Kart Club, daily 9–9, moderate).

steer you through the surreal landscape of vines and reeds.

➕ 199 E2

**TAT**
✉ Ratchadamnoen Road ☎ 07 534 6515

## 7 Songkhla

Perched on a tongue of land between the Gulf of Thailand and the Thalay Sap lagoon, Songkhla is aptly known as the "big town of two seas". As capital of the province, it has a small fishing port and some historic buildings built during the Na Songkhla dynasty.

A splendid Chinese mansion built in 1878 houses the **National Museum**, which has exhibits ranging from local agricultural implements to Chinese furniture.

An elegant Reclining Buddha at the
National Museum in Songkhla

**Wat Matchimawat** temple is set in
stately gardens and ornately decorated.
**Khao Tung Kuan**, a hill on the northwest edge of town, has a royal pavilion
and good views. To the
south, **Khao Saen**
has a lively fish
market every after-
noon except Friday.

➕ 199 E2
**National Museum**
✉ Thanon Jana
🕐 Wed–Sun 9–noon,
1–4 💲 Inexpensive

**TAT**
✉ 1/1Soi 2 Thanon
Niphatuthit 3,
Ampoe Hat Yai,
Songkhla
☎ 07 424
3747

## 8 Malaysia

The best route across the border
into Malaysia is by train from Padang
Besar (four hours to Butterworth).
Although Malaysia is slightly closer
to the Andaman Coast, it is only
50km (31 miles) or so from
Songkhla on the Gulf Coast.

Another train route (two hours)
hugs the Gulf Coast further south,
starting from Bangkok and ending
at Sungai Kolok, not far from the
border. Take a taxi to Golok Bridge
in Thailand for immigration and
another to Rantau Panjang in
Malaysia. Neither Sungai Kolok nor
Rantau Panjang are worth hanging
around in – it's best just to use them
as entry points to Malaysia.

Alternatively, there are lots of
buses to Malaysia from Hat Yai
(and they are comfortable and air-
conditioned), as well as from other
important transport hubs such as
Phuket, Krabi and Bangkok.

Tourists from the west can usually
spend 30 days in Malaysia without a
visa. Watch out for unscrupulous bus
companies who try to charge you a
visa or border crossing fee.

### Korlae

*Korlae* are hand-crafted wooden
fishing boats used by Muslim fishermen in the Gulf. They take four
months to construct. You can watch
craftsmen carve and paint intricate
designs in Ban Pasey Yawo, 2km
(1.2 miles) north of Saiburi, and in
Pattani. The design is hundreds of
years old and has changed little,
although engines are now the practical replacement for the original sails
of the ancient craft. Favourite
animals to decorate the wooden hulls
include lions, mythological birds and
sea serpents.

# Where to... Stay

## Prices

Expect to pay per double room
£ under 1,000 baht ££ 1,000–4,000 baht £££ over 4,000 baht

The Gulf Coast, especially around Hua Hin, specialises in health resorts. Some of the best in the world are here, offering unparalleled rest and relaxation. Although Ko Samui has developed at a remarkable rate, it is still possible to find small bungalow bargains with comfortable rooms.

## HUA HIN

### Anantara Resort and Spa £££

This resort is a virtual palace, blending traditional Thai architecture, landscaped gardens and modern conveniences. Special spa packages are available. All rooms have large private terraces which overlook lagoons and have stunning rattan and teak furniture. The Baan Thalia restaurant, in keeping with the general healthy manifesto of the Anantara, provides a well-balanced and delicious menu. Facilities include a pitch-and-putt course.

➕ 198 B3 ✉ 43/1 Phetkasem Beach Road ☎ 03 252 0250, fax: 03 252 0259, www.anantara.com

### Chiva Som International Health Resort £££

Winner of the Condé Nast Traveller magazine's "World's Best Destination Spa" award, the Chiva Som, (which means "Haven of Life") is a health resort par excellence. Every conceivable type of pampering a stressed body could need is available. The resort is set in 3ha (7.5 acres) of gardens next to the beach. Pleasant pools (both decorative and for swimming) and even the odd waterfall surround the 57 deluxe rooms and suites. Healthy activities include *tai chi*, canoeing, mountain biking and horse riding.

➕ 198 B3 ✉ 73/4 Thanon Phetkasem ☎ 03 253 6536, fax: 03 251 1154, www.chivasom.com

### Hilton Hua Hin £££

Formerly the Meliá Hua Hin, this huge high-rise hotel sits squarely in the middle of the beach. All 296 rooms and suites have stunning sea views, satellite TV, in-house movies and mini-bar. Amenities include squash courts, a fully equipped gym, disco, children's playground and a swimming pool with water slide. It's also the best-placed hotel for visiting Hua Hin's famous seafood restaurants on the pier. The hotel has a restaurant that serves excellent Italian, Chinese and Thai food.

➕ 198 B3 ✉ 33 Thanon Naretdamri ☎ 03 251 2888, fax: 03 251 1135, www.hilton.com

### Sofitel Central £££

This fine old Colonial-style hotel opened in 1923 and was originally known as the Railway Hotel. At the time it was the most luxurious hotel for miles around. The interior still evokes the 1920s, with high ceilings and wood panelling. It is next to the beach, with gardens that have a wonderful topiary section. The hotel played the part of the French Embassy in neighbouring Cambodia in Roland Joffe's powerful 1984 film *The Killing Fields*. Facilities include three swimming pools, a croquet lawn and tennis courts. It is also justly famous for its excellent restaurants, which include the Railway Restaurant (▶ 144).

➕ 198 B3 ✉ 1 Thanon Damnoen Kasem ☎ 03 251 2021, fax: 03 251 1014, www.sofitel.com

## KHAO SAM ROI YOT PARK

### Dolphin Bay Resort £

This is the closest comfortable accommodation to Khao Sam Roi Yot National Park. The resort is set in pretty Phu Noi Bay on the coast, about 35km (21.7 miles) south of Hua Hin. It's not a big place – there are only 10 bungalows and 24 rooms in the main building – but the management and staff are very friendly and there are two swimming pools and great sea views. All rooms are air-conditioned with satellite TV and mini-bar. The restaurants provide both Thai and European dishes.

🕂 198 B3 🖾 223 Moo 4, Phu Noi Beach ☎ 03 255 9333, fax: 03 255 9361, www.dolphinthailand.com

## KO SAMUI ARCHIPELAGO

### Central Samui Beach Resort £££

This resort has been beautifully designed to fit naturally into its tropical surroundings. Situated towards the centre of Chaweng Beach, it is just 15 minutes from the local airport. The property is built in neo-Colonial style with 208 superbly proportioned rooms and suites, each with cable TV and mini-bar. The resort's Centara Spa is probably the best on the island, and has a range of health treatments and massages. Try out the large swimming pool, tennis courts, gymnasium and outdoor jacuzzi. Most of Chaweng's best bars and restaurants are a short stroll away.

🕂 198 C2 🖾 38/2 Moo 3 Borpud, Chaweng Beach ☎ 07 723 0500, fax: 07 742 2385, www.centralhotels resorts.com/samuibeach

### Coral Cove Chalets ££

In a cove between Chaweng and Lamai beaches, Coral Cove is framed by coconut palms. The beach here is usually very quiet and private. If you are a snorkelling enthusiast, the cove is an excellent place to go exploring; there are a number of reefs offshore. The traditional Thai-style bungalows are comfortable and all offer superb ocean views.

🕂 198 C2 🖾 210 Coral Cove Beach, Lamai ☎ 07 742 2242, fax: 07 742 2496, www.coralcovechalet.com

### Imperial Boat House £££

This is one of Thailand's unique resorts, and a real gem. It comprises 34 beautifully decorated old teak rice barges and a boat-shaped swimming pool set on an unspoiled section of Hat Choeng Mon in the northeast of Ko Samui. The rice barges have been converted into luxury suites with skylit bathrooms and separate dining areas. There is also a low-rise hotel with 176 deluxe rooms which all have satellite TV and mini-bar. The All Scuba Adventures Diving School is attached to the resort and offers courses depending on your diving proficiency. The Vietnamese restaurant is first class, and there are also Japanese and Thai restaurants.

🕂 198 C2 🖾 83 Moo 5, Hat Choeng Mon ☎ 07 742 5041, fax: 07 742 5460, www.imperialboathouse.com

### Natural Wing Resort ££

Hotels and resorts on Ko Samui often ignore the environment, and very few take the time at the design and planning stage to consider their situation. This is not the case with the Natural Wing, at Bang Po Beach on the northwest of Ko Samui. The villas nestling unobtrusively into the hillside have satellite TV and internet access. Tree-house accommodation is also available. A good spa and a restaurant serving Thai, Vietnamese and Japanese dishes complete this excellent resort.

🕂 198 C2 🖾 11/5 Moo 6, Hat Bang Po ☎ 07 742 0871, fax: 07 742 1368, www.naturalwing.com

### Pavilion Resort ££

Probably Lamai's top property, the Pavilion is located slightly south of the noisier part of the beach. The staff are very helpful and friendly. It

# Where to...
## Eat and Drink

### Prices

Expect to pay per person for a three-course meal, excluding drinks and service
£ under 200 baht ££ 200–500 baht £££ over 500 baht

### HUA HIN

#### Brasserie de Paris £

This excellent French restaurant has a terrace overlooking the sea. Seafood specialities include crab Hua Hin, and the fresh scallop dish *coquille Saint-Jacques*. There are classic French main dishes, appetisers and desserts. French management keeps standards high. The terrace affords a lovely view of Hua Hin's brightly painted fishing fleet. There is also a good selection of French wine, and it's not too expensive.

🚹 198 B3 ☒ 3 Thanon Naretdamri
☎ 03 253 0637 ⓖ Daily 12–10.30

#### Railway Restaurant £££

A few years ago the Railway Hotel (now Sofitel Central, ➤ 142) was thoroughly renovated, and one splendid offshoot was the Railway Restaurant. It is decorated and furnished in the style of Hua Hin Railway Station during the 1920s, with old station clocks and other railway paraphernalia. Apart from the regular Thai dishes they have various speciality buffets including French, Italian and Chinese. An extensive wine list is also available.

🚹 198 B3 ☒ Sofitel Central Hotel,
1 Thanon Damnoen Kasem ☎ 03 251
2031 ⓖ Daily 6:30 am–11:30 pm

---

also has one of the best swimming pools on the island, large and attractively landscaped. Accommodation is in rooms in the main hotel and 36 Thai-style cottages. All rooms have air-conditioning, mini-bar and balconies. The beachside Blue Marlin restaurant serves excellent seafood and standard Thai fare.

🚹 198 C2 ☒ 124/24 Moo 3, Hat
Lamai ☎ 07 742 4420, fax: 07 742
4029, www.pavilionsamui.com

### CHA-AM

**Most people stay in Cha-am when visiting Phetchaburi.**

#### Regent Cha-am £££

Not far from Cha-am on the road to Hua Hin, this large, self-contained resort is ideal if you have limited time. About 185km (115 miles) south of Bangkok and set in 16ha (39.5 acres) of beautifully landscaped gardens, the Regent, with more than 700 rooms, is actually made up of three parts: The

Regent Cha-Am, The Regency Wing and The Regent Chalet. An unspoiled, quiet beach fronts the whole resort. All rooms overlook one of the three swimming pools, the well-kept garden or the ocean. Facilities include a gym and sauna, squash courts, tennis courts and an outdoor jacuzzi.

🚹 198 B4 ☒ 849/21 Thanon
Phetkasem ☎ 03 245 1240–9, fax: 03
247 1491–2, www.regent-chaam.com

#### Pineapple Garden Beach Hotel and Resort ££

Pineapples grow in the garden of this attractive and friendly little resort on Cha-Am's beachfront. Bungalows are modern with tiled-floors, and each has its own patio with views of the gardens and the sea. Young guests are particularly well catered for, with water sports equipment, a playground and a games room.

🚹 198 B4 ☒ 335/1 Tambon Cha-
Am ☎ 02 231 3671, www.cha-am-
resorts.com/pineapple-garden-beach

## Saeng Thai ££

Hua Hin's fishing fleet lands its daily catch just along the pier from this popular, old seafood restaurant, in fact the oldest restaurant in Hua Hin. Reliable fresh food accompanied by good service is the draw at this large, open-air spot on the seafront. The smell of the sea and the faint aroma from the fish market only add to the overall atmosphere.

**➕ 198 B3 ✉ Thanon Naretdamri (near the pier) ☎ 03 251 2144 🕒 Daily 11 am–10.30 pm**

## Suan Guang ££

Another old Hua Hin favourite, Suan Guang is very popular with visiting Thais, and for good reason – the food is superb. With live classical Thai music as an accompaniment, savour excellent Thai dishes such as *kaeng khiaw wan* (green curry) served in a traditional Thai setting. There are also a number of hot southern curries on the menu, which can be spicy.

**➕ 198 B3 ✉ 43/1 Phetkasem Beach Road ☎ 03 252 0250 🕒 Daily 11 am–11 pm**

## KO SAMUI ARCHIPELAGO

## Ali Baba ££

This restaurant serves mainly Indian dishes, but also a few Thai and European standards. It's rightly regarded as the best Indian restaurant on Ko Samui, and with a real tandoori oven is able to produce some great tikka and tandoori dishes. It's also well known for Indian-style seafood. A large selection of fine coffees helps round off any meal.

**➕ 198 C2 ✉ Chaweng Beach Road (opposite the Samui Hot Club), Chaweng ☎ 07 741 8237 🕒 Daily 10 am–11 pm**

## Ban Thai Food Garden & Antique House ££

The largest lobsters you're ever likely to encounter are a specialty of this spectacular Thai restaurant, a short walk from Chaweng Beach. They're known as "Dragon lobsters" and are prepared to a European recipe that's a secret of the chef. Other seafood is laid out buffet-style on ice for you to select personally. Thai traditional dancing is presented nightly.

**➕ 198 C2 ✉ Chaweng Beach Road, 157 Moo 2, Bophut, Chaweng Beach ☎ 07 723 1123 🕒 Daily noon–11 pm**

## Betelnut £££

The cuisine at Betelnut, the trendiest and best, independent restaurant on the island, begun by well-known Californian chef Jeffrey Lord, is a fusion of Thai and Californian traditions. The menu constantly changes and is full of delightful surprises such as boneless rib-eye steak with potato crisps and green curry pepper sauce. Some of the desserts are divine – try amaretto cheesecake with cashew cinnamon crust. There is limited space so reservations are advisable. Jeffrey provides

an admirable wine list, with labels from France, Italy and, of course, California.

**➕ 198 C2 ✉ 46/27 Chaweng Boulevard, Central Chaweng ☎ 07 741 3370 🕒 Daily 6 pm–midnight**

## Captain's Choice £££

This beach restaurant, part of the Imperial Boat House hotel complex (▶ 143), is one of Ko Samui's very best. Lunches tend to be light, with plenty of fresh salads and fish. Evening meals are grander affairs consisting mainly of seafood delicacies such as prawns, squid, crab, lobster and crayfish – all caught locally. If it's available then this is also a good place to enjoy shark. An extensive wine list complements the meal.

**➕ 198 C2 ✉ Imperial Boat House, 83 Moo 5, Hat Choeng Mon ☎ 07 742 5041 🕒 Daily noon–10 pm**

## Happy Elephant ££

The Happy Elephant is just like it sounds, offering a friendly, cosy atmosphere next to Bophut Beach on Ko Samui. There are some very good Thai specialities, such as grilled prawns and sweet tamarind sauce with prawn cakes grilled on fresh sugarcane sticks. The menu is mostly fresh seafood with a few international staples like pizza, pasta and burgers. For drinks there is a wide variety of fruit shakes and an admirable selection of wines.

➕ **198 C2** ✉ **78/1 Moo 1, Bophut Beach** ☎ **07 724 5347** ⏰ **All day**

### Jing £££

Samui's top Chinese restaurant has been compared by the critics with favoured dining destinations in Bangkok and even Hong Kong. Not surprising, since the menu – comprising 70 dishes – was prepared by the head of the Bangkok Culinary Circle, Peter Lei. Head chef Chan Liu Lam is a Hong Kong veteran who also worked for 14 years at the Bangkok Hilton and Shangri-La Hotels. His Cantonese

dishes are the real thing, but he also brings to the table such rarities as Mongolian lamb. He and his sous-chefs work in full view of the diners, who are treated to a fantastic show of culinary dexterity.

➕ **198 C2** ✉ **Soi Calibri, South Chaweng (opp Central Resort)** ☎ **07 741 3462** ⏰ **Daily 11.30–2.30 and 6–midnight**

### Pakarang ££

Pakarang is in a great location, away from the bustle of Chaweng Beach, in quiet, beautiful surroundings, with a choice of dining areas. Sit indoors surrounded by paintings of Ko Samui, or outside under a huge bougainvillaea trellis. The chef makes no attempt to tone down the spices and subtle flavours of Thai food, unless requested to do so. The menu revolves around traditional curries, most of which use coconut milk to enhance the creaminess. There's also an extensive cocktail list to accompany the delicious food.

➕ **198 C2** ✉ **9 Moo 2, Tambon Bophut** ☎ **07 742 2223** ⏰ **Daily 11:30–3, 5.30–11:30**

### Poppies ££

Poppies gives a choice of dining locations. Try the lovely teak pavilion, set in a verdant tropical garden, or the beachside marquee. The food is mainly dishes from central Thailand and seafood, and standards are very high. There's a fine selection of wines and cocktails. Live musical entertainment is provided by a classical guitarist on Tuesday, Thursday and Friday. Saturday is Thai night, with traditional Thai dancing.

➕ **198 C2** ✉ **South Chaweng Beach Road** ☎ **07 742 2419** ⏰ **Daily 7 am–11 pm**

### Sala-Thai ££

Lamai Beach on Ko Samui does not have a particularly great selection of eating places, but Sala-Thai is one of the better ones. It's in a romantic setting dotted with small waterfalls

and fountains. The menu features Thai and international dishes. Specialities include *tom kha gai* (chicken cooked in coconut milk) and *kung pao* (grilled prawns).

➕ **198 C2** ✉ **Lamai Beach Road (opposite the Full Moon Bar)** ☎ **07 723 3180** ⏰ **Daily 2 pm–midnight**

### Vecchia Napoli ££

The pasta and breads served at this very authentic Neapolitan restaurant are home-made and delicious. Portions are generous – the pizzas alone are a record-setting 30cm (12 inches) in diameter. And you eat in a dining room that could have been transported straight from Naples itself.

➕ **198 C2** ✉ **Center Point, Chaweng** ☎ **07 723 1229** ⏰ **Daily 12–11**

## PHETCHABURI

### Rabieng Rim Nam £

Centrally located by the Chomrut Bridge on the banks of the River

Phet, this popular and attractive restaurant (there's also a guest house) has a Thai and English menu with a listing of over 100 dishes. Seafood is a speciality, as are spicy *yam* salads. A good choice to try a local dish is *khanom jiin thawt man* (noodles with spicy fish cakes). The restaurant/guest house is a useful source of local information for travellers, and it has the added advantage of offering internet access.

+ 198 B4 ⊠ 1 Thanon Chisa ln
☎ 03 242 5707 ⓒ Daily 7 am–11:30 pm

## NAKHON SI THAMMARAT

### Nok Chan ££

This is a large, friendly, open-air place with a great atmosphere. It is decorated with southern Thai folk art and shaded by a large banyan tree. Local dishes worth a try are *khao yam* (rice salad) and *kaeng tai plaa* (spicy fish curry), among others. The Hao Coffee Shop

next door serves excellent coffee which can be ordered at Nok Chan.

+ 198 B1 ⊠ Bovorn Bazaar ☎ 07 534 3476 ⓒ Daily 11 am–midnight

### Wang Inn Kitchen £

In the same compound as the Nakhon Garden Inn, this cosy, atmospheric diner serves excellent breakfasts and an unusual selection of Thai and European fare. A wide range of ice creams includes a great local version of a banana split.

+ 198 B1 ⊠ 1/4 Thanon Pak Nakhon ☎ 07 534 4831 ⓒ Daily 7 am–11 pm

## SONGKHLA

### Naiwan £

Catch of the day at this outstanding fish restaurant on Samila beach includes lobster, squid, giant prawns and clams, all imaginatively prepared in southern Thai style. The *pla muek khai sai sai* (squid caviar in a lemon sauce) is a truly local speciality, but if it's not to your taste then try something simple such as the sea bass or

prawns straight from the grill, which are wonderfully fresh and delicious.

+ 199 E2 ⊠ 8/13-16 Rachadamnoen Road, Muang Songkhla ☎ 07 431 1295 ⓒ Daily 10.30 am–10 pm

### Big John's Seafood Restaurant ££

Regarded as the finest seafood restaurant on Ko Samui, Big John's also serves the island's finest margaritas, best enjoyed at a waterfront table with a sunset view. The seafood platter with rice baked in pineapple is legendary.

+ 199 E2 ⊠ 95/4 Moo 2, Lipanoi ☎ 07 742 3025 ⓒ Daily 11–11

### Shades ££

Reserve a table overlooking the bay at this stylish restaurant on Bophut's main street. Service is friendly, attentive and very knowledgeable. Recommendations include seafood dishes such as tartar or fresh tuna, prawns and avocado.

+ 199 E2 ⊠ Bophut high street ☎ 07 724 56889 ⓒ Daily 11–11

# Where to...
# Shop

The Gulf Coast is not known for its shopping opportunities. Hua Hin is especially bereft of anything decent to buy, and is overrun with tacky souvenirs. Ko Samui has a slightly better selection, with a few gem shops, but you should exercise real caution, especially regarding unmounted cut stones.

## KO SAMUI

Ko Samui's main beach areas, **Chaweng** and **Lamai**, are dotted with **supermarkets** providing everyday essentials.

If you need swimwear, try **Life's A Beach** (Chaweng Beach Road, tel: 07 742 2630), which advertises the latest Australian imports.

**Oriental Gallery Arts and Antiques** (Chaweng Beach Road, tel: 07 742 2200) has a fine collection of teak furniture and crafts, and can arrange shipping to anywhere in the world.

**Joop! Tailors** (Choeng Mon beach, tel: 07 742 4011 and Chaweng Beach, tel: 07 741 3237) is the best tailor on the island and can knock up a suit or dress within 24 hours.

Ko Samui has an international reputation for the handmade shoes produced by local craftsman **Nimit Meefuang**. You'll find his creations in the boutiques of all the top luxury hotels: the Anantara, Poppies, Meridien and Santibury.

Hua Hin has a lively night market and a good selection of boutiques along Thanon Naret Damri.

On Ko Samui there's a bewildering array of shopping outlets, ranging from arts and crafts stalls to designer boutiques, all under one roof at the **Central Shopping Arcade**, Chaweng Beach.

# Where to...
# Be Entertained

Most nightlife and entertainment along the Gulf Coast is on Ko Samui and Ko Phangan. Hua Hin has a strip of beer bars between Thanon Naretdamri and Thanon Phunsuk.

## GOLF

**Hua Hin** is home to the 18-hole **Royal Hua Hin Golf Course** (tel: 03 251 2475), the oldest in Thailand. Established in 1924, it has been followed by a number of top-quality rivals, making Hua Hin and nearby Cha-am a major golfing destination. Green fees at most courses are about US$25 weekdays and US$50 weekends. Caddies are required at most courses and cost about US$6 with an additional US$4–8 tip, depending on their experience and help. Electric carts cost about US$25, which usually includes a caddy.

## NIGHTLIFE

### Ko Samui

One of Chaweng Beach's favourite venues, the **Green Mango Disco** (Soi Green Mango, north end of central Chaweng), rarely gets going until after midnight.

Also on Chaweng Beach, the **Reggae Pub** continues to be popular, with a large open-air dance floor swinging to the latest sounds and reggae. Irish ex-plumber **Paul Waton** has created a corner of Ireland in the center of Chaweng (Chaweng Beach Road). Irish regulars and visitors love its laid-back atmosphere, the on-tap Irish beers, the live music and the friendly banter at the bar. It's open daily from 9 am until after midnight.

Over on **Big Buddha Beach**, look out for the **Secret Garden Festival** (22/1 Moo 4, Ban Bangrak, tel: 07 742 5419) on from December to April, Sunday 2–10 pm. What began as an impromptu jam session among friends has now become a major scene, with international stars dropping in on occasion. Even so, it still retains a pleasant, friendly feel.

The main nightlife venue on **Lamai Beach** is **Bauhaus**, a large entertainment complex with giant screens showing various sporting fixtures from around the world, and a busy dance floor. There are also occasional drag shows and Thai boxing exhibitions.

### Ko Phangan

One of the biggest social events in Thailand happens every full moon on Ko Samui's smaller sister island, Ko Phangan. The **Full Moon Party** (Hat Rin, ▶ 135) has become a world-famous rave venue.

# Andaman Coast

Getting Your Bearings 150 – 151
In Seven Days 152 – 153
Don't Miss 154 – 163
At Your Leisure 164 – 167
Where To 168 – 172

# Getting Your Bearings

Thailand's Andaman coast wriggles down the western side of its skinny peninsula, and features spectacular scenery all the way down from the famous island of Ko Phuket to the border with Malaysia. The area's delights include stunning white beaches, calm turquoise sea, vertical limestone islands, tumbling waterfalls and renowned seafood.

Island jewels off the Andaman coast are all around. Choose sophisticated Ko Phuket, with its international airport and good travel connections; idyllic and justly popular Ko Phi Phi; or the remote peace of Thalay Ban National Park further south. Transport to the islands is by colourful wooden longtail boats, and sea gypsies dive for pearls in the traditional way. Beneath the surface, coral harbours exotic fish, providing excellent diving and snorkelling.

On the mainland the spectacle continues with the beautiful coastline at Krabi, exciting tours of Ao Phang Nga, coffee and cashew plantations, lush green rainforests and tropical mangroves.

The exotic varied plant and wildlife found here are protected in Khao Sok National Park, a wild and magical place and home of one of the largest flowers in the world, the *Rafflesia kerri meyer* (wild lotus).

The monsoon hits this coast more heavily than the Gulf side, and is most intense between May and October. More time is also needed to enjoy this part of the country, where the pace of life is unhurried.

Ko Surin
National
Park

Khao Lak,
Ko Similan
and Ko Surin
**5**

Left: Rocky outcrops are a feature of the Krabi coast

Previous page: A typical scene at Hat Thram Phra Nang

## ★ Don't Miss

1 **Khao Sok National Park**
➤ 154
2 **Ao Phang Nga** ➤ 156
3 **Krabi** ➤ 159
4 **Ko Phi Phi** ➤ 162

## At Your Leisure

5 Khao Lak, Ko Similan and Ko Surin ➤ 164
6 Ko Phuket ➤ 164
7 Ko Jam ➤ 165
8 Ko Lanta Yai ➤ 166
9 Trang Province ➤ 166
10 Ko Tarutao ➤ 167
11 Thalay Ban National Park ➤ 167

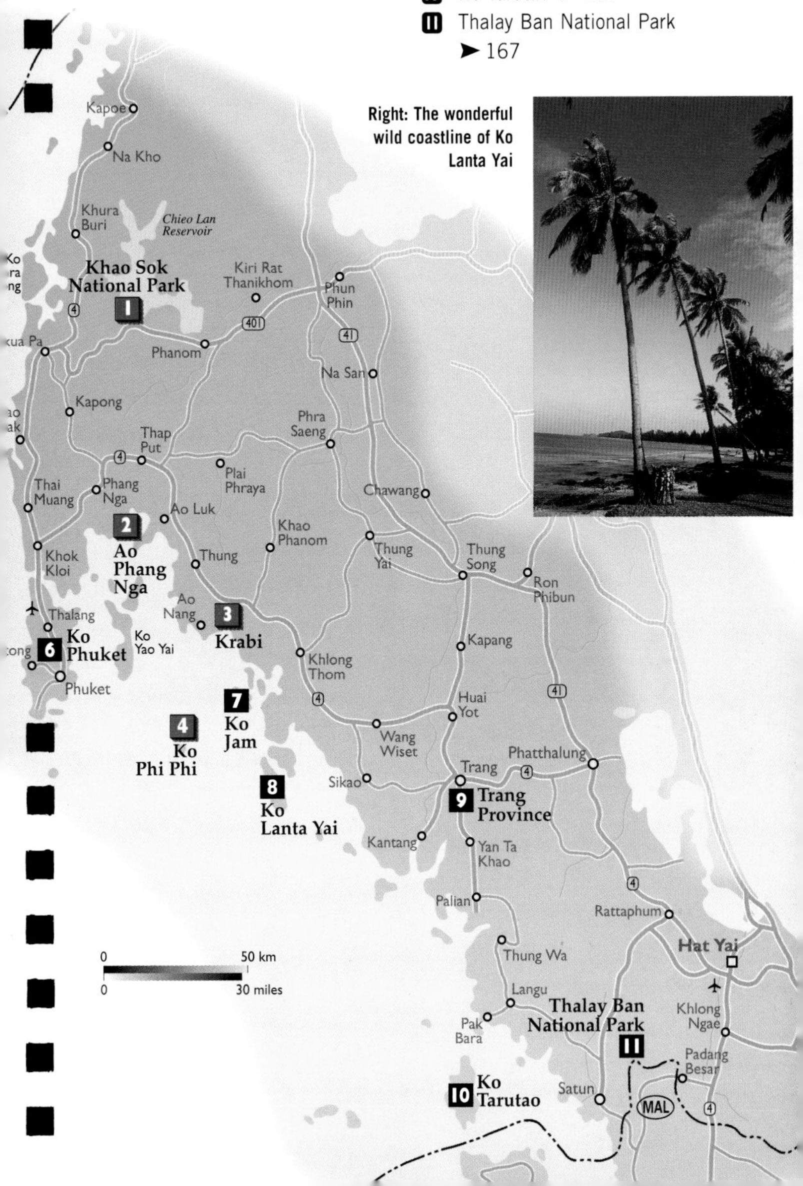

Right: The wonderful wild coastline of Ko Lanta Yai

Kapoe
Na Kho
Khura Buri
Chieo Lan Reservoir
Ko ra ng
**Khao Sok National Park** 1
Kiri Rat Thanikhom
Phun Phin
(401)
(41)
Phanom
Na San
kua Pa
Kapong
Phra Saeng
Thap Put
Plai Phraya
Chawang
Thai Muang
Phang Nga
Ao Luk
Khao Phanom
Thung Yai
Thung Song
Ron Phibun
2 **Ao Phang Nga**
Khok Kloi
Thung
ao ak
Thalang
Ao Nang
Ko Yao Yai
3 **Krabi**
Kapang
6 **Ko Phuket**
ong
Khlong Thom
(4)
Phuket
7 **Ko Jam**
Huai Yot
(41)
4 **Ko Phi Phi**
Wang Wiset
Phatthalung
8 **Ko Lanta Yai**
Sikao
Trang
9 **Trang Province**
Kantang
Yan Ta Khao
Palian
Rattaphum
**Hat Yai**
0 50 km
0 30 miles
Thung Wa
Langu
**Thalay Ban National Park** 11
Khlong Ngae
Pak Bara
Padang Besar
10 **Ko Tarutao**
Satun
(MAL)
(4)

Work your way down the west coast, zigzagging across the Andaman's emerald waters. This is an island hop interspersed with a jungle trip, a scenic cruise and a guided jeep tour and ending with a relaxing beach retreat.

# Andaman Coast in Seven Days

## Day One

### Morning
Take the 1.5-hour flight to **6 Ko Phuket** (➤ 164–165) from Bangkok (avoid the long train and bus journeys). Flights are inexpensive (if you come from the east coast, they're even more of a bargain from Pattaya, ➤ 120). Flights also go from Ko Samui, Chiang Mai, Hat Yai and Surat Thani. Have lunch in one of the noodle and curry restaurants in Phuket – try Thai Naan (➤ 171).

### Afternoon and Evening
Spend the rest of the day at **Ao Patong** (➤ 164), the most popular of Ko Phuket's beaches, and the evening and night at one of the luxury resorts (such as Le Royal Meridien, right ➤ 170).

## Day Two

### Morning
Drive or take a bus to **1 Khao Sok National Park** (left, ➤ 154–155) via Takua Pa. The trip should take about four hours.

### Afternoon and Evening
Relax in a hammock hanging from a treehouse and listen to the sounds of the jungle. Take a night safari (➤ 155). When darkness falls, you have a better chance of spotting the shyer inhabitants.

# Day Three

Set off on a guided lake tour (► 155). This takes you deep into the Khao Sok National Park to explore the stunning **Chieo Lan Reservoir**, with its impressive limestone towers and river-fed caves. Stay in scenic raft accommodation at the lake.

# Day Four

### Morning

Drive or take the bus to **2 Ao Phang Nga** (left, ► 156–158), a spectacular bay studded with islets. Change at Takua Pa if you are going by bus. The journey will take about half a day.

### Afternoon

From the bus station, take the tour of **Ao Phang Nga**. Sayan Tours have a trip leaving at 2 pm that includes a seafood supper and overnight accommodation at a floating Muslim village (► 156).

# Day Five

### Morning

Drive or take an early bus to **3 Krabi** (below, ► 159–161), a journey of about 1.5 hours. Spend the rest of the day doing the road tour of **Krabi province** (► 181). Visit the forest temple of **Wat Tham Seua** (► 161) before skirting the scenic coast and having lunch at one of the beach restaurants (► 161).

### Afternoon and Evening

If you have time, take a boat to one of the scenic beaches at **Laem Phra Nang** (► 160). Complete the loop by driving back to Krabi for dinner at the night market. Or treat yourself to an Italian meal at Viva (► 170).

# Days Six and Seven

Catch a boat from the pier at Krabi to the island of **4 Ko Phi Phi** (► 162–163). Spend two days relaxing on the idyllic beaches or embark on a black shark boat trip (most of the agencies offer them). Sharks measuring 2m (6.5 feet) long can be found hanging around off the rocks and reef.

# Khao Sok National Park

This national park forms one of the oldest ecosystems on earth. Mist-shrouded limestone towers rise out of the pristine jungle fed by a network of freshwater rivers, which tumble into waterfalls. A Communist hideout in the 1970s, wild elephants, bears and even tigers now lurk in the dense trees. More visible are monkeys, lizards, wild pigs, barking deer and flashing fireflies. Gibbons call from the rainforest canopy and cicadas produce a daily cacophony.

The best way to enjoy the park is to immerse yourself in the unique environment. There are short walks to waterfalls from the visitor centre, which provides a free leaflet showing the trails. These take you past thick buttress roots, vine-tangled umbrella palms and towering bamboo. You may not come across some of the larger mammals, but you'll be able to see dancing butterflies, huge dragonflies and exotic *rambutan* fruit trees.

The star attraction is the huge *rafflesia*, the largest flower in the world, measuring 1m (3.28 feet) across and weighing 7kg (15.4 pounds). It only blooms in January and February.

**Left: Signs near the park entrance fight for attention**

**Below: Bamboo rafting; just one of the many ways to enjoy the river**

➕ 198 A1　✉ 40km east of Takua Pa　🕐 Visitor Centre: Daily 8–4　☎ 07 727 8230, www.khaosok.com　💲 Expensive

## KHAO SOK NATIONAL PARK: INSIDE INFO

**Top tips** Kilometre marker 109 is the stop for buses from Surat Thani to the park, but if you just ask for "Khao Sok", the driver will know where to stop. Here you will be met by touts waiting to take you to the various lodges.

• The **wet season** (June to September) can be very wet. Trails are often slippery, and leeches can be a problem, but you may see more wildlife.

• The park has **no phone or email services** (apart from the odd satellite phone) and intermittent electricity, so if you need to communicate with the outside world do it before you get there.

• *Waterfalls and Gibbon Calls* by Thom Henley is on sale in the visitor centre. Its simple illustrations and accessible style provide a detailed background to the park and can act as a guide along the trails.

**Hidden gem** Chieo Lan Reservoir has limestone outcrops rising to 960m (3,148 feet) – three times higher than those in Ao Phang Nga (► 156–158). You need to take an overnight guided tour, which usually includes accommodation in one of the floating lodges on the shore (if not, it is easy to arrange your own accommodation, ask at the visitor centre). The lake is especially beautiful in the early morning when hornbills, eagles, gibbons and even elephants gather.

Much of the **accommodation** in the park is in simple but atmospheric wooden huts on stilts overlooking the rainforest or river. This is a good place to relax in a hammock in the day or by candlelight at night. All guest houses have guides offering **day and night safaris** – the guides usually speak good enough English to point things out along the way. Elephant rides, canoeing and "tubing" (floating down the river in a rubber ring – in the rainy season only) can all be arranged. Highly recommended is the **overnight lake tour**, which is usually combined with a spot of caving.

**Below: A panoramic view of one of the world's most ancient landscapes**

### TAKING A BREAK

All the lodges have restaurants with very similar menus – traditional Thai food and some Western basics.

# 2 Ao Phang Nga

With more than a hundred spectacular vertical islets, this huge bay forms an extraordinary landscape. Buzzing longtail boats take you through tangled mangroves, and past limestone outcrops to hidden white-sand beaches, semi-submerged caves dripping with stalactites, a floating Muslim village and Ko Phing Kan, or James Bond Island, made famous by its appearance in *The Man with the Golden Gun*.

**A tourist boat approaching a sea cave is dwarfed by the cliffs**

**Tours** of the bay, which is a national park, start from the bus terminal of the nondescript town of Phang Nga. **Sayan Tours**, which have been established for nearly 20 years, provide a friendly and efficient service and are timed to miss the Phuket crowds. Half-day trips to the main islands and caves run in the morning and afternoon; full-day trips offer more islands and a chance to swim.

An overnight option combines the half-day itinerary with accommodation in the floating Muslim village of **Ko Panyi** and a seafood supper. This is the more leisurely, recommended option, if you don't mind basic accommodation. It gives you a glimpse of the community without the

**The charmingly ramshackle floating village of Ko Panyi**

tourist crowds and there is not much reason to spend the night in Phang Nga town.

Ko Panyi was established more than 200 years ago, and now has a population of 2,000, consisting of just four or five families. It's best seen in the evening when the seafood restaurants and souvenir shops wind down and the daytime tourists have left. Wander around the floating labyrinth of corrugated iron and wood, which is crowded with crab and lobster pots and fishing nets, where chickens, cats and children somehow manage not to fall into the water. Sit on the western side to watch the sun set over the water. Branches sticking out of the water become makeshift moorings for the weathered wooden longtail boats that serve as fishing boats for the traditional community. There is a call to prayer five times a day at the green and gold mosque.

It is a short journey by road from the town of Phang Nga to the pier where a brightly coloured **longtail boat** takes you across green waterways with high, mangrove-covered banks. Boats sail through the large water cave of **Tahm Lod**. You pass **Kao Marjoo** (Dog Island), so-named because of its shape, and **Kao Khien** (Writing Island) which features rock drawings that date back at least 3,000 years. The final stop is Ko Phing Kan, or **James Bond Island**, which has souvenir shops on the small white-sand beach.

**Tiny fishing settlements huddle on the shores**

Ko Khao Tapu,
or Nail Island,
viewed from
James Bond
Island

Shell souvenirs
are on sale at
James Bond
Island

## TAKING A BREAK
Tours include **lunch at a
seafood restaurant** in a
floating village and dinner in
a house if you are staying
overnight.

➕ 199 D2  ✉ Sayan Tours, 209 Phang Nga bus terminal, Phang Nga
☎ 07 643 0348/01 979 0858, www.sayantours.com  ♿ Moderate

## AO PHANG NGA: INSIDE INFO

**Top tips** Although you can go on a **tour round the bay** from Phuket, it is better
to do it from Phang Nga as numbers will be smaller and it costs less.
• In the Muslim village of Ko Panyi **respect the locals**, who dress conservatively
and don't drink alcohol.
• Pick up the **information leaflet** at Sayan Tours' office. It gives information
about the route and points of interest. Guides speak little English, although
Sayan's owner comes and chats after dinner and will answer any questions.

# ③ Krabi

When visitors talk of Krabi, they tend to mean the beautiful coast as much as the fishing town itself, which is a major jumping-off point for the area's superb white-sand beaches and emerald waters. Most of Krabi province's attractions are offshore. The snaking coastline shelters deep bays, many of which are only accessible by boat, circled by coral reefs. They are backed by sheer limestone cliffs which offer some of the best rock climbing in the world.

Krabi town is in a peaceful riverside setting with a tree-lined grass promenade and the charmingly named Ko Maew and Ko Nu, "**Cat and Mouse Islands**", on its eastern side. As well as being in some ways the capital of the Andaman coast, Krabi is also a culinary capital. At the lively **night market**, illuminated glass cabinets line a string of pavement tables where streetside chefs roll out dough for deep-fried pastry and toss just-caught sizzling seafood. An amazing range of international food, from Thai curry, pizza and Mexican food to American burgers and Greek salads, is served in the town's restaurants and cafés.

Lying under a limestone cliff is a 15m-long (50-foot) **Reclining Buddha**. In a kink in Route 404 it is easy to miss, but it is close to the 7km marker, which indicates its distance from Krabi. The image is part of **Wat Sai Thai**, although there are hardly any monks living in the temple here.

Some 18km (11 miles) northwest of Krabi, **Hat Noppharat Thara** is a beautiful, clean stretch of pine-fringed beach, part of a national park of the same name. Its name means "Beach of the Nine-Gem Stream" but it was previously called "Dry Canal Beach" because of the pretty canal which flows into the sea here. The tide retreats far into the bay, making swimming

There's curry galore at Krabi's night market

Restaurants and shops vie with the palms on Ao Nang's beach road

impossible at low tide, but it is a lovely, tranquil place for a stroll on the sand. There are picnic areas, and **boat and snorkelling trips** are available to islands such as Chicken and Poda, which stud the large scenic bay. No need to reserve, someone will probably offer you one at Hat Noppharat Thara.

**Ao Nang** is a developed stretch along a roadside beach that attracts package holidaymakers. Just south of here, the little headland of **Laem Phra Nang** is named after a local princess (*phra nang* means "revered lady"). Although reached only by boat – longtails leave from near Krabi's pier – it is very popular and famous for its **rock climbing**, offering hundreds of world-class routes. Beginners are catered to as well, and even if you are not participating, it's a good spectator sport. Other activities on offer include kayaking through the mangroves, and snorkelling and diving trips to nearby islands. The beach is packed with places offering all these activities.

There are three beaches: **Ao Phra Nang** at the centre and **East** and **West Rai Lai** on either side, which are separated by a few rows of bungalow accommodation. The east beach has rock climbing shops and

Below: rock climbing on Laem Phra Nang is a popular spectator sport

➕ 199 D2
TAT
✉ Utrakit Road ☎ 07 561 1381

mangroves and mudflats rather than a real beach, but cheaper accommodation. At the main west beach, snorkelling, diving and kayaking are available as well as rock climbing.

Most people pass by **Wat Tham Seua** (Tiger Cave Temple, free), on their way to the beaches. In a beautiful setting on the northeast reaches of Krabi, it is one of southern Thailand's most important forest temples, where monks live in meditation huts in caves among the trees. The first and main cave is full of paraphernalia – nuns can be seen making bracelets and Thais come to worship. Behind the altar, stairs lead to a smaller cave, featuring a **giant Buddha footprint**. If you walk through the temple grounds to the statue of the Goddess of Mercy, the first set of steps is a near-vertical route. It takes about an hour to get to the top, but there are good views as far as the coast. The second series of steps leads to the meditation huts and a temple with a **Big Buddha** with a mirror in its palm. You can follow a marked loop through ancient trees, including one that is said to be 1,000 years old. Although you can reach the temple by *songthaew* from Utrakit Road, the best option is to rent a jeep or motorbike.

Above: The view from Hat Thram Phra Nang beach on Laem Phra Nang

Above right: A longtail ferry at East Rai Lai

## TAKING A BREAK

The **Kiang Lay** restaurant at Krabi's Aonang Villa Resort (113 Ao Nang Beach, tel: 07 563 7270–4, 6–9 pm) is a very romantic spot for a candlelit dinner. From its airy terrace you can watch the ferries leave for the islands in the bay beyond.

## KRABI: INSIDE INFO

**Top tips** Ao Nang is also sometimes called **Ao Phra Nang**, especially on road signs, which makes it easily confused with the beach on the cape.
• Most of the **accommodation** on Ao Nang is closed between May and October when the beach tends to be covered in debris brought in by the tide. At this time of year, the beaches around **Laem Phra Nang** are a much better bet.

**One to miss** Although all signs seem to point to the **Shell Cemetery of Su-San Hoi**, and trips are offered from Krabi, unless you are particularly interested in geology, you might feel you are just looking at slabs of concrete. The blocks are made up of 75-million-year-old mollusc shell fossils.

# 4 Ko Phi Phi

The horrifying tsunami of December 26, 2004 hit the idyllic island of Phi Phi particularly badly, killing over a thousand people, many of them tourists, and demolishing its double-sided seafront area, called The Village. This strip of beach-fringed land, joining the higher north and south, was the heart of the island's holiday trade, with bars, budget hotels, restaurants and guest houses. Virtually everything was destroyed and complete rebuilding will take until at least 2007, but don't let that put you off a visit to this enchanting island.

The hotels and resorts on the higher ground in the north and south survived the tsunami untouched, and they are as welcoming as ever, their bays and beaches unscarred and beautifully maintained. At the time of writing, more than a dozen top-end hotels and resorts were back in business.

**Left: Pleasure craft and long-tail boats moor in Ao Ton Sai**

**Below: The island's twin beaches from a popular viewpoint**

The Village is slowly taking shape again, and some bars, restaurants, guest houses and resorts will be open if you visit. In fact, this is an excellent time to visit, as the island is relatively quiet and not overrun by the peak season crowds, who are sure to return before long.

Phi Phi is actually two islands – Phi Phi Don and the smaller, virtually uninhabited Phi Phi Ley. Phi Phi Don is the

tourist island, two upland tracts of jungle joined by a narrow strip of of beach-lined land, known before the tsunami as The Village. Two very pretty bays emanate from this strip, Loh Dalum Bay and the better-known and more developed Tonsai Bay. Some of the hotels and resorts on these two bays can only be reached by boat, a very romantic way of starting a holiday.

For a fine view of the island, climb the well signposted path from The Village, which passes a tiny Thai settlement and leads after a mile or two to the deserted beaches of Ao Lanti and Ao Koh Bakao.

**The white sands of Ao Ton Sai give way to rocks at its eastern end**

## TAKING A BREAK

The **Chao Koh Phi Phi Lodge** (53 Moo 7), under the same management as the popular **Carlito's Bar**, has an excellent restaurant overlooking central Tonsai Village beach. Early risers can breakfast there from a large a la carte menu, while evening diners can enjoy a cocktail or crisp Chardonnay watching the lights flick on along Tonsai Village beachfront.

You can escape the Tonsai Beach crowds by heading to the northeastern side of the island, to the **Phi Phi Island Village Beach Resort and Spa** (tel: 07 562 8900–3). At the resort's hillside **Wana Spa** you can enjoy a jacuzzi in a petal-strewn tub overlooking the ocean.

➕ 199 D2
TAT
✉ The nearest office is at Krabi or Phuket (➤ 159)

---

## KO PHI PHI: INSIDE INFO

### Top tips

- The website **www.phi-phi.com** carries up-to-date information about Ko Phi Phi. Other tourist information is provided by the TAT offices in Phuket or Krabi.
- Sunrise and sunset are magical times. Watch the sun rise over the Andaman Sea in front of the Beach Club at Tonsai Village, or sunset from the island's View Point.

# At Your Leisure

## 5 Khao Lak, Ko Similan and Ko Surin

The village of **Khao Lak** (part of the national park of the same name), has a laid-back atmosphere and is home to just 30 or so fishing families. Snorkelling, diving trips and jungle treks take you deeper into the spectacular surrounding scenery in the national park.

Khao Lak is a departure point for **Ko Similan** (a group of nine islands) and **Ko Surin** (five islands). These archipelagos offer some of the world's best diving among vast networks of spectacular coral teeming with exotic fish. Both groups of islands are remote, with only basic accommodation. Practically inaccessible during the monsoon season (between May and October), the islands are best visited as part of an organised tour during the rest of the year. One company organising tours is **Sea Dragon Dive Centre** in Khao Lak (tel: 07 642 0420). The tour lasts three days and includes the boat trips, accommodation, food and equipment.

➕ 198 A1

## 6 Ko Phuket

The island once called "Junk Ceylon" was a resting place for sailors travelling between India and China. Now called "Pearl of the Andaman", it is famed for its cuisine, yachting, fishing and world-class diving. Thailand's largest island, and its wealthiest province, everything is on a grand scale, with sweeping beaches, huge luxury resorts and high mountain roads.

Commercial developments are centred on the west coast. Glitzy **Ao Patong** is the most built up and the centre for diving operations. Its

### For Kids

● **Snorkelling** – Seatran Travel run day trips to Ko Phi Phi. The Holiday Diving Club at Ao Patong on Ko Phuket (tel: 07 621 9391-2, expensive), runs tours including lunch and equipment

● **Fantasea** in Phuket (near Hat Kamala, tel: 07 638 5100, www.phuket-fantasea.com, daily except Tue 5:30–11:30 pm, expensive) is a spectacular night-time show combining modern light and sound technology, traditional Thai dance and a buffet.

● **Phuket Butterfly Garden and Aquarium** (Yaowarat Road, north of Phuket town, daily 9–5:30, expensive) has a wide variety of butterflies and reef fish.

● **Whale- and dolphin-watching trips** (information from the visitor centre tel: 07 478 1285, trips leave from Ko Taratuo and last all day, moderate).

● **Boat trip at Ao Phang Nga** (➤ 156).

seafront was badly hit by the December 2004 tsunami but swiftly reconstructed, and today is again Phuket's principal entertainment scene, a glittering strip of seafood restaurants, souvenir shops and bars.

Neighbouring **Ao Karon** and **Ao Kata** are

quieter. Upmarket hotels dominate the other beaches here, though at Kamala buffalo still come to the beach to cool down. Hat Mai Khao is a national park beach on the north coast. "Water-people" communities (➤ panel) are centred around the south and east coast, where the landscape has been destroyed by tin mining.

The centre of Phuket Town is pretty unexciting, although it does have traditional Sino-Portuguese mansions, upmarket antiques shops and a tucked-away Chinese Taoist Temple, the **Shrine of the Serene Light** (free). There are Chinese and Portuguese influences, and around a third of Phuket's population is Muslim.

Phuket is expensive compared to the rest of the country. Because of the Sarasin Bridge linking it to the mainland, there are more cars here than on other islands. During the monsoon the water can be rough, so look for red flags when swimming.

➕ 199 D2

**TAT**

✉ 73–75 Phuket Road ☎ 07 621 2213 ⏰ Daily 8:30–4:30

## 🟧 Ko Jam

This remote fishing island has a mangrove-lined shore, cashew nut plantations and little else. A real get-away-from-it-all spot, the northern section is almost impenetrable due to

**A long sweep of beach at Karon resort in the southwest of Ko Phuket**

### Cultural Connections

The west side of Thailand which works its way down to Malaysia was once at the heart of trading routes with the countries that surround it – China, India and Malaysia. It's a history that can be seen everywhere; in the architecture of the minarets of Muslim mosques, in the traditional wooden Chinese shophouses and in the cuisine, with Chinese, Malay and Indian influences. Chinese merchants settled in the cities here, while Thais who are closely related to Malays live in the rural interior. In the far south, locals speak a dialect and a language close to both Malay and Indonesian. Muslim influences can be seen, too, in the fishing families of *Chao Ley*, or "water people", who dive for pearls, fish and shells with makeshift equipment. Different in appearance to other Thais, the *Chao Ley*, who often have dark skin and red hair, are thought to have originally come from Indonesia and speak their own language. Although many communities have been forced out by tourist development, they continue to fish the coast of the Andaman and live their unique lifestyle.

thick forest. Less than a handful of rustic bungalows operate here, sending out longtail boats to meet the Krabi and Ko Lanta ferries.

⊞ 199 D2

## 8 Ko Lanta Yai

This remote island is wild and peaceful. It is the largest of a group of 52 islands known as Ko Lanta. If you do the Krabi tour (► 181), you could continue to Ko Lanta Yai by car (around 100km/62 miles). There are two very short ferry crossings from Krabi that take vehicles to the island, and a newly constructed road bridge.

**Fishing boats are tied with good-luck talismans in Ko Lanta Yai**

Boats dock at a ramshackle village with tourist facilities and wooden thatched restaurants perched on stilts over the water.

There are avenues of rubber trees, prawn farms and lush rice fields in the southern section, which has little tourist development, just the occasional water buffalo.

During the monsoon season, Ko Lanta Yai is practically deserted. The wide, open beaches can be windswept and much of the beach accommodation is closed.

⊞ 199 D2
**TAT**
✉ Utrakit Road, Krabi ☎ 07 561 1381

---

### Five Island Retreats
Ko Jam (► 165)
Ko Similan (► 164)
Ko Surin (► 164)
Ko Lanta Yai (► 166)
Ko Tarutao (► 167)

---

## 9 Trang Province

The capital, Trang, once known as the "City of Waves", was an important sea-trading and shipping centre. Today its wealth comes from rubber and the influence is mostly Chinese. It has a wealth of Chinese noodle restaurants, Muslim curry houses, traditional coffee shops and an annual **Vegetarian Festival** held every October.

The coast of Trang Province is dotted with islands, long, wide sandy beaches and towering limestone mountains. **Hat Jao Mai** is a 5km (3-mile) stretch of sand that is part of the national park of the same name. Islands offshore – **Ko Hai**, **Ko Muk** and **Ko Kradan** – offer white-sand beaches and excellent snorkelling. **Hat Pak Meng** is another long stretch of beach which also has a long promenade pier and limestone caves to explore.

⊞ 199 E2
**TAT**
✉ Sanon Na Meuang city park, Nakhon Si Thammarat
☎ 07 534 6515

## ⑩ Ko Tarutao

The Tarutao National Marine Park is made up of 51 islands – most of which are uninhabited. There are idyllic beaches, limestone caves and mangrove-fringed shores to explore, along with more than 100 species of birds, including sea eagles and reef egrets. Wild pigs, macaques and dusky langurs (a type of monkey) roam the rainforest, four species of turtles lay their eggs on the sands, and dolphins, whales and a variety of fish swim in the waters. Three of the islands, Ko Tarutao, Ko Adang and Ko Lipe, offer accommodation. The park is only accessible from November to April and is closed to visitors the rest of the year due to the monsoon (check with the visitor centre for exact dates, which vary from year to year).

➕ 199 E2  ✉ Ferries from Pak Bara

**Visitor Centre**
✉ Pak Bara  ☎ 02 579 0529
🏷 Inexpensive (donation to park)

## ⑪ Thalay Ban National Park

Sitting on the border with Malaysia, this national rainforest park is home to rare birds such as booted eagles as well as honey bears and clouded leopards. There are guided trails (book at the park headquarters, expensive)

**Thalay Ban National Park is definitely a step off the beaten track**

### Malaysia

Many people who get to the southern end of Thailand's tail feel the pull of Malaysia (► 141), and even Singapore. It's a very well-connected route and a simple procedure; plenty of visitors make this popular crossing just to renew their Thai visas. Probably the easiest way is to travel by rail across the border from Padang Besar (reserve a sleeper in advance if you're travelling at a weekend or on a public holiday). You will have to disembark with your luggage to clear immigration before getting back on the train.

through lush green valleys to a lily-covered lake; you can swim in tiered waterfalls and wonder at panoramic views from the limestone outcrops.

As the park receives heavy rainfall, it is best visited between December and March, outside the monsoon season.

➕ 199 E1  ✉ 40km (25 miles) northeast of Satun, 90km (56 miles) south of Hat Yai

**Thalay Ban National Park Headquarters**
☎ 02 735 0644

# Where to... Stay

**Prices**
Expect to pay per double room
£ under 1,000 baht  ££ 1,000–4,000 baht  £££ over 4,000 baht

## Krabi Meritime ££

Beside the meandering Krabi River, this large hotel has some impressive views of the surrounding limestone pinnacles. Its proximity to the nature of the area sets it apart. Trips into the mangrove forests can be arranged on longtail boats. All rooms overlook the lagoon and surrounding forest and have satellite TV, air-conditioning and mini-bar. Other facilities include a large swimming pool and spa.

➕ 199 D2 ⬜ 1 Tungfah Road, Muang Krabi ☎ 07 562 0028, fax: 07 561 2992, email: meritime@krabi-hotels. com, www.krabi-hotels.com

## Rayavadee £££

Overlooking one of the world's most beautiful beaches, Rayavadee is the only accommodation on Ao Phra Nang. The surrounding limestone cliffs seal the resort from the rest of the world; it's only accessible by boat or two tortuous footpaths. There are more than 100 luxury pavilions and villas nestling amid a large coconut plantation. The resort is completely self contained with its own video and CD library, a body and mind retreat and a spectacular swimming pool.

➕ 199 D2 ⬜ 214 Moo 2, Tambon Ao Nang ☎ 07 562 0740, fax: 07 562 0630, email: rayavadee@rayavadee.com, www.rayavadee.com

## Tipa Resort ££

This extensive resort complex sits on a hillside site a short walk from Ao Nang beach. Choose between deluxe rooms furnished in dark woods, bamboo and rattan and cheaper timber-built bungalows. It's an ideal holiday destination for families, with two pools, playground, bike and boat rental and even a "music corner" with Thai musical instruments.

➕ 199 D2 ⬜ 121/1 Moo 2, Ao Nang, Muang Krabi ☎ 07 563 7527–31, www.krabi-hotels.com/tipa resort

## Phi Phi Island Cabana £££

One of the first places you'll see on sailing into Ko Phi Phi's small harbour, this hotel is beautifully situated between the island's two famous bays, Ao Ton Sai and Ao Lo Dalam. In a jungle setting, the large, comfortable bungalows offer great sea views and a good place to retreat to. There is also a hotel with air-conditioned rooms. Facilities include a nightclub, snooker club and swimming pool.

➕ 199 D2 ⬜ Ton Sai Bay ☎ 07 561 1496, fax: 07 561 2132, email: info@phiphicabana-hotel.com, www.phiphicabana-hotel.com

## Holiday Inn Resort £££

A boutique-style resort with 80 bungalows, the Holiday Inn group's Phi Phi Hotel is self-contained and away from the more hectic Ao Ton Sai area of the island. Bungalows cater to a maximum of three people, or there are family units comprising two bungalows with interconnecting doors. All have good views across to the adjoining islands of Ko Yung (Mosquito Island) and Ko Mai Phai (Bamboo Island). This is a great place to get away from the rest of the world and bask in the delights of an open-air jacuzzi, windsurfing, tennis courts, a sauna and the island's only freshwater swimming pool.

➕ 199 D2 ⬜ Laem Tong Beach ☎ 07 562 1334, fax: 07 562 0798, www.holiday-inn.com

## KO PHUKET

### Amanpuri Resort £££

This is Ko Phuket's most exclusive resort. Isolated and tranquil, its name means "Place of Peace". There are 40 beautiful pavilions and 30 classic Thai villas. The villas vary in size and each has its own live-in maid and cook. The resort also has a library with more than 1,000 books. The Amanpuri provides a fleet of over 20 vessels (the largest professionally crewed fleet in Thailand) available for cruises in the beautiful waters..

➕ 199 D2 ⊠ 118/1 Moo 3, Cherngtalay, Pansea Beach ☎ 07 632 4333, fax: 07 632 4100, www.amanresorts.com

### Chedi Resort £££

The Chedi has 108 luxury, secluded cottages near the shore of Pansea Beach. Set in a stunning landscaped environment, each cottage has its own veranda and sundeck. Interiors feature beautiful panels of specially woven palm fronds, teak floors and soothing natural fabrics. The rooms all have king-size beds, satellite TV and air-conditioning. An unusual feature of the Chedi is its distinctive diamond-shaped, black swimming pool. There's also a spa, tennis courts and watersports. The resort is within a 30-minute drive of five golf courses.

➕ 199 D2 ⊠ 118 Moo 3, Choeng Talay, Pansea Beach ☎ 07 632 4017/20, fax: 07 632 4252, www.phuket.com

### Diamond Cliff Resort £££

Situated on the hillside in extensive grounds at the quiet, northern end of Patong Beach, this fine resort and spa overlooks the clear waters of Ao Patong. All rooms have a sea view and satellite TV. Facilities include two restaurants and a spa offering Thai, Swedish and sports' massages. Activities range from Thai cooking lessons, fruit and vegetable carving and free tennis lessons to miniature golf competitions.

➕ 199 D2 ⊠ 284 Prabaramee Road, Patong Beach ☎ 07 634 0501–6, fax: 07 634 0507, www.diamondcliff.com

### Dusit Laguna Resort £££

The Dusit Laguna is part of a resort system that includes the Sheraton Grande Laguna Beach, Banyan Tree, Allamanda and Laguna Beach Resort. If you're staying at one of the five hotels you can use the facilities of the others. The Dusit Laguna offers every amenity along with superb restaurants and health facilities. All 226 rooms have a private balcony that faces either the sea or the lagoons. The swimming pool has a water slide and there's a putting green and tennis courts. You can also learn traditional Thai crafts such as fruit and vegetable carving.

➕ 199 D2 ⊠ 390 Thanon Sri Sunthorn, Thalang ☎ 07 632 4324, fax: 07 632 4174, www.dusit.com

### Felix Karon Phuket £££

The 121-room Felix Karon is a short stroll from Ao Karon's popular shopping and nightlife area. The rooms have satellite TV, mini-bar and in-house movie channels. The hotel is particularly popular with families as the children's facilities are very good. There's a children's swimming pool with slides and a supervised playground. Other facilities include a fitness centre and two curvy swimming pools. The View Point restaurant is renowned for its southern Thai cuisine.

➕ 199 D2 ⊠ 4/8 Thanon Patak, Ao Karon ☎ 07 639 6666–75, fax: 07 639 6853, www.felixphuket.com

### Marina Phuket ££

The Marina Phuket is a collection of Thai-style cottages in a stunning natural environment, with coconut palms and a garden teeming with life. Fruit trees, ferns, palms and orchids provide a relaxing atmosphere. All rooms are attractively decorated with traditional Thai crafts and have either an ocean view or a jungle view. Enjoy the split-level pool and Sala Thai, one of the

# Where to...
# Eat and Drink

## Prices

Expect to pay per person for a three-course meal, excluding drinks and service

£ under 200 baht  ££ 200–500 baht  £££ over 500 baht

best restaurants on the island (➤ 171).

🔼 199 D2 ☒ 119 Thanon Patak, Ao Karon ☎ 07 633 0625, fax: 07 633 0516, www.marinaphuket.com

### Le Royal Meridien Phuket Yacht Club £££

Phuket's exclusive Yacht Club is situated at Ao Nai Harn, with good swimming and beautiful sunsets. It's a great place to be for the annual King's Cup Regatta in early December, when the bay is filled with brightly coloured yachts. This superb hotel overlooks the bay at its northern end and offers every luxury imaginable, coupled with picture-perfect views. All rooms have views of the bay, a CD system, mini-bar and in-house movies. Sports facilities include yachting, a fitness centre, tennis courts and Le Royal Spa. The Regatta is a renowned restaurant (➤ 171).

🔼 199 D2 ☒ 23/3 Thanon Viset, Ao Nai Harn ☎ 07 638 0200, fax: 07 638 0280, www.phuket-yachtclub.com

### Reuan Mai £–££

This attractive, traditional-style Thai "Suan Ahaan" (Garden Restaurant) serves excellent southern and central Thai food in a garden setting. It's 1.5km (1 mile) north of the town, but worth the small effort. The seafood selection is extensive and excellent.

🔼 199 D2 ☒ Thanon Maharat ☎ 07 563 1796–7 ☻ Daily 11:30–2:30, 6–10:30

### Tamarind Tree £

The Tamarind Tree restaurant is part

of KR Mansion, a popular guest house and useful source of tourist and traveller information. It's enduringly good and offers Thai and Western dishes. The house specialities are healthy salads and macrobiotic dishes using organic produce. There's a rooftop bar offering fine evening views across the mountains.

🔼 199 D2 ☒ KR Mansion, Thanon Chao Fa ☎ 07 561 2761, fax 07 561 2545 ☻ Daily 7 am–11 pm

### Viva £

Viva, run by Italians, serves homemade ciabatta bread, a fantastic choice of 40 kinds of real Sicilian pizza, fresh spinach pasta and even imported Italian cheeses. It is well appointed with attractive bamboo furniture and seating inside and out.

🔼 199 D2 ☒ Thanon 29 Pruksa Uthit ☎ 07 563 0517 ☻ Daily noon–11:30

### Marlin Restaurant ££

The Phi Phi Island Village Beach Resort's restaurant is one of the finest on the island, an elegant, open-sided venue for romantic evening dining on the terrace under the stars. The menu is an imaginative mix of Thai and finely presented international dishes.

🔼 199 D2 ☒ Phi Phi Island Village Resort and Spa ☎ 07 625 8185 ☻ Daily 6 pm–11 pm

### Sun Set Satay Bar £

Malaysian-style satays and sunsets make a great combination at this popular bistro-bar at the Holiday Inn Resort. It's only open for two hours every evening, coinciding with sunset, but the neighbouring Mong Talay bar continues until midnight and has live music.

➕ 199 D2 ⊠ Holiday Inn Resort ☎ 07 562 1334 Sun Set Satay Bar ⏰ Daily 5.30–7.30 Mong Talay Bar ⏰ Daily 12–midnight

## KO PHUKET

### Krajok Si ££

Located in a 19th-century shop-house in the heart of Phuket Town, this most popular of eating establishments serves traditional Phuket cuisine. *Krajok si* means "coloured glass" and that's what you need to look out for to find the restaurant, as there is no English sign – the coloured glass is over the door. Numerous antiques scattered about give the interior an agreeable atmosphere. Specialities include the delightful *haw mok thaleh* (seafood mousse) and green mango salad.

➕ 199 D2 ⊠ 26 Thanon Takua Pa, Phuket Town ☎ 07-6217903 ⏰ Tue–Sun 6 pm–midnight; closed Mon

### Mom Tri's Boathouse £££

Romantic views of Ao Kata from the terrace make this one of Phuket's best restaurants, with Thai and European food. Renowned for its choice of quality wines, the cellar has more than 350 different labels. Live music makes for a pleasant atmosphere right on the beach.

➕ 199 D2 ⊠ Boathouse Inn, 2/2 Patak Road, Ao Kata ☎ 07 633 0015 ⏰ Daily 7 am–10:30 pm

### Old Siam ££

Old Siam offers a choice of either the beautiful old teak house or the rooftop terrace overlooking the ocean. Dishes tend towards central Thai cooking and if you like things spicy you may need to tell the staff to pop in an extra chilli. Entertainment includes Thai dancing Wednesday and Sunday and nightly Thai music.

➕ 199 D2 ⊠ Karon Beach Road at the Thavorn Palm Beach Hotel ☎ 07 639 6554 ⏰ Daily noon–3, 6–11

### The Regatta £££

This is a fine Italian restaurant found in the exclusive Le Royal Meridien Phuket Yacht Club (▶ 170). Dishes tend towards simple Italian home cooking, with lots of great pasta dishes and seafood. The resident European chef makes regular changes to the menu. A great place to sit and watch the sun set over Ao Nai Harn and sip one of the many delicious cocktails on offer.

➕ 199 D2 ⊠ Le Royal Meridien Phuket Yacht Club, Ao Nai Harn ☎ 07 638 0300 ⏰ Daily 7–11 pm

### Sala Thai £££

Marina Phuket has two excellent restaurants, Sala Thai or "Thai Room", with its remarkable adaptation of traditional Thai architecture and splendid views of the jungle and swimming pool, is one of Ko Phuket's most famous restaurants. At night, diners can enjoy fine Thai cuisine to the accompaniment of traditional Thai music and dance in airy, open spaces defined by beautiful woods, tiles and carved panels. The second restaurant, On the Rock, is famous for its seafood and southern Thai dishes and presents some of Ko Phuket's finest cuisine in a luxurious setting with sweeping views of the sea at Ao Karon.

➕ 199 D2 ⊠ 119 Thanon Patak, Ao Karon ☎ 07 633 0625, fax: 07 633 0516, e-mail: info@marinaphuket.com, www.marinaphuket.com

### Thai Naan ££

Reputed to be the largest teak restaurant in southern Thailand, Thai Naan serves a spectacular lunchtime buffet with numerous Thai dishes and more than 20 types of *dim sum*. Royal Thai cuisine (prepared so that the food does not need to be cut by the diner!) and traditional Phuket favourites are presented in the special Srivichai set dinner. There is also a sophisticated cultural show each evening.

➕ 199 D2 ⊠ 16 Thanon Vichitsongkhram, Phuket Town ☎ 07 622 6164 ⏰ Daily 6 am–9:30 pm

# Where to...
# Shop

## PHUKET TOWN

### Antiques and Crafts

Most of the antiques and craft shops are clustered around the Yaowarat, Thalang and Ratsada roads area in the old Sino-Portuguese part of town. **Ban Boran Textiles** (51 Thanon Yaowarat, tel: 07 621 2473) showcases gorgeous fabrics from six countries in the Southeast Asia region. The fabrics are made into shirts, trousers, skirts and dresses.

The **Jim Thompson Silk Company** has six outlets in Phuket, five of them in luxury hotels such as the Marriott at Mai Khao beach and one in the centre of Phuket town (The Courtyard, tel. 07 626 4468).

For art and antiques, visit **Soul of Asia**, a gallery converted from two old Chinese shophouses (39 Ratsada Road, tel: 07 621 1122) or Chan's Antique House (99/42 Moo 5, Chalermprakiat Road, tel: 07 626 1416–7).

**Touch Wood Antique Furniture** (12–14 Thanon Ratsada, tel: 07 625 6407), has Colonial antique items from Myanmar and Thailand, such as refurbished plantation chairs.

### Pearls

Phuket is a good source of fine-quality pearls and the **Pearl Centre** (83 Thanon Ranong, Soi Phutorn, Phuket Town, tel: 07 621 1707) has some good bargains.

## AROUND PHUKET TOWN

**Baanboonpitak** (30 Thanon Prachanukroh, Patong Beach, tel: 07 634 1789) has traditional Thai and Burmese furniture. At **Siam Arts** (382/5 Thanon Srisoonthorn, Cherngtalay, Thalang, tel: 07 632 5207) you'll find teak furniture, woodcarvings and antiques.

# Where to...
# Be Entertained

## NIGHTLIFE

### Ko Phuket

**The Star Club Entertainment Discotheque** (1984 Thanon Ratuthit, Patong Beach, tel: 07 634 6187) is the island's largest disco. **Banana Discotheque** (96 Thanon Thawiwong, Patong Beach, tel: 07 634 0301) has a pub attached and live music. **Otawa** (100/7 Kalim Beach Road, Patong Beach, tel: 07 634 4254) offers the Raw Jazz Quartet most nights. **Simon Cabaret** (100/6–8 Moo 4, Patong– Karon Road, Patong, tel: 07 634 2114) stages one of the best transvestite cabaret shows in Thailand.

### Ko Phi Phi

**Carlito's Bar**, on the beach at Ton Sai Bay, is open again after being hit by the tsunami, it has become a kind of information centre for the island. Many nearby bars are rapidly being rebuilt, often under new management and names.

## OUTDOOR PURSUITS

The limestone cliffs of the Krabi coast offer **rock climbs** of various degrees of difficulty, with professional instructors.

The area around Ao Phang Nga is ideal for **kayaking**. Canoes enter narrow crevices, sometimes passing beneath overhangs so low that the canoeist has to lie flat to enter.

Ko Phuket is famous for **big-game fishing**. Charter a fully equipped fishing vessel or hire a small boat. Fish for marlin, sea bass, barracuda, king mackerel and yellowfin tuna.

# Walks and Tours

1 Bangkok's Chinatown 174 – 176
2 Mae Hong Son Loop 177 – 180
3 Krabi 181 – 183
4 Khao Sam Roi Yot
  National Park 184 – 186

# 1 BANGKOK'S CHINATOWN

*Walk*

This walk guides you around the tiny alleyways of Chinatown, which is situated between Thanon Charoen Krung (New Road) and the river. The area takes in exotic produce, hidden temples, shops selling gold and wood-lined apothecaries. Be warned: the crowds, smells and sights here are not for the squeamish. Try to set off mid-afternoon, stopping for cocktails at dusk at the revolving restaurant of the Grand Chinese Princess Hotel to see the lights of the city and ending with a taste of Little India. Avoid doing this walk at the weekend when many of the stalls are closed, and bear in mind that River Express boats do not run in the evening.

**DISTANCE** 2.5km/1.5 miles (one way)
**TIME** 2–3 hours depending on whether you stop for reflexology, cocktails or dinner
**START/END POINT** River Express Stop, Tha Ratchawong/Thanon Chakraphet ✚ 200 C2

## 1–2

Take the River Express boat to the Tha Ratchawong pier and walk up the road of the same name for about 300m (327 yards), past the gangs of motorcycle couriers and taxis. Turn right at the cluster of food stalls where a blue sign announces **Soi Wanit 1**. This tiny alley, also known as **Sampeng Lane**, is at the heart of Chinatown. Although barely wide enough for two people, load-bearing carts and motorbikes weave their way hazardously down here. Once the highlight for opium dens and gambling

**A food vendor in Chinatown dishes up delicacies both familiar and exotic**

### Taking a Break

On the 25th floor of the **Grand Chinese Princess Hotel** (215 Thanon Yaowarat) is a **revolving restaurant** (5 pm–1 am, expensive) and "club lounge" with a bird's-eye view of the city. Order a cocktail and gaze at the floodlit riverside *wats* and illuminated high-rises of Siam Square. A full revolution takes three hours, so if you want to see the whole lot without walking around, consider having dinner here – they serve Thai, sushi and some international dishes.

### Places to Visit

**Wat Mangkon Kamalawat**
✚ 200 C2 ☒ Thanon Charoen Krung 🎫 Free

**Sikh temple**
✚ 200 B2 ☒ off Thanon Chakraphet 🎫 Free

houses, now it has tourist commercialism at its heart and is a good place to buy Chinese silk and computer games.

## 2–3

Walk for two blocks past the 100-year-old **Tang To Kang gold shop** before turning left down **Soi 16**. This alley is lined with giant sacks of rice crackers, tea and dried mushrooms, and stalls selling local delicacies such as dried fish, plucked ducks, pigs' heads and sea horses.

Cross the main road of Thanon Yaowarat and turn left along Thanon Charoen Krung (New Road). Half-way down this block on the right is the bustling temple of **Wat Mangkon Kamalawat** (Dragon Flower Temple). Combining elements of Buddhism,

## Safety in Numbers

Crossing the road in Chinatown can be difficult and hazardous. Cars, buses, motorbikes and *tuk-tuks* seem unwilling to stop even at pedestrian crossings. Do what the locals do and wait until at least two other people are ready to stride out at the same time.

0 ———— 250 metres
0 ———— 250 yards

Chao Phraya

THANON CHAROEN KRUNG

Wat Mangkon Kamalawat ③

THANON MANGKON

THANON SUAPA

THANON CHAROEN KRUNG

SOI 16

THANON MANGKON

④

THANON RATCHAWONG

THANON YAOWARAT

Old Market

THANON NUPPAK

Tang To Kang gold shop

SOI ISARA 1

SOI WANIT 1

THANON SONGWAT

Grand Chinese Princess Hotel

Sampeng Lane ②

CHINATOWN

THANON ①

Tha Ratchawong

Thieves' Market

THANON MAHA CHAI

THANON BORIPHAT

THANON CHAKKRAWAT

Saphan Han market

SOI WANIT 2

THANON

Royal India

THANON CHAKRAPHET

LITTLE INDIA

⑤

THANON PHAHURAT

Sikh temple

THANON

⑥

THANON CHAK PHET

PHRA POK KLAO BRIDGE

Tha Saphan Phut

Confucianism and Taoism, the temple features both Chinese characters and Buddhist images.

It's normally a bustling place, filled with praying devotees clutching huge bunches of incense or clipping notes as offerings to a brightly coloured money tree while monks sell amulets or dispense medicine from the temple apothecary.

## 3–4

Turn right as you come out of the temple and take the first left down the side street of Thanon Mangkon..

On the corner of its junction with Thanon Yaowarat, the **Old Market** is actually a modern complex of shopping stalls. Take the escalator upstairs for a highly professional reflexology

or head and neck massage, lasting as long or as short as you like.

## 4–5

Turn right on to the main street of Thanon Yaowarat. Walk straight down this road past shops selling electrical goods and sunglasses. After five blocks, **Nakhon Kasen** (Thieves' Market) on your left on the corner with Thanon Boriphat sounds much more exciting than it actually is. Antiques have replaced the stolen goods that were traditionally sold here.

On the right is the subterranean **Saphan Han market**. Dark, cramped and next to a festering canal, the market has a kind of Dickensian appeal. You can cut through here if you are interested. Otherwise, cross over the bridge and turn left at the major road junction on to Thanon Chakraphet.

## 5–6

Now you are in **Little India**. Follow the green sign to the **Sikh temple** (said to be the largest outside India) via a small tangle of market stalls. Then return to **Thanon Chakraphet** with its Indian restaurants and confectionery shops.

**Some of Chinatown's streets could be mistaken for downtown Hong Kong**

## Local Treasures

This area is full of specialities not found in the rest of the city. Look for shops featuring candlelit Chinese shrines and selling green or jasmine tea in decorative containers. Sample some *dim sum*, Chinese ice cream or lychee juice and wander around traditional wood-lined apothecaries crammed with fascinating ancient remedies.

# 2 Mae Hong Son Loop

*Tour*

**DISTANCE** 600km (372 miles)
**TIME** 3 days
**START/END POINT** Chiang Mai ⊞ 196 B4

This neat loop makes a highly scenic drive through the beautiful mountainous region known as the "Roof of Thailand". The circuit takes in hill-tribe villages, a city of "three mists" and the country's highest mountain, but the journey itself is the inspiration. The route avoids spots that get swamped by tour buses and as few tourists make this trip independently, you will have the roads to yourself.

## 1–2

Leave Chiang Mai on the 107 following the signs to **Mae Rim**. At Mae Rim, route 1096 leads to a tourist trail of commercial elephant camps, butterfly parks and orchid farms. Mobbed by tour groups, they are not worth a special detour, unlike the **Queen Sirikit Botanic Garden**, 12km (7.5 miles) along this road. Built with the help of London's Kew Gardens at a cost of £1 million, highlights include a magnificent Tropical Rainforest House.

## 2–3

Continue north of Mae Rim on the 107 and turn left on to the 1095, which wriggles all the way to Pai. If you feel like a hot bath, call in at the clearly signposted **Pong Ron Hot Springs** about 10km (6.2 miles) before the village.

**Pai**, once a remote village and now a comfortable traveller centre, with international cuisine and even jazz bars, is a good place to spend the night (Rim Pai Cottage, 17 Moo 3, Viang Tai, tel: 05 369 9133, has log cabins, hot showers and riverside treehouses, ££). For a more authentic village experience, consider staying in **Soppong** village, a couple of hours further on (Jungle Guest House is on the main road west, tel: 05 361 7099, ££).

## 3–4

From Pai, continue on the 1095 for one of the most picturesque stretches of the journey. After around 20km (12.5 miles) the marked "scenic area" gives spectacular views over the valley. Just before Soppong, look for the sign

to **Lod Cave**, a series of caves with stalactites and stalagmites and a river running through it. The landscape is particularly scenic here, with agricultural terracing. Drive through a tribal Lahu village and over the river and take the right fork at the Karen village of **Ban Tham**, with its houses on stilts. At the car park for Lod Cave (which is in Ban Tham)

## Employing a Driver

There is no need for a guide to do this tour, but if you don't feel like doing all the driving yourself (around four hours a day), a driver can be employed for about the same daily rate as a car – ideally a 4WD. You could also do half the loop from Chiang Mai to Mae Hong Son in either direction if you had the car collected and flew back to Chiang Mai. Before you set off, get hold of the Mae Hong Son Loop map (with the red cover) from a Chiang Mai newsagent.

there's an information board telling how to get a guide, and providing some history and a map of the caves. A guide with a lantern (moderate) is necessary unless you have a powerful torch. Continue northwest of here to join up with the 1095, as long as rain hasn't made the road impassable. If it has, return the way you came (8km/5 miles).

### 4–5

Once you're back on the 1095 turn right. Around 15km (9.3 miles) after Soppong turn right on to the 1226 to **Mae Lana Cave**, with its interesting rock formations. With a 12km (7.5 mile) river running through it, it is said to be the longest cave in Asia. Before the Black Lahu (hill-tribe) village of Jabo, look to the right for beautiful views.

Take the right fork to Mae Lana village in the pretty valley below. Drive through the village to its lovely temple where figures from Burma act as protectors. The Mai Lun people who live here are half-Burmese and half-Thai. The village is close to the border with Burma, although there is no crossing for tourists.

If you want to see another cave, return to where you took the right fork and turn right to **Pa Puek Cave** (rock formations) behind the village of the same name.

### 5–6

Return to the 1095 and turn right. After 40 km (25 miles), you reach the mysterious **Fish Cave**, which attracts masses of mountain carp for no apparent reason. Continue on the 1095 all the way to **Mae Hong Son**. Turn right at the town's only traffic lights on the outskirts and bear right to **Wat Doi Kong Mou**, the temple on the hill. It's the view rather than the temple itself that is special, but note the Burmese-style Buddhas with their red lips and white faces. The temples by **Jong Kham Lake** in the centre of town are much prettier. At their entrance, the twisted trunk of a sacred Bodhi tree shelters ageing spirit houses which cannot be destroyed because they are a sacred object to Buddhists. The Bodhi tree is sacred because it is believed that the Buddha gained enlightenment under one.

### Places to Visit

**Queen Sirikit Botanic Garden**
➕ 196 B4 ⬛ Mae Rim, Chiang Mai ☎ 5329 8171 🕐 Daily 8:30–5 💰 Expensive

### 6–7

After spending the night in Mae Hong Son (➤ 105), continue south along the 108 through Mae Surin. On the edge of the village of **Khun Yuam**, a ramshackle, dusty and low-key **war museum** commemorates the Japanese troops who poured into the area in September 1945 on their retreat from Allied forces in Burma. If you don't want to take a look here, turn left along the 1263 before the village.

### 7–8

The road passes valleys of bright green rice fields, winding its way to the next major settlement of **Mae Chaem**.

Between the villages of Thung Yao and Mae Chaem look for a wooden hut hung with flowers on the left-hand side just before the bridge. A **spirit house**, it was built when road construction was besieged with problems. Locals beep their horns in respect driving past.

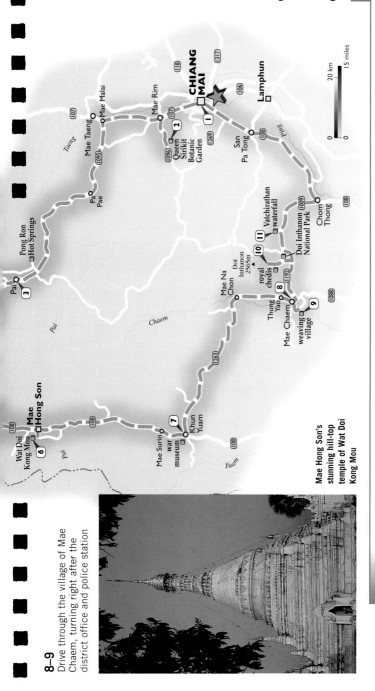

**8–9**
Drive through the village of Mae Chaem, turning right after the district office and police station

Mae Hong Son's stunning hill-top temple of Wat Doi Kong Mou

and over the large bridge. Turn left at the T-junction at the sign for the **weaving village**. Once you have driven through the gate at the

**The Vatchirathan waterfall is just one of the many impressive cascades to be seen at Doi Inthanon National Park**

village entrance, look for looms and textiles and bags for sale outside some of the houses. Although on a very small scale, this is one of Queen Sirikit's projects, established to try and preserve traditional local weaving that is in danger of dying out. The queen sponsors and supports the project.

## 9–10

Return to Mae Chaem and turn left at the sign for Chiang Mai onto the 1192. You may spot water buffalo or wild mushrooms in the wet season by the roadside. After 22km (13.6 miles) at the T-junction turn left at the sign to **Doi Inthanon National Park** (➤ 99). At the end of the road you can walk up to the summit of Doi Inthanon, Thailand's highest mountain. Just below the summit are two **royal *chedis*** built to honour the present king and queen (➤ 99), a small information centre and a short circular walking trail.

## 10–11

Return to the 1192 and turn left. Around 20km (12.4 miles) along this road, the **Vatchirathan waterfall** makes a pretty stop close to the road before returning to **Chiang Mai.**

### Taking a Break

Eat fresh mountain trout at the restaurant of the royal project gardens next to the National Park headquarters, and then stroll to the foot of the nearby Siriphum waterfall.

# 3
## KRABI
*Tour*

**DISTANCE** 80km (49.6 miles)
**TIME** Half a day
**START/END POINT** Krabi Town ⊞ 199 D2

Some of Krabi province's most interesting sights are difficult to see by public transport. This gentle tour makes a convenient loop from the popular riverside town of Krabi. It passes through dramatic limestone scenery to the remote forest temple of Wat Tham Seua (Tiger Cave) and a Buddha reclining at the roadside, calling in on the way at beautiful beaches, with boat trips as additional extras.

## 1–2

Leave **Krabi** town following Highway 411 north along the river. After about 4.5km (3 miles) turn right following the signs to Trang. After a few kilometres you will see a big outcrop on the right-hand side of the road.
Turn left here and follow the signs to the **Wat Tham Seua** (Tiger Cave Temple, ► 161).

**Wat Tham Seua's community of monks (in orange) and nuns (seated, in white)**

turning left to go back to Krabi, continue to the next major junction, turning left along route 4200. After around 20km (12.4 miles) turn right at the traffic lights at the sign for Hat Noppharat. Follow the wriggling route from where it is easy to miss the roadside

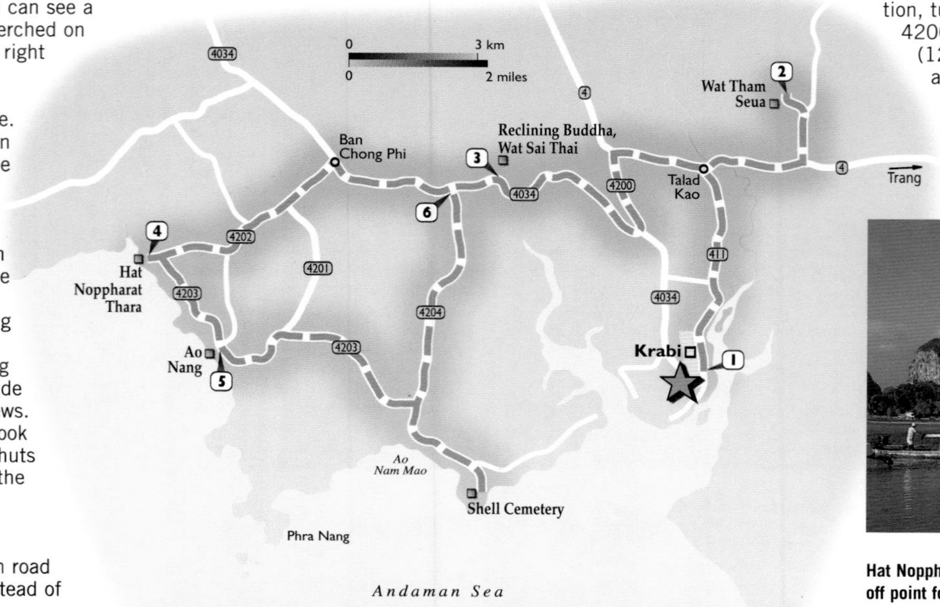

**Hat Noppharat Thara is the jumping-off point for Chicken Island**

Dancing elephants adorn the lamp posts down the centre of this road and on a clear day you can see a temple building perched on top of a mountain right ahead of you.

Take time to explore this temple. Start with the main cave and follow the stairs up to the cave behind, with its giant Buddha footprint, and then wander through the temple grounds.

If you are feeling energetic you can make the hour-long climb up the hillside for spectacular views. Otherwise take a look at the meditation huts and walk through the ancient forest.

**2–3**
Return to the main road and turn right. Instead of

[Map labels: Trang, 4, Wat Tham Seua 2, 411, Talad Kao, Krabi 1, 4034, 4200, Reclining Buddha, Wat Sai Thai 3, 4034, 6, Ban Chong Phi, 4204, Shell Cemetery, 4200, 4203, Ao Nam Mao, 4034, 4202, Phra Nang, 4203, Hat Noppharat Thara 4, Ao Nang 5, Andaman Sea, 0 3 km, 0 2 miles]

**Reclining Buddha** at Wat Sai Thai, nestled into a limestone outcrop in a kink in the road. There is not too much to look at here, but you might want to stretch your legs.

## 3–4

Follow the signs to Hat Noppharat, turning left down the 4202 at the Muslim village of **Ban Chong Phi**. You may see women selling coconuts at the side of the road here and a green turreted mosque.

Follow the road until it stops at the sea at **Hat Noppharat Thara** (➤ 159). This 2.5km (1.5 mile) beach is a tranquil spot backed by pine trees, where a pretty canal joins the sea. Take a walk along the wide stretch of sand or relax at one of the picnic tables under the trees. As soon as you get out of your car here, a boat-man will probably appear to offer you a snorkelling trip (moderate) to Chicken or Poda islands, sitting out in the bay.

## 4–5

The road vaguely hugs the coast to **Ao Nang** – a developed and not particularly attractive stretch of beach packed with shops and restaurants. Here the road swings inland. There's no road access to the headland of Phra Nang – if you want to visit its pretty

A roadside limestone outcrop hangs precariously over passing cars

### Taking a Break

At Ao Nang follow the road until it forks inland. Here a dirt track leads to simple beach restaurants offering Thai and Western food and a seafood dinner menu.

beaches (➤ 161), you need to walk or take a boat trip.

The little headland of **Laem Phra Nang** is named after a local princess (*phra nang* means "revered lady"). Although reached only by boat – longtails leave from near Krabi's pier – it is very popular and something of a rock-climbing mecca, with hundreds of world-class routes. Beginners are catered to as well, and if you are not participating, it's a good spectator sport.

Other activities on offer include kayaking through the mangroves and snorkelling and diving trips to nearby islands.

## 5–6

You can return to Krabi by following the 4203, then the 4204 and then turning right on to the 4034.

# 4 KHAO SAM ROI YOT NATIONAL PARK

**Tour**

**DISTANCE** 150km/93 miles (one way)
**TIME** One day
**START/END POINT** Hua Hin ⊞ 198 B3

This leisurely tour explores peaceful coastal marshland and deserted golden beaches fringed by pine trees where there are hidden caves, scenic boat trips and forest trails. Shrimp farmers and fishermen eke out a living in this isolated, atmospheric backwater and thousands of birds from around the world come to breed. Known as "the mountain with 300 peaks", the park's forested interior provides challenging climbs with excellent views.

## How To Visit

Although you can take organised tours of the park, by far the most enjoyable way to see it is to rent a car. Part of the park's charm is its isolation and taking a taxi or public transport isn't feasible because you need to be able to get around the park once you arrive. Try to catch either sunset or sunrise for the best chances of seeing birdlife. If you are very lucky you may also see a monkey-like, long-tailed macaque or a dusky langur which usually only appear at night.

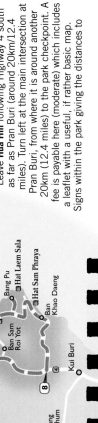

### 1–2

Leave **Hua Hin** following Highway 4 south as far as Pran Buri (around 20km/12.4 miles). Turn left at the main intersection at Pran Buri, from where it is around another 20km (12.4 miles) to the park checkpoint. A fee is payable here (moderate) which includes a leaflet with a useful, if rather basic map. Signs within the park giving the distances to

Sam Roi Yot National Park confusingly refer only to the park headquarters.

### 2–3

Turn left at the signs to Hat Laem Sala past the entrance to **Tham Kaew Cave** and land given over to shrimp farming. You will need to rent a lamp and probably a guide (moderate)

to explore the Jewel Cave of Tham Kaew, with its glittering stalactites and crystal. Follow the road to the end. You cannot enter the village of **Bang Pu**, instead leave your car in the car park just past the village entrance. At the eastern side of the deep horseshoe bay you may see villagers disentangling small catches from their nets.

## 3–4

To reach **Hat Laem Sala** (the beach) from here, you can either take the half-hour walk over the steep headland or one of the fishing boats (moderate) for a five-minute journey around the coastline. You may have to take your shoes off to wade through the mud to the shore. At Laem Sala there's a small visitor centre, basic accommodation and a restaurant. From here it's a half-hour walk to the cave with the famous royal pavilion of **Tham**

**Phraya Nakhon** (► 133, free). Despite its secluded position, the pavilion is the most visited spot in the park and is included in most tours.

## 4–5

Return to the car in the car park at Bang Pu, and then to the main intersection and follow the road to **Hat Sam Phraya**. This pretty beach has a restaurant, visitor centre, binoculars for rent

## Taking a Break

The beach at **Hat Sam Phraya** is a lovely place to have lunch. Eat at the café here or bring a picnic to have in one of the wooden pavilions on the sand, shaded by a thick band of pine trees.

(moderate) and bird hideaways. You'll see ibis, heron, spotted eagle and whistling duck. The cave of **Tham Sai** at its northern end can be reached by a trail from the road.

## 5–6

Continue south, following the signs to **Khao Daeng**, the park headquarters. The headquarters have some information about the plants and wildlife in the park, but it is no more detailed than that found in the visitor's centre at Hat Sam Phraya and not worth a special visit.

The headquarters is the start of the Horseshoe Trail and the Mangrove Trail –

both badly marked and maintained. In fact you are more likely to see wildlife on the road approaching the headquarters where monkeys tend to gather. Near by, the **Khao Daeng hill** is worth the steep 30-minute climb for the views it offers.

Continue following the road south and cross over the bridge. If you turn right along the river you will come to a collection of *wats*, grazing cattle and a boatman offering to take you on an hour-long scenic ride down the **Khlong Khao Daeng** canal (moderate).

## 6–7

Follow the road out of the park (via Ban Somrong) and through the checkpoint to a scenic area of blue-hued mountains.

Cross the railway line, watching out for trains that steam through with no warning. A few metres on, just before the major junction, look out for a **shop** on the left-hand side selling delicious **banana leaf packages** filled with sweet sticky rice and fruit.

Turn right to Pran Buri and then back to Hua Hin on Highway 4.

**Shrimp farms are a common sight in Khao Sam Roi Yot National Park, and although important for the local economy, the practice is damaging to the environment**

**Practicalities**

**Websites**
- Thailand Tourist Authority: www.tat.or.th

**In the UK**
Tourism Authority of Thailand
49 Albemarle Street
London W1X 3FE
☎ 0839 300800/
020 7499 7679

**In the USA**
Tourism Authority of Thailand
611 North Larchmont Boulevard, 1st Floor,
Los Angeles CA 90004
☎ (323) 461-9814

## BEFORE YOU GO

### WHAT YOU NEED

| | | UK | Germany | USA | Canada | Australia | Ireland | Netherlands | Spain |
|---|---|---|---|---|---|---|---|---|---|
| ● Required | Some countries require a passport to remain valid for a minimum period (usually at least six months) beyond the date of entry – check before you travel | | | | | | | | |
| ○ Suggested | | | | | | | | | |
| ▲ Not required | | | | | | | | | |
| Passport (valid for at least six months) | | ● | ● | ● | ● | ● | ● | ● | ● |
| Visa (only for periods over one month) | | ● | ● | ● | ● | ● | ● | ● | ● |
| Onward or Return ticket | | ● | ● | ● | ● | ● | ● | ● | ● |
| Health inoculations (diptheria, tetanus, hep A & B, typhoid) | | ○ | ○ | ○ | ○ | ○ | ○ | ○ | ○ |
| Travel Insurance | | ○ | ○ | ○ | ○ | ○ | ○ | ○ | ○ |
| Driving licence (national) and international driving permit | | ● | ● | ● | ● | ● | ● | ● | ● |

Note that proof of funds is sometimes required.

### WHEN TO GO

| | Peak season | | Off-season |

| JAN | FEB | MAR | APR | MAY | JUN | JUL | AUG | SEP | OCT | NOV | DEC |
|---|---|---|---|---|---|---|---|---|---|---|---|
| 26°C | 28°C | 29°C | 30°C | 30°C | 29°C | 29°C | 28°C | 28°C | 28°C | 27°C | 26°C |
| 79°F | 82°F | 84°F | 86°F | 86°F | 84°F | 84°F | 82°F | 82°F | 82°F | 81°F | 79°F |

Very wet — Wet — Cloud — Sun — Sun/Showers

The temperatures above are the **average daily maximum** for each month in Bangkok. Thailand has three seasons – wet (Jun–Oct), cool (Nov–Feb) and hot (Mar–May). **Temperatures** are generally warm, but it can get cold in the north, especially at night, and very hot in April and May. There are **three monsoons** – in the north, northeast and central parts of the country.

**High season**, when the weather is at its most pleasant and when prices are higher and accommodation and transport are fully reserved, is November to February, July and August. **Low season** is March to June, September and October. Monsoon can be a good time to go but it mostly depends on luck; temperatures are more conducive to travel, it is easier to get accommodation and transport and there are fewer people around.

**In Australia**
Level 2
National Australia
Bank House
255 George Street
Sydney NSW 2000
☎ (02) 9247 7549

**In Canada**
1393 Royal York Road
#15, Toronto
Ontario M9A 4Y9
☎ (416) 614-2625 or
1-800-THAILAND

**In New Zealand**
Floor 2
87 Queen Street
Auckland
☎ 09 379 8398

## GETTING THERE

**By Air** The best way to get to Thailand is to **fly direct to Bangkok**.
For the **cheapest flights**, you will need to go to travel agents rather than contacting the airlines direct. You can save even more money if you are willing to make stopovers.
The following **airlines** all fly to Bangkok and other major cities in Thailand:

**Thai Airways International**
www.thaiair.com
UK: 020 7499 9113
USA: 1-800 426-5204

**British Airways**
www.britishairways.com
Australia: 13 1960
UK: 0345 222111

**Malaysia Airlines**
www.mas.com.my
Australia: 13 2476
New Zealand: 09 357 3000
USA: 1-800 522-9264

**Qantas**
www.qantas.co.au
Australia: 13 1211
New Zealand: 09 357 8900
UK: 0345 747767

**Singapore Airlines**
www.singaporeair.com
Australia: 02 9350 0100
New Zealand: 09 379 3209
USA: 1-800 742-3333

## TIME

There is only one time zone throughout the country. Local time is seven hours ahead of GMT and 12 hours ahead of New York (Eastern Standard Time).

## CURRENCY AND FOREIGN EXCHANGE

**Currency** The monetary unit in Thailand is the **baht** (B) and **satang** (100 satang = 1 baht).
    **Notes** come in 10 (brown), 20 (green), 50 (blue), 100 (red), 500 (purple) and 1,000 (beige) denominations; the bigger the value, the larger the note.
    **Coins** come in denominations of 25 and 50 satangs (rarely used because of their low value; most prices are rounded up to the nearest baht) and 1, 5 and 10 baht.

All major **credit cards** are widely accepted and can be used for cash advances in certain branches of major banks. However, many restaurants, guest houses and businesses on the islands and in mainland towns accept only cash.

**Exchange rates** tend to fluctuate, so it is worth keeping your eye on them.
    Sterling or dollar **travellers' cheques** are widely accepted (commission rates vary) and offer better rates of exchange than cash. This is a safe means of carrying money, but keep details of cheque numbers, the original receipt and contact details of the issuer in case of loss or theft. **Cash withdrawals** can conveniently be made at 24-hour ATMs (cash dispenser machines) throughout the country. Make sure you have your pin number with you and check with your bank at home for details of compatible banks. A 1.5 per cent handling fee is normally charged.

## TIME DIFFERENCES

**GMT**
12 noon

**Bangkok**
7 pm

**USA (New York)**
7 am

**USA (Los Angeles)**
4 am

**Australia**
10 pm

**New Zealand**
11 pm

## WHEN YOU ARE THERE

### CLOTHING SIZES

| UK | USA | |
|----|-----|--|
| 36 | 36 | |
| 38 | 38 | |
| 40 | 40 | |
| 42 | 42 | Suits |
| 44 | 44 | |
| 46 | 46 | |
| 7 | 8 | |
| 7.5 | 8.5 | |
| 8.5 | 9.5 | |
| 9.5 | 10.5 | Shoes |
| 10.5 | 11.5 | |
| 11 | 12 | |
| 14.5 | 14.5 | |
| 15 | 15 | |
| 15.5 | 15.5 | |
| 16 | 16 | Shirts |
| 16.5 | 16.5 | |
| 17 | 17 | |
| 8 | 6 | |
| 10 | 8 | |
| 12 | 10 | |
| 14 | 12 | Dresses |
| 16 | 14 | |
| 18 | 16 | |
| 4.5 | 6 | |
| 5 | 6.5 | |
| 5.5 | 7 | |
| 6 | 7.5 | Shoes |
| 6.5 | 8 | |
| 7 | 8.5 | |

### NATIONAL HOLIDAYS

| | |
|--|--|
| 1 Jan | New Year's Day |
| Feb | (full moon) Maha Puja commemorates the Buddha preaching to 1,250 monks |
| 6 Apr | Chakri Day |
| Apr | Songkran (Thai New Year) |
| 5 May | Coronation Day |
| Early May | Royal Ploughing Ceremony |
| May | Visakha Puja commemorates the Buddha's birth, enlightenment and death |
| Jul | Asanha Puja – the Buddha's first sermon |
| Jul | Start of Buddhist "lent" |
| 12 Aug | Queen's birthday |
| 5 Dec | King's birthday |
| 10 Dec | Constitution Day |

Shops, tourist offices and tourist services remain open on these days.

### OPENING HOURS

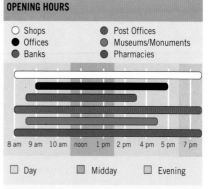

○ Shops       ● Post Offices
● Offices      ● Museums/Monuments
● Banks       ● Pharmacies

8 am  9 am  10 am  noon  1 pm  2 pm  4 pm  5 pm  7 pm

☐ Day    ▨ Midday    ☐ Evening

**Shops** Daily 8–8, although in tourist areas they may remain open until late at night and all weekend. Department stores usually open 10–9.
**Banks** Mon–Fri 8:30–3:30.
**Post offices** Main branches Mon–Fri 8–8, Sat and Sun 8–1.
**National museums** 8:30–4:30. Close lunchtime, Mon, Tue and public holidays.
**Pharmacies** 8 am–9 pm, and later in some parts of Bangkok such as Kao San Road.

POLICE: 1155

POLICE: Chiang Mai 05 327 6040

POLICE: Ko Phuket 07 621 9878

POLICE: Ko Samui 07 742 1282

## PERSONAL SAFETY

Violent crime is rare, but take the following precautions:

- Lock your hotel room doors and windows at night.
- Don't accept food and drink from strangers on trains and buses as there have been cases of passengers being drugged and robbed.
- The Bangkok headquarters of the **Tourism Authority of Thailand**, TAT (tel: 02 694 1222) or the Tourist Police (tel: 1155) will contact the relevant emergency service as well as deal with complaints about services and products. The operators speak English.

## TELEPHONES

International calls can be made from black and yellow public call boxes, but calls abroad can be made from most internet outlets for very low rates, where you don't have to feed coins into a call box. National calls from any call box cost as little as 5 baht. To make an international call from a public phone, feed in a 10 baht coin and have a lot ready to use if you make your connection. Drop the zero from a Thai phone number when calling from abroad, but include it when calling within the country. Phone cards are sold by stationers and some convenience stores. **Directory enquiries:** Dial 13 for Bangkok numbers, and 183 for the rest of the country. Thailand's international dialing code is 66.

**International dialling codes from Thailand: 00, then UK: 44, USA/Canada: 1, Aust: 61, NZ: 64.**

## POST OFFICES

Stamps are available from post offices, and from some shops and hotels, although hotels will usually charge you a bit extra.

Major hotels will often post letters and packages for you. Post takes around seven days to Europe or the USA.

## ELECTRICITY

The power supply is 220 volts, 50 cycles.

Two pole pins are the usual plug sockets with some additionally taking two flat-blade pins. You'll find that adaptors and voltage converters are available in most electrical shops.

## TIPS/GRATUITIES

Some hotels and restaurants add a service charge. Simple Thai restaurants don't expect a tip but it's usual to round the bill up to the next 10 baht or so. In other restaurants, leave 10 per cent or more if the service is good. It's also customary to tip tour guides, porters, masseurs and masseuses, hairdressers, hotel concierges and taxi drivers with a 20 baht note. Self-service petrol stations are unknown in Thailand, so it's usual to tip the attendant 5 or 10 baht. In hotels and guest houses with daily room service, a 20 baht note for each night stayed is appreciated.

**UK**
(02253 0191)

**USA**
02205 4000

**Australia**
02287 2680

**Canada**
0263 60560

**Netherlands**
02254 7701

## HEALTH

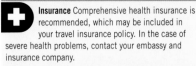
**Insurance** Comprehensive health insurance is recommended, which may be included in your travel insurance policy. In the case of severe health problems, contact your embassy and insurance company.

**Dental Services** Dental treatment is best carried out in Bangkok. Ask at your hotel for names and qualifications of dentists in your area. Alternatively, your health insurance company should be able to supply details of dentists.

**Weather** Avoid the sun during the middle of the day. Excessive exposure can cause heat rash, severe dehydration and diarrhoea. It is best to wear a sunhat and cover up whenever possible. Drink plenty of water.

**Drugs** Both prescription and non-prescription drugs, international and local brands, are available from chemists or pharmacies, and are normally much cheaper than in countries outside Thailand. Most pharmacies (whatever size the town) have highly trained, English-speaking pharmacists.

**Safe Water** Never drink tap water, it may carry diseases such as hepatitis or typhoid. Always drink bottled water (the still variety), which is inexpensive and widely available throughout the country.

## CONCESSIONS

**Students/Youths** Discounted entrance to tourist attractions is rare, but it may still be worth carrying your international student identity card with you. Some organisations offer discounts to children.

There are several useful websites with information on budget travelling. Try the **Internet Travel Information Service** on www.itisnet.com, a useful resource with up-to-date information on current budget tips. The **Open Directory Project**, www.dmoz.org/Recreation/Travel/Budget_Travel/Backpacking, has backpacker information and message boards; and www.travel-library.com has informative travelogues on student/budget options.

## TRAVELLING WITH A DISABILITY

There is little provision for travellers with disabilities, but Thai people are helpful. Contact the following organisations: In the UK, **RADAR**, the Royal Association for Disability and Rehabilitation, tel: 0207 250 3222. In the US, **The Society for the Advancement of Travel for the Handicapped**, tel: (212/) 447-7284, or from the US, **Access-Able Travel Source**, www.access-able.com.

## CHILDREN

Your children will, quite literally, be welcomed with open arms everywhere you go, and there are practically no restrictions on where you can take them.

## TOILETS

Western-style flush toilets and toilet paper are in most hotels. Restaurants and tourist facilities may have squat toilets and no toilet paper. Always dispose of paper in the bin provided as Thai toilets are not equipped for dealing with paper waste.

## CUSTOMS

The import of wildlife souvenirs sourced from rare or endangered species may be illegal or require a special permit. Check your home country's customs regulations.

Thai is a complex language written in an elaborate script containing more than 80 letters. It has five tones, or pitches, (mid, high, low, rising and falling) which help determine the meaning of words. Although Thai is a difficult language to master, learning a few simple words will usually endear you greatly to the locals and can be very useful when bargaining for goods. However, English is widely used in tourist areas and many Thais know enough to communicate on a basic level. In polite speech, or to show particular respect, men add the word *krup* to the end of sentences; women add *ka*. Note that the words below are transliterated to give as clear a guide to pronunciation as possible. Spellings may vary on different signs, maps and menus.

## GREETINGS AND COMMON PHRASES

Yes  **Chai or krup/ka**
No  **Mai**
Thank you  **Korb-koon (krup/ka)**
Hello/Goodbye  **Sawat dee (krup/ka)/ laa gorn**
How are you?  **Sabai dee ru?**
Fine, thank you  **Sabai dee (krup/ka)**
Excuse me/sorry  **Kor tort (krup/ka)**
What is your name?  **Khun chu arai?**
My name is...  **Pom chu... (male), chun chu... (female)**
Do you speak English?  **Koon poot pah sah Angrit?**
I don't understand  **Pom (chun) mai kowjai**
I speak a little Thai  **Pom (chun) puut pasa Thai nitnoy**
See you later  **Pop gan mai**

## EMERGENCY!

Help!  **Chuay dooay!**
Fire!  **Fai mai!**
Call the police!  **Reeuk dtum roout hai noy!**
Call an ambulance!  **Reeuk rot payah-bahn hai noy!**
I need a doctor  **Tong haa mor**
I need a dentist  **Tong haa mor fun**
Hospital  **Rong payabarn**

## DIRECTIONS

Where are you going?  **Pai nai?**
I'm going to...  **Jai pai...**
Where is...?  **...yu thii nai?**
We want to go to...?  **...rao yahk bpai**
How do I get to...?  **Bpai...yung ngai?**
How long does it take?  **Chai way-lah tao-rai?**
Please drive slowly  **Prot put cha cha**
Turn right  **Lieo khwa;** Turn left  **Lieo sai**
Straight on  **Trong pai**
Stop here  **Jop tinni**

## TRANSPORT AND PLACES

Air-conditioned bus  **Rot tooa**
Ordinary bus  **Rot tammada**
Bus station  **Sattani rot may**
Minibus  **Rot dtoo**
Car  **Rot keng**
Ticket  **Tua**
Timetable  **Talang Waylar**
Railway station  **Sattani rot fai**
Train  **Rot fai**
Express  **Duan**
Sleeper  **Rot nawn**
Seat  **Tee nung**
Airport  **Sanam bin**
Aeroplane  **Krueng bin**
Boat  **Rua**
Longtail boat  **Rua harng yao**
Ferry  **Rua doy sarn**
Ferry pier  **Tha**
Taxi  **Teksi**
Bicycle  **Rot jakrayan**
Motorcycle  **Rot motorsai**
Bank  **Tanakaan**
Beach  **Hat**
Embassy  **Sa-tantoot**
Island  **Ko**
Market  **Talaht**
Museum  **Pipitapun**
Police station  **Satanee tamruat**
Post office  **Prai-sanee**
Street  **Thanon**
Town  **Meung**
Village  **Ban**

## HOTELS AND RESTAURANTS

Do you have a vacant room?  **Mee horng wahng mai?**
Air-conditioned room  **Horng air**
Guesthouse  **Guest how**
Hotel  **Rong raem**
Key  **Goon jair**
Shower  **Fuk boo-a**
Swimming pool  **Sa wai nahm**
Toilet/bathroom  **Hong nahm**

A table for two please **Kor dto sum-rup sorng kon**
Please bring me the menu **Kor doo menu**
May I have…? **Kor…?**
The food is delicious **Ahan arroi**
The bill, please **Kor check bin**
Restaurant **Raan aahaan**
Café **Raan garfay**
Breakfast **Ahan chow**
Hot (spicy) **Pet**
Mild **Mai pet**
I can't eat… **Kin…mai dai**
I'm vegetarian **Kin jeh**
Water **Nam**
A glass of water **Nam plao**
Bottled water **Nam deum kuat**
Tea **Chaa**
Coffee **Cafee**
Beef **Neua**
Chicken **Gai**
Duck **Phet**
Fish **Pla**
Pork **Moo**

## SHOPPING

How much is this? **Nee taorai?**
Do you have…? **Mee…mai?**
Cheap **Tuk**
Very good/No good **Dee mak/Mai dee**
Too expensive **Paeng pai**
Too big **Yai pair**
Too small **Lek pai**
A little **Nid noi**
Night market **Talaat toh rung**

## TIME AND DAYS

| | |
|---|---|
| Today | **Wan nee** |
| Tomorrow | **Proong nee** |
| Yesterday | **Meua wan nee** |
| Now | **Diao nee** |
| Later | **Tee lang** |
| This week | **Atit ni** |
| Next week | **Atit na** |
| Minute | **Na tee** |
| Hour | **Chua mong** |

| | |
|---|---|
| Monday | **Wan jun** |
| Tuesday | **Wan ungkahn** |
| Wednesday | **Wan poot** |
| Thursday | **Wan pryhart** |
| Friday | **Wan sook** |
| Saturday | **Wan sao** |
| Sunday | **Wan aathit** |

## GLOSSARY

Ao **Bay**
Ban **Village or house**
Bot **Main sanctuary of a Buddhist temple**
Celadon **Porcelain with a greyish green glaze**
Changwat **Province**
Chedi **Tower for relics in a Buddhist temple**
Doi **Mountain**
Farang **Foreigner**
Garuda **Half-man, half-bird mythical Hindu creature**
Hang yoa **Longtail boat**
Hat **Beach**
Hin **Stone**
Khao **Hill or mountain**
Khlong **Canal**
Ko **Island**
Laem **Headland**
Mahathat **A *chedi* (see above) containing relics of the Buddha**
Mondop **A square temple containing religious texts or small artefacts**
Nielloware **Metalwork engraved with design**
Prang **A central tower in a Khmer temple**
Soi **Alley**
Songthaew **Pickup taxi**
Thanon **Road**
That **another word for chedi (see above)**
Viharn **Assembly hall in the temple, usually with the main Buddha image**
Wang **Palace**
Wat **Temple**

## NUMBERS

| | | | | | | | |
|---|---|---|---|---|---|---|---|
| 0 | soon | 8 | bpairt | 16 | sip-hok | 50 | hah-sip |
| 1 | neeung | 9 | gao | 17 | sip-jet | 60 | hok-sip |
| 2 | sorng | 10 | sip | 18 | sip-bpairt | 70 | jet-sip |
| 3 | sahm | 11 | sip-et | 19 | sip-gao | 80 | bpairt-sip |
| 4 | see | 12 | sip-sorng | 20 | yee-sip | 90 | gao-sip |
| 5 | hah | 13 | sip-sahm | 21 | yee-sip-et | 100 | neung roy |
| 6 | hok | 14 | sip-see | 30 | sahm-sip | 101 | roy-et |
| 7 | jet | 15 | sip-hah | 40 | see-sip | 500 | hah roy |

# Atlas

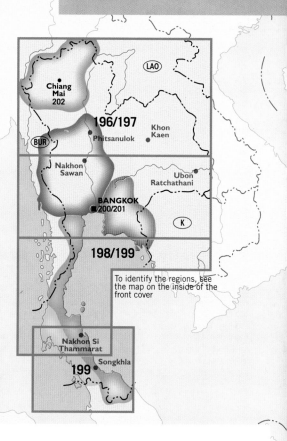

To identify the regions, see the map on the inside of the front cover

**Regional Maps**

- –·–·– International boundary
- —— Major route
- —— Main road
- —— Other road
- Built-up area
- ✈ Airport
- ☐ City
- ☐ Major town

- ● Large town
- ● Town, village
- ■ Featured place of interest
- ■ Place of interest

**196/199**
```
0   20   40   60   80   100 km
0   20        40        60 miles
```

**City Plans**

- ■ Important building
- ■ Park

- ⓘ Information
- ■ Featured place of interest

**200/201**
```
0   200  400  600  800  1000 metres
0   200  400  600  800  1000 yards
```

**202**
```
0      300      600      900   1200 metres
0          400      800      1200 yards
```

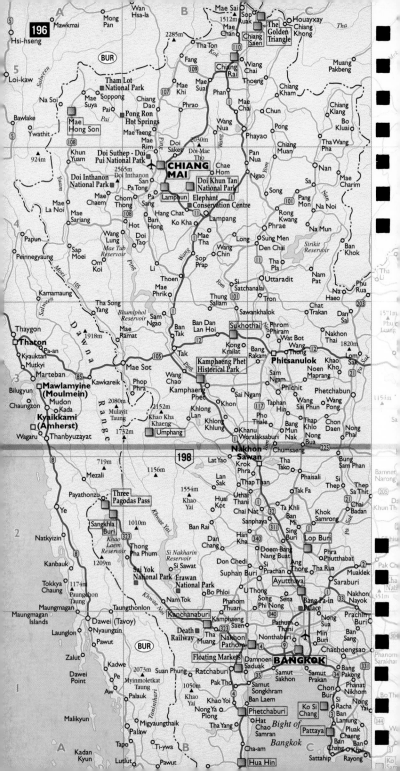

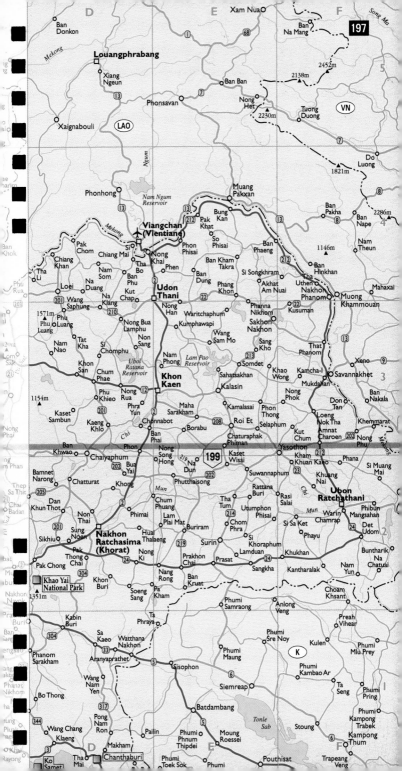

Song Ma

Ban Donkon

Louangphrabang

Xiang Ngeun

13

Xaignabouli

LAO

Mekong

Xam Nua

68

Ban Na Mang

2452m

2138m

Ban Ban

7

Phonsavan

Nong Het

2230m

Tuong Duong

VN

1821m

Do Luong

8

Phonhong

13

Nam Ngum Reservoir

Muang Pakxan

Ban Pakha

8

Ban Nape

2286m

13

Bung Kan

212

Pak Khat

13

So Phisai

Ban Phaeng

212

Ban Hinkhan

Nam Theun

Viangchan (Vientiane)

Si

Nong Khai

Tha Bo

Chiang Mai

Phon Phisai

Ban Kham Takra

Si Songkhram

1146m

Tha Uthen

Nakhon Phanom

Muong Khammouan

Pak Chom

Chiang Khan

Tha Li

Nam Som

Ban Phu

Phen

2

Ban Dung

Phang Khon

Akhat Am Nuai

Mahaxai

Loei

Na Duang

Na Klang

Kut Chap

Udon Thani

Nong Han

Waritchaphum

Phanna Nikhom

Sakhon Nakhon

22

Kusuman

That Phanom

13

Xeno

9

201

Wang Saphung

210

Phu Luang

Nong Bua Lamphu

Non Sang

Kumphawapi

Wang Sam Mo

Sang Kho

Savannakhet

1571m

Phu Luang

Nam Nao

Tat Kha

Si Chomphu

Nam Phong

Lam Pao Reservoir

213

Somdet

Khao Wong

Kamcha-I

Mukdahan

Ban Nakala

Khon San

Chum Phae

Ubol Ratana Reservoir

Khon Kaen

Sahatsakhan

Nong Phok

Don Tan

Khemmarat

1154m

Phu Khieo

Nong Rua

12

Phra Yun

Maha Sarakham

Kalasin

Kamalasai

Phon Thong

Selaphum

Loeng Nok Tha

Amnat Charoen

202

Nong Phu

Kaset Sambun

Kaeng Khlo

Chi

Chonnabot

Ban Phai

Borabu

208

Roi Et

Chaturaphak Phiman

Kut Chum

Yasothon

Mekong

Ban Khwao

Phon

Nong Song Hong

219

Na Dun

199

202

Kaset Wisai

Kham Khuan Kaeo

212

Phana

Si Muang Mai

Chaiyaphum

202

Bua Yai

Phutthaisong

Suwannaphum

23

Khuang Nai

Bamnet Narong

Khong

Mun

Rattana Buri

Rasi Salai

Chatturat

Chum Phuang

Tha Tum

214

Utumphon Phisai

Ubon Ratchathani

205

Dan Khun Thot

Phimai

Lam Plai Mat

Buriram

Chom Phra

Si Sa Ket

Phayu

Mun

Warin Chamrap

Phibun Mangsahan

Det Udom

2

201

Non Thai

Sung Noen

Huai Thalaeng

219

Surin

Si Khoraphum

Lamduan

Khukhan

Sangkha

Kantharalak

Nam Yun

Buntharik Na Chatuai

Sikhiu

Nakhon Ratchasima (Khorat)

Nong Ki

Prakhon Chai

Prasat

24

Pak Chong

24

Khon Buri

Nang Rong

Ban Kruat

Pa Kham

Choam Khsant

Khao Yai National Park

1351m

Soeng Sang

Phumi Samraong

Anlong Veng

Preah Vihear

Kabin Buri

Ta Phraya

Phumi Sre Noy

Kulen

Phumi Mlu Prey

304

Sa Kaeo

Watthana Nakhon

33

Phumi Maung

K

Phumi Kambao Ar

Ta Seng

Phumi Pring

Phanom Sarakham

Aranyaprathet

5

Sisophon

6

Siemreap

Phumi Kampong Trabek

Wang Nam Yen

317

Bo Thong

Pong Nam Ron

Batdambang

5

Phumi Phnum Thipdei

Moung Roessei

Tonle Sab

Stoung

6

Phumi Kampong Thum

344

Wang Chang

Klaeng

3

Tha Mai

Chanthaburi

Makham

Pailin

Phumi Toek Sok

Phumi

Pouthisat

Trapeang Veng

Ko Samet

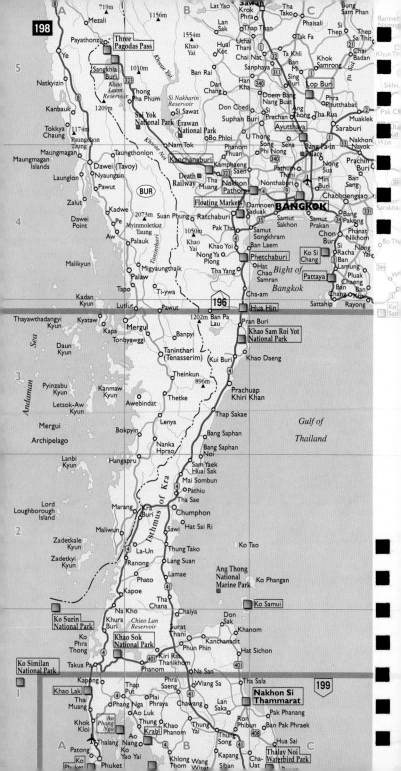

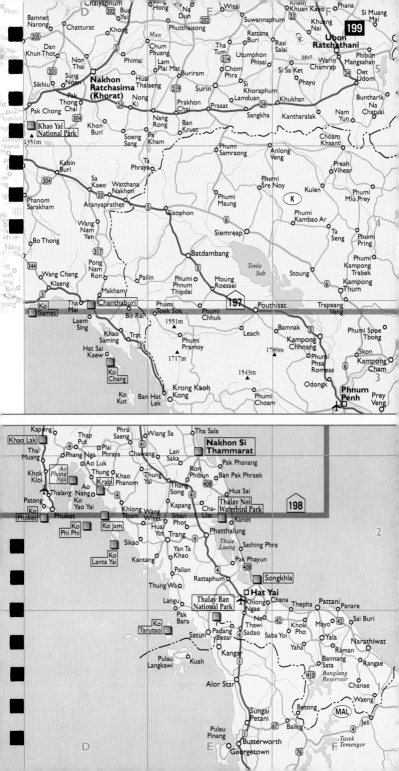

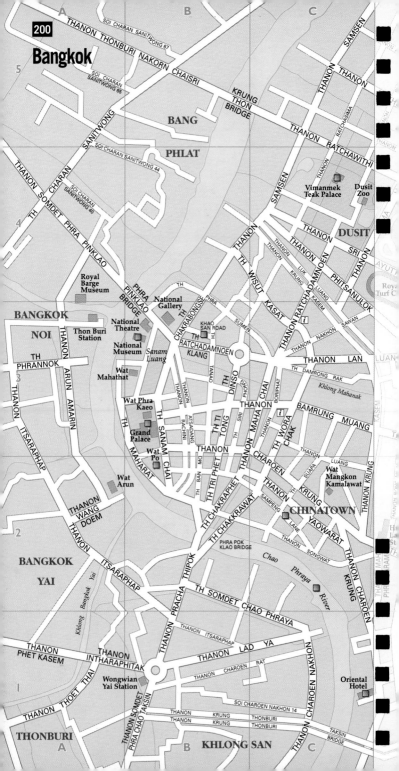

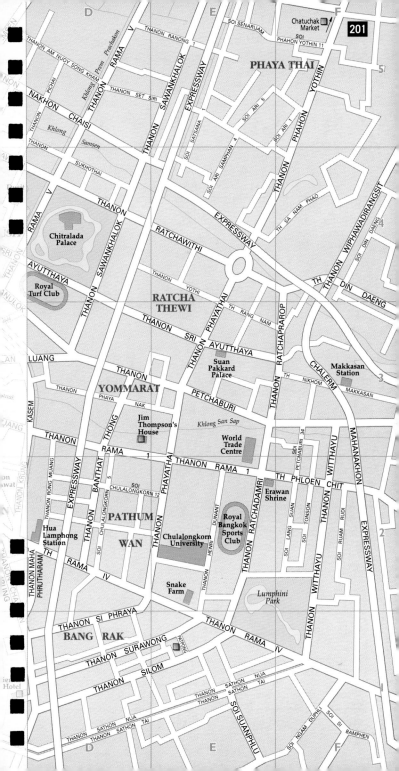

**PHAYA THAI**

Chatuchak Market

SOI SENARUAM

SOI PHAHON YOTHIN 11

THANON AM NUOY SONG KHAM

Khlong Prem Prachakon

THANON PICHAI

THANON RAMA V

THANON RANONG 1

THANON SAWANKHALOK

EXPRESSWAY

THANON SET SIRI

SOI ARI 5

SOI ARI 1

PHAHON YOTHIN

NAKHON CHAISI

THANON NON

THANON

Khlong Samsen

SUKHOTHAI

SOI SATSANA

SOI ARI SAMPRAN 9

SOI ARI SAMPRAN 1

TH SA NAM PHAO

THANON WIPHAWADIRANGSIT

RAMA V

THANON

THANON SAWANKHALOK

RATCHAWITHI

EXPRESSWAY

SOI DIN DAENG

Chitralada Palace

AYUTTHAYA

Royal Turf Club

THANON YOTHI

TH DIN DAENG

RATCHA THEWI

THANON SRI AYUTTHAYA

TH RANG NAM

RATCHAPRAROP

CHALERM

Makkasan Station

LUANG

THANON

THANON PHAYATHAI

TH NIKHOM

MAKKASAN

YOMMARAT

THANON

PHAYA NAK

Suan Pakkard Palace

PETCHABURI

KASEM

THANON THONG

Jim Thompson's House

Khlong San Sap

World Trade Centre

SOI PETCHABURI 34

MAHANAKHON

THANON

RAMA 1

THANON PHAYATHAI

THANON RAMA 1

TH PHLOEN CHIT

THANON WITTHAYU

EXPRESSWAY

THANON RONG MUANG

BANTHAT

THANON CHULALONGKORN

SOI CHULALONGKORN 12

THANON HENRI DUNANT

THANON RATCHADAMRI

Erawan Shrine

SOI LANG SUAN

SOI TONSON

SOI RUAM RUDI

THANON KRUNG

EXPRESSWAY

PATHUM

WAN

Hua Lamphong Station

SOI CHULALONGKORN 5

Chulalongkorn University

Royal Bangkok Sports Club

TH RAMA IV

THANON MAHA PHRUTHARAM

Snake Farm

Lumphini Park

THANON WITTHAYU

THANON SI PHRAYA

THANON RAMA IV

BANG RAK

THANON SURAWONG

PATPONG

THANON SILOM

SOI SUANPHLU

Hotel

THANON SATHON NUA

SATHON TAI

THANON SATHON NUA

THANON SATHON TAI

SOI NGAM DUPHLI

SOI SI BAMPHEN

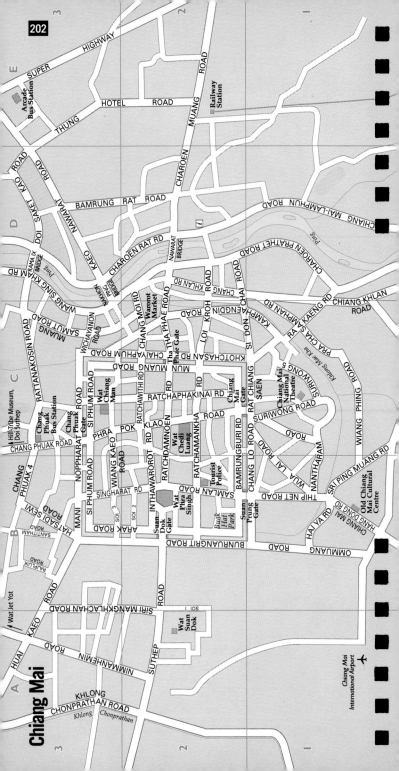

# Index

**A**ccommodation 34–35
  see also individual areas
admission charges 33
airport and air services
  30–31, 32, 189
Andaman Coast 149–172
  accommodation 168–170
  Ao Phang Nga 156–158
  children's entertainment 164
  eating out 170–171
  entertainment 172
  Khao Lak 164
  Khao Sok National Park
    150, 154–155
  Ko Jam 165–166
  Ko Lanta Yai 151, 166
  Ko Phi Phi 162–163
  Ko Phuket 164–165
  Ko Similan 164
  Ko Surin 164
  Ko Tarutao 167
  Krabi 159–161
  map 150–151
  seven-day itinerary
    152–153
  shopping 172
  Thalay Ban National Park
    167
  Trang Province 166
Ang Thong National Marine
  Park 134
Ao Phang Nga 7, 156–158
ATMs 189
Ayutthaya 7, 64, 72–74
  Bang-Pa-In Palace 64, 74
  Chan Kasem Palace 74
  Chao Sam Phraya National
    Museum 74
  Phra Mongkonbophit 73
  Wat Chaiwatthanaram 74
  Wat Lokayasutharam 74
  Wat Mahathat 73
  Wat Phra Si San Phet 73–74
  Wat Ratchaburana 73

**B**an Tham 177
Bang-Pa-In Palace 64, 74
Bangkok 39–62
  accommodation 56–57
  Chao Phraya River 7, 41,
    49–50
  Chatuchak Market 6, 36, 51
  children's entertainment 55
  Chinatown 55, 174–176
  Dusit Zoo 55
  eating out 58–60
  Emerald Buddha 45

entertainment 62
Grand Palace 44–46
Ice Skating Rink 54
Jim Thompson's House
  53–54
Khao San Road 52
Little India 176
Lumphini Park 54
maps 40–41, 175
National Museum 6–7, 52
Oriental Hotel 54–55, 57
Patpong 54
Rama IX Bridge 50
shopping 61
Skytrain 40
three-day itinerary 42–43
Vimanmek Teak Palace
  52–53
walk 174–176
Wat Mangkon Kamalawat
  175–176
Wat Phra Kaeo 45
Wat Po 7, 12, 40, 47–48
banks 190
big-game fishing 172
boat trips 49–50, 100, 102,
  140, 156, 157, 186
Bridge Over the River Kwai
  68–69
Buddha images 6, 13, 14,
  37, 93
Buddhism 18–19
buses 31–32
Butterfly Garden and
  Aquarium 164

**C**ambodia 121
camping 119
car rental 33
cave temples 138–139
caves 99, 157, 177–178,
  184–185
Central Plains 63–86
  accommodation 82–84
  Ayutthaya 7, 64, 72–74
  Bridge Over the River Kwai
    68–69
  children's entertainment 79
  Damnoen Saduak Floating
    Markets 70–71
  eating out 85
  entertainment 86
  JEATH War Museum 69
  Kamphaeng Phet
    Historical Park 80–81
  Kanchanaburi Allied War
    Cemetery 69
  Kanchanaburi Province
    78–79

Kanchanaburi Town 64,
  68–69
Lop Buri 79–80
map 64–65
Nakhon Pathom 79
Sangkhla Buri 81
scenic journeys 79
shopping 86
Sukhothai 7, 64, 75–77
three-day itinerary 66–67
Three Pagodas Pass 81
Umphang 81
Chan Kasem Palace 74
Chanthaburi 120
Chao Phraya River 7, 41,
  49–50
Chatuchak Market 6, 36, 51
Chiang Mai 88, 92–94
  Chiang Mai Zoo 102
  cookery and cultural
    courses 102
  drive 177–180
  Hill-Tribe Museum 94
  night bazaar and markets
    93, 108
  Viharn Lai Kam 93
  Warorot Market 94
  Wat Chedi Luang 93
  Wat Chiang Man 13, 93
  Wat Doi Suthep 89, 92
  Wat Phra Singh 12, 93
Chiang Rai 97, 101
Chiang Saen 101
Chieo Lan Reservoir 155
children 192
children's entertainment
  see individual areas
Chinatown, Bangkok 55,
  174–176
Chung Kai Allied War
  Cemetery 69
climate and seasons 188
clothing sizes 190
concessions 192
credit cards 37, 189
crime and personal safety 191
currency 189
customs regulations 192

**D**amnoen Saduak Floating
  Markets 70–71
Death Railway 64, 68–69,
  78–79
dental services 192
disabilities, travellers with 192
diving and snorkelling 7, 38,
  119, 136–137, 160, 164
Doi Inthanon National Park
  6, 88, 99, 102, 180

Doi Khun Tan National Park 103
drinking water 192
driving 33
drugs, illegal 22, 100
drugs and medicines 192
Dusit Zoo 55

**E**ast Coast 109–124
  accommodation 122
  Chanthaburi 120
  children's entertainment 120
  eating out 123
  entertainment 124
  five-day itinerary 112–113
  Khao Yai National Park 110, 121
  Ko Chang 114–116
  Ko Samet 117–119
  Ko Si Chang 121
  map 110–111
  Pattaya 120
  shopping 124
eating out 35–36
  see also individual areas
electricity 191
Elephant Conservation Centre 102
Elephant Village 124
embassies 192
Emerald Buddha 6, 14, 45, 80, 93, 101
emergency telephone numbers 191
entertainment 38
Erawan National Park 65, 78
etiquette
  social 9, 17, 26
  temple 13
  tribal 95

**F**ake goods 26
Fantasea 164
festivals 10–11, 38, 77, 86
Fish Cave 99, 178
food and drink 35–36
  cookery courses 102
  see also eating out
foreign exchange 189
full-moon parties (Ko Phangan) 135, 137, 148

**G**em trade 120
go-karting 124, 140
Golden Triangle 88, 100
golf 148
Grand Palace 44–46
Gulf Coast 125–148
  accommodation 142–144

children's entertainment 140
eating out 144–147
entertainment 148
Hua Hin 130–131
Khao Sam Roi Yot National Park 126, 132–133
Ko Samui archipelago 126, 134–137
  map 127
Nakhon Si Thammarat 126, 139–140
Phetchaburi 126, 138
seven-day itinerary 128–129
shopping 147–148
Songkhla 140–141
Thalay Noi Waterbird Park 140

**H**air-braiding 120
health 188, 192
Hellfire Pass 78–79
henna tattoes 120
hill tribes 20–22, 94, 95–97
Hill-Tribe Museums 94, 101
Hindu religion 14
Hua Hin 130–131
  Klai Klangwon Palace 131
  "monkey island" 130

**I**ce skating 54
insurance 192
islands 6
  see also entries beginning "Ko"

**J**ames Bond Island 7, 157, 158
JEATH War Museum 69
Jim Thompson's House 53–54

**K**amphaeng Phet Historical Park 80–81
  National Museum 80
  Provincial Museum 80
  San Phra Isuan Shrine 80
  Wat Phra Kaeo 80
  Wat Phrathat 80
Kanchanaburi Province 78–79
  Erawan National Park 65, 78
  Hellfire Pass 78–79
  Sai Yok National Park 79
Kanchanaburi Town 7, 64, 68–69
  JEATH War Museum 69

war cemeteries 69
  World War II Museum 69
Kao Khien 157
Kao Marjoo 157
Karen people 81, 94
kayaking 172
Khao Lak 164
Khao Sam Roi Yot National Park 126, 132–133, 184–186
  Hat Laem Sala 132, 185
  Hat Sam Phraya 185–186
  Khao Daeng 133, 186
  Khlong Khao Daeng 186
  map 184–185
  Tham Kaew Cave 184–185
  Tham Phraya Nakhon 133, 185
  tour 184–186
Khao San Road, Bangkok 52
Khao Sok National Park 6, 150, 154–155
Khao Wang 138
Khao Yai National Park 110, 121
Kheuan Khao Laem Reservoir 81
kick boxing 38
Klai Klangwon Palace 131
Ko Chang 114–116
  Hat Kai Bae 116
  Hat Khlong Phrao 115
  Hat Sai Kaew 115
  Khlong Phu waterfall 115
Ko Hai 166
Ko Jam 6, 165–166
Ko Kham 116
Ko Kradan 166
Ko Kut 116
Ko Lanta Yai 151, 166
Ko Mae Ko 134
Ko Mak 116
Ko Muk 166
Ko Panyi 156–157, 158
Ko Phangan 134–136
  Ao Chaloaklam 136
  Ban Tai 136
  full-moon parties 135, 137, 148
  Hat Rin Nai 135
  Hat Rin Nok 135
  Pang Waterfall National Park 136
Ko Phi Phi 6, 162–163
Ko Phuket 6, 164–165
  Ao Karon 164
  Ao Kata 164
  Ao Patong 164

Butterfly Garden and Aquarium 164
Fantasea 164
Shrine of the Serene Light 165
Ko Samet 117–119
  Ao Hin Kok 118
  Ao Kiu 118
  Ao Phrao 118
  Ao Thian 118
  Ao Wong Duan 118
  Hat Sai Kaew 117
Ko Samui 134
  Ban Chaweng 134
  Big Buddha 134
  Hat Lamai 134
Ko Samui archipelago 126, 134–137
Ko Si Chang 121
Ko Similan 164
Ko Surin 164
Ko Tao 7, 136–137
  Ao Chaloke Ban Kao 136
  Hat Sai Ree 136
  Mae Hat 136
Ko Tarutao 167
Ko Wua Talub 134
korlae 141
Krabi 159–161
  Ao Nang 160, 183
  Cat and Mouse Islands 159
  drive 181–183
  Hat Noppharat Thara 159–160, 182, 183
  Laem Phra Nang 160, 183
  night market 159
  Reclining Buddha 159, 183
  rock-climbing 160
  Wat Tham Seua 12–13, 161, 181–182

Laem Phra Nang 160
Lamphun 103
Laos 100
Lod Cave 177
long-neck women 94, 99
longtail boat trips 49, 100, 140, 157
Lop Buri 79–80
  monkeys 79
  Narai National Museum 79
  Wat Phra Phutthabat 80
  Wat Phra Si Ratana Mahathat 79–80

Mae Hat 136
Mae Hong Son 7, 97, 98–99, 178
Mae Lana Cave 178

Mae Sai 103
malaria 116, 133
Malaysia 141, 165, 167
markets 6, 36–37, 51, 61, 70–71, 93–94
massage 7, 24, 25, 48
meditation retreats 23
Mini Siam 120
Mon people 80, 81
money 189
monks 13, 18, 19
museums
  Chan Kasem Palace 74
  Chao Sam Phraya National Museum 74
  Elephant Museum 55
  Hellfire Memorial Museum 79
  Hill-Tribe Museum, Chiang Mai 94
  Hill-Tribe Museum, Chiang Rai 101
  JEATH War Museum 69
  Narai National Museum 79
  National Museum, Bangkok 6–7, 52
  National Museum, Chiang Saen 101
  National Museum, Kamphaeng Phet 80
  National Museum, Lamphun 103
  National Museum, Songkhla 140
  Opium Museum 100
  Phra Pathom Museum 79
  Provincial Museum 80
  Ramkhamhaeng Museum 75–76
  Ripley's Believe It Or Not! 124
  Viharn Kien Museum 139
  Wat Phra Kaeo Museum 45, 46
  World War II Museum 69
Myanmar (Burma) border 64, 81, 103

Nakhon Pathom 79
  Phra Pathom Chedi 79
  Phra Pathom Museum 79
Nakhon Si Thammarat 126, 139–140
  shadow puppets 139–140
  Viharn Kien Museum 139
  Wat Mahathat 139
national holidays 190
National Museum, Bangkok 6–7, 52

national parks 6
night safaris 120, 155
nightlife 38
the North 87–108
  accommodation 104–105
  Chiang Mai 88, 92–94
  Chiang Rai 97, 101
  Chiang Saen 101
  children's entertainment 102
  Doi Khun Tan National Park 103
  eating out 106–107
  entertainment 108
  Golden Triangle 88, 100
  Lamphun 103
  Mae Hong Son 7, 97, 98–99, 178
  map 89
  shopping 108
  six-day itinerary 90–91
  trekking 95–97, 108

Opening hours 37, 190
opium 100
Opium Museum 100
Oriental Hotel 54–55, 57

Pa Puek Cave 178
Pai 97, 99, 177
Pang Waterfall National Park 136
passports and visas 188
Patpong 54
Pattaya 7, 120
Payathonzu 81
pharmacies 190, 192
Phetchaburi 126, 138–139
  Kaho Banda-it 139
  Khao Luang 139
  Khao Wang 138
  Phra Nakhon Khiri 138
  Wat Borom 138
  Wat Kamphaeng Leang 138
  Wat Mahathat 138
  Wat Trailok 138
  Wat Yai Suwannaram 138
Phra Mongkonbophit 73
Phra Nakhon Khiri 138
Phra Pathom Chedi 79
police 191
post offices 190, 191
public holidays 17
public transport 31–33

Queen Sirikit Botanic Garden 177

Rafflesia 154
Rama IX Bridge 50

Reclining Buddha 47, 48, 159
rock-climbing 160, 172, 183
royal family 8, 15–17, 131, 139

Sai Yok National Park 79
Sangkhla Buri 81
sea gypsies 165
sex industry 54, 120
shadow puppets 139–140
Shell Cemetery 161
shopping 36–37, 190
  see also individual areas
shrimp farming 186
snake farm 55
Songkhla 140–141
  Khao Saen 141
  National Museum 140
  Wat Matchimawat 141
Sop Ruak 100
Soppong 99, 177
spa hotels 23–25
spirits and superstitions 8–9, 178
sports 38
Sri Sawai 76
student/young travellers 192
Sukhothai 7, 75–77
  Ramkhamhaeng Museum 75–76
  Sri Sawai 76
  Thuriang Kiln 76–77
  Wat Mahathat 76
  Wat Phra Pai Luang 76
  Wat Saphan Hin 77
  Wat Si Thon 77
  Wat Sra Sri 76
  Wat Trapang Ngoen 76
  Wat Trapang Thong 76
Sukhothai Historical Park 75
sun safety 192

Tamh Lod 157
Tarutao National Marine Park 167
taxis 30, 32
telephones 191
temples 12–13
  see also entries beginning "Wat"
Thalay Ban National Park 6, 167
Thalay Noi Waterbird Park 140
Tham Kaew Cave 184–185
Tham Lot 99
Tham Phraya Nakhon 133, 185
Three Pagodas Pass 81
Thuriang Kiln 76–77
tiger farm 124
time differences 189, 190
tipping 34, 36, 191
toilets 34, 192
tourist information 31, 188–189
trains 31, 32
Trang Province 166
transvestism 26, 62
travel documents 188
travellers' cheques 189
trekking 7, 95–97, 108
tuk-tuks 32–33

Umphang 81

Viharn Lai Kam 93
Vimanmek Teak Palace 52–53

Wat Borom 138
Wat Chaiwatthanaram 74
Wat Chedi Luang 93
Wat Chiang Man 13, 93
Wat Doi Suthep 89, 92
Wat Kamphaeng Leang 138
Wat Kukut 103

Wat Lokayasutharam 74
Wat Mahathat, Ayutthaya 73
Wat Mahathat, Nakhon Si Thammarat 139
Wat Mahathat, Phetchaburi 138
Wat Mahathat, Sukhothai 76
Wat Mangkon Kamalawat 175–176
Wat Matchimawat 141
Wat Phra Kaeo 45
Wat Phra Kaeo, Chiang Rai 101
Wat Phra Kaeo, Kamphaeng Phet 80
Wat Phra Pai Luang 76
Wat Phra Phutthabat 80
Wat Phra Si Ratana Mahathat 79–80
Wat Phra Si San Phet 73–74
Wat Phra Singh 12, 93
Wat Phra That Doi Tong 13, 101
Wat Phra That Haripunchai 103
Wat Phra That Phu Khao 100
Wat Phrathat 80
Wat Po 7, 12, 40, 47–48
Wat Ratchaburana 73
Wat Saphan Hin 77
Wat Si Thon 77
Wat Sra Sri 76
Wat Tham Seua 12–13, 161, 181–182
Wat Trailok 138
Wat Traimit 6
Wat Trapang Thong 76
Wat Yai Suwannaram 138
website 188
whale- and dolphin-watching 164
wildlife 79, 132, 134, 140, 154, 167, 186

# Picture Credits

The Automobile Association wishes to thank the following photographers, libraries and museums for their assistance with the preparation of this book.

Front and back cover: All images AA Photo Library/Rick Strange.

CHIVA-SOM INTERNATIONAL HEALTH RESORT, HUA HIN 23t, 23c, 23b, 24/5, 25; BRUCE COLEMAN COLLECTION 7ct, 136/7; CPA MEDIA/OLIVER HARGREAVE 76c; JANE EGGINGTON 8bl, 14ct, 19tl, 24t.

The remaining photographs are held in the Association's own photo library (AA Photo Library) and were taken by DAVID HENLEY, with the exception of the following pages: BEN DAVIES 91t, 95l, 96/7, 97b, 187; JIM HOLMES 49 inset, 174, 176; RICK STRANGE 2i, 2v, 3v, 5, 6t, 15, 19tr, 19bc, 19br, 26, 27tr, 27c, 27b, 87, 102, 113b, 165.

# SPIRAL GUIDES

# Questionnaire

## Dear Traveler

Your comments, opinions and recommendations are very important to us. So please help us to improve our travel guides by taking a few minutes to complete this simple questionnaire.

**Send to:** Spiral Guides, MailStop 66, 1000 AAA Drive, Heathrow, FL 32746–5063

## Your recommendations...

We always encourage readers' recommendations for restaurants, nightlife or shopping – if your recommendation is added to the next edition of the guide, we will send you a FREE AAA Spiral Guide of your choice. Please state below the establishment name, location and your reasons for recommending it.

_____

_____

_____

_____

_____

**Please send me AAA Spiral**_____

(see list of titles inside the back cover)

## About this guide...

**Which title did you buy?**

_____ **AAA Spiral**

**Where did you buy it?** _____

**When?** mm/ y y

**Why did you choose a AAA Spiral Guide?** _____

_____

_____

_____

**Did this guide meet your expectations?**

Exceeded ☐   Met all ☐   Met most ☐   Fell below ☐

**Please give your reasons** _____

_____

_____

_____

continued on next page...

Were there any aspects of this guide that you particularly liked?

_______________________________________________

_______________________________________________

_______________________________________________

_______________________________________________

_______________________________________________

Is there anything we could have done better?

_______________________________________________

_______________________________________________

_______________________________________________

_______________________________________________

_______________________________________________

## About you...

Name (Mr/Mrs/Ms) _______________________________

Address _______________________________________

_______________________________________________

_______________________________ Zip ____________

Daytime tel nos. ________________________________

Which age group are you in?

Under 25 ☐ 25–34 ☐ 35–44 ☐ 45–54 ☐ 55–64 ☐ 65+ ☐

How many trips do you make a year?

Less than one ☐ One ☐ Two ☐ Three or more ☐

Are you a AAA member? Yes ☐ No ☐

Name of AAA club ________________________________

About your trip...

When did you book? m m/ y y When did you travel? m m/ y y

How long did you stay? __________________________

Was it for business or leisure? ____________________

Did you buy any other travel guides for your trip? ☐ Yes ☐ No

If yes, which ones? ______________________________

_______________________________________________

Thank you for taking the time to complete this questionnaire.

All information is for AAA internal use only and will NOT be distributed outside the organization to any third parties.